Letters of a Javanese Princess

LETTERS

OF A *Javanese*

Princess

RADEN ADJENG KARTINI

TRANSLATED FROM THE DUTCH BY

Agnes Louise Symmers

EDITED AND WITH AN INTRODUCTION BY

Hildred Geertz

PREFACE BY

Eleanor Roosevelt

The Norton Library

W · W · NORTON & COMPANY · *New York*

FIRST PUBLISHED IN THE NORTON LIBRARY 1964

UNESCO COLLECTION OF REPRESENTATIVE WORKS
INDONESIAN SERIES

This work has been accepted in the Indonesian Translation
Series sponsored by the United Nations Educational, Scientific and Cultural Organization (UNESCO).

PREFACE   *by Eleanor Roosevelt*

[MRS. ROOSEVELT READ KARTINI'S *Letters* IN 1961.]

These letters are, I think, just as important today as they were when written. To those who read them in Holland I am sure they gave the first little bit of insight into the lives of the people whom the Dutch were ruling at that time. The girl who wrote the letters happened to have a father who, as she says, was liberal and had a tremendous understanding of the longings in the hearts of the young Javanese. He allowed his daughters to go to a foreign school until they were twelve and then they had to return to the cloistered homelife, but among themselves there was a freedom of communication and a closeness which did not exist in many of the Javanese families of the day.

The translator, Agnes Louise Symmers, said of Kartini, "The influence of her life and teachings is perhaps greater than that of any other woman of modern times because it reaches all the millions of Javanese and extends to some extent throughout the entire East." Therefore, even though she died young, this young woman began the liberation of women and to a great extent pointed the way for their education.

Kartini's letters are fascinating for the picture they give of the life and spirit of the times and I imagine that much of it, as far as the general attitude goes, has not changed through the years. In many ways they will help us to understand what we of the Western world must understand if we are to be helpful to nations emerging from old customs into new. Much there is of value to be preserved but in the modern world much has to be changed. This is so over and over again in infinite variety in every country that begins to touch other countries. If we are to become cognizant of the oneness of humanity, regardless of race or creed or color, this book will be one of the ways that we will learn.

I am delighted to gain the insight which these letters offer. One little remark in one of the letters is something I think we might all remember. Kartini says: "We feel that the kernel of all religion is right living, and that all religion is good and beautiful. But, O ye peoples, what have ye made of it?" Instead of drawing us together, religion has often forced us apart and even this young girl realized that it should be a unifying force.

ELEANOR ROOSEVELT

KARTINI: AN INTRODUCTION

> Welcome, O life! I go to encounter for the millionth time the reality of experience and to forge in the smithy of my soul the uncreated conscience of my race.
>
> —James Joyce, A *Portrait of*
> *The Artist as a Young Man*

To cross the terrain between innocent childhood and self-reliant maturity is a difficult transit at all times—but it is all the more painful when one is forced, by temperament or circumstances, to question the validity of the accepted routes and destinations. Kartini, who came of age just as Java was on the verge of undergoing its most intimate contact with modern Western civilization, left in these letters a graphic record of the conflicts, inner and outer, that were stirred up when a sensitive young Javanese encountered the peculiarly disturbing ideals of the West. She learned enough of Western culture to criticize and reject the course of life which her family expected her to take, and yet she eventually found it inadequate as a guide for solving the many problems her new ideals themselves had created.

Kartini was by nature one of those unhappy few who can never contentedly drift with the current of their culture, who cannot accept as given the world around them, who won't surrender themselves to the role that society sets for them. Refusing to see one's self as others do means that one's inner sense of who one is, one's assurance of personal identity, is severely shaken. However, unless there follows a total retreat from human intercourse, the search for one's true self does not entail fabrication of an entirely unique mode of being, but is rather a trying-on of various existing philosophies to see how they fit. A new conception of personal purpose and a novel style of life may result, but they can be based only on the cultural traditions that one knows. In Kartini's case, the adolescent fumbling for a style of life which could simultaneously satisfy all of her competing desires and ideals was paralleled by a series of social changes in Java which just as urgently needed new formulations of societal purpose and style. Kartini's individual crisis of identity both responded to, and, as her writings became known, contributed to a crisis in Javanese cultural identity.

Where Kartini stood as she wrote these letters—where she was located socially, what emotional state she was in, and what kinds of ideas and ideals she held—must all be seen in terms of the confrontation of the Javanese with the Dutch: the traditional society of rice-growing peasants and highly civilized aristocrats, over against the bourgeois, economically-expanding colonial system introduced by Holland; and the profound mystical philosophy of the Javanese over against the practical, activist ethic of social welfare and progress of the nineteenth century Westerners. When the letters begin Kartini is twenty, still caught in the alternating optimism and despair of a thoughtful, rebellious adolescent. When the letters abruptly end with her death four years later, she has become a woman. She has discovered for herself who she is, whom she loves, and for whom she must fight. She has made her choices.

At the end of the nineteenth century, the time when Kartini wrote, the colonial system which had enveloped Java for more than two centuries was undergoing sharp criticism, not as yet so much from the Indonesians themselves, as from within its ranks of colonial officers and from humanitarian Dutch political thinkers, for its neglect of the social and economic welfare of the Indonesian people. Most of the Dutch persons who befriended Kartini, who encouraged her to learn Dutch, to strive for further education, and to search for a new kind of vocation for herself, were proponents of the—at that time very new—colonial policy which was later to be labeled the "Ethical Policy." This program, which emphasized the increased education of the Indonesians, fuller participation by them in their own local government as civil servants, efforts to raise the peasants' standard of living through agricultural improvements and the promotion of indigenous handicrafts (none of which had concerned the Dutch up to that time), was put into effect after Kartini's death during the first decades of the twentieth century. These high-minded efforts on the part of the Dutch had, in the end, some unforeseen results: on the one hand there was some improvement in the native welfare but on the other hand, the deepening penetration of Western ideas among the Indonesian peoples resulted ultimately in their demand for self-determination, and, in 1945, the collapse of the colonial system itself.

During Kartini's time, however, these changes were still in the future. The fundamental internal contradictions within a colonial system itself—the mistaken idea that profitable development of a country by foreigners would at the same time redound to the welfare of the natives, who could only be grateful for the efforts on their behalf—were not yet fully apparent. And yet, in many ways, Kartini experienced a kind of abbreviated preview of what was to happen in the twentieth century, not only to the Javanese but to colonial peoples elsewhere in Asia and Africa as well. She was among the first Javanese to acquire some Western education, and the deductions which she drew from it—more or less on her own— were the same ones which would be made over and over again in other countries in the coming century. The Western progressive tradition that Kartini enthusiastically absorbed led her inevitably to the realization that her position as inferior to the Dutch was neither just nor irremediable, and that it was not merely her own social position as an individual that needed revision but that of her entire people. She was forced to the conclusion that some basic changes had to be made in Javanese society in order to bring it into accord with the ideals of social equality and progress, but at the same time, the more she understood Western culture, the more she became convinced that her own ancient Javanese civilization was in itself of the highest value and should not be abandoned for a shallow modernity.

The implications for practical action, for effecting immediate changes in her own social milieu and in her own personal life, were much more difficult for her to draw. The interest of these letters lies not so much in a story of a determined girl fighting against unyielding traditional demands, but rather in her internal struggles, between the forces of tradition and modernity as parts of her own personality, between the pull of abstract ideas and the pressure of her affections for her family. Should she go to Holland and become a great writer, should she study medicine, should she establish a school for girls, should she flaunt her unconventionality in the face of her reactionary community and become a shining example of what a Javanese girl could become, or should she attempt to undermine tradition and vested interests inconspicuously but steadily as a teacher or as a simple midwife? These were the con-

crete alternatives she considered, but underlying them was a conflict of loyalties: to her historic destiny as she saw it, to her various
—and contradictory—Dutch friends, and above all, to her father,
whose love and approval were overwhelmingly necessary to her.

Kartini spoke often in these letters of the stiflingly protected life
she led, yet in terms of intellectual exposure it was an extremely
open one. She came from a family which had not only unusually
close contacts with the Dutch—for Javanese—but also was uncom-
monly receptive to Western ideas. Although her title, "Raden
Adjeng," means literally "princess," she was not actually one in
the proper sense of the word, for her father was not sovereign over
a royal domain. He was a servant of the Dutch, who made him a
"Regent" or governor, in nominal charge of an administrative district, where his royal blood and familial traditions of governing
gained for him, and thus for them, the allegiance of the peasants.
Almost literally at his side was a Dutch advisor, the Assistant Resident, who made all decisions that concerned Dutch interests, and
most of his Javanese inferiors also had their Dutch counterparts.
He was stationed in Japara, not because he had inherited a throne,
but because the Dutch had transferred him there. However, unlike
many of the other Javanese Regents of the time, who held themselves personally aloof from foreign influence, preferring to act as
much as possible as if the Dutch did not exist, Kartini's father spoke
Dutch fluently and read extensively in Western literature. In 1902
there were only three other Regents out of more than 80 in all
of Java who could speak Dutch as well as he, and one of them was
his brother.

Kartini's father and uncles had had some Dutch education, an
almost unique experience in Java of the 1860's. Her grandfather,
an eminent and farseeing man, had had a young tutor brought to
them from Holland, for at that time there were few Western
schools in Java. This young Dutchman no doubt taught them much
more than his language, for he later became chief editor of a
progressive-minded newspaper, *De Locomotief*, published in Java,
which crusaded for the Ethical Policy. One of the brothers became
a writer, writing a travel book in Javanese as early as 1862, and later
a series of scholarly critiques of Veth's book on Javanese society.
They all made sure that their own children, both sons and daughters, had similar educational opportunities. One of Kartini's brothers, Kartono, graduated with honors from a colonial Dutch high

school and continued with higher education in Holland and Vienna, stopping just short of a doctoral degree in literature and languages. It was this brother who, together with her father, continued to encourage Kartini's reading after she was drawn out of school.

For Kartini, her early school experience, from her sixth year to her twelfth, set the pattern of cultural confrontation which was to dominate her life. It was in a Dutch elementary school, established in Japara for the benefit of the children of the rubber and sugar plantation operators and the civil servants of the region. A handful of Javanese children were admitted, but only those who were of exceedingly high status, and willing to learn Dutch. The building was directly across the road from Kartini's home and the schoolmaster's house was built within the grounds of the Regent's estate. Kartini and her brothers and sisters played and studied daily with the schoolmaster's children. It was then that she acquired in addition to her easy command of Dutch, an intense feeling for the difference between Western and Javanese ways of life. As Kartini herself relates in these letters, what impressed her the most was the freedom from social restraint of the Dutch children, and the expectant attitude they had toward their own personal futures, the sure knowledge that they could look forward to directing the course of their careers themselves, and to choose among many different, alluring ways of life.

This glimpse into the exotic ways of another society came to an abrupt end for her when, with the onset of adolescence, Kartini was required to withdraw again entirely into her own culture, to take on her prescribed role as a noble Javanese girl. No longer permitted even to cross the road into the Dutch school, she was expected now to hold herself demurely out of sight of everyone but her closest family, to be in readiness for the high-born suitors who might petition her father for her hand. This period of seclusion within the grounds of her father's estate was not so much an Islamic custom as Kartini thought, but rather an indigenous Javanese way of demonstrating the high rank and pure blood of her family. Unlike the practices in Middle Eastern countries, where women are kept in seclusion throughout their lives, in Java it was only the women of the nobility, and especially the young unmarried girls who were expected to hide themselves from the eyes of outsiders. Javanese women do not wear veils, and after marriage and the birth of their children, even the noblest women are permitted considerable freedom of movement.

For Kartini, restless, alert, and proud, confinement to her home was virtual imprisonment. She felt oppressed by her family, particularly by her mother, her oldest brother and an older sister, all of whom were highly conventional persons who demanded her conformity to the rigid etiquette required of younger persons toward their elders. Their enforced companionship was made all the heavier to bear when, in that same year, her Dutch playmates, the schoolteacher's daughters, returned with their father to Holland, and her brother, Kartono, with whom she felt closest, left for high school in another city. She had a special affinity to Kartono: they were close in age, very similar in temperament and intellectual brilliance, and the interesting course of Kartono's later career was to be curiously foreshadowed in Kartini's. Moreover, they too, probably alone among the other children of the Regent, had a different mother, one of his secondary wives. The similarity in their names, Kartini and Kartono, reflects this common maternal tie. Kartini never mentions her real mother (perhaps she died when Kartini was very young?) and the woman that Kartini calls Mother throughout these letters is actually her foster mother, the first and most purebred wife of the Regent. This fact, perhaps, in part explains the chilly aloofness that she held toward Kartini—but only in part—for there were fundamental differences between Kartini and her foster mother in cultural background, and especially in education. Where Kartini's father stood largely for the world of modern ideas, her foster mother stood for old Java, for the courtly customs and, even more, for the ancient Javanese mystical outlook on the world. When Kartini finally was able to reconcile within herself these two traditions, she and her foster mother drew much closer together. Nonetheless, throughout her life, it was to her father that Kartini looked for affection and guidance, and during those periods that she was estranged from him by her actions, she felt intense regret. As a Javanese father, however, he had to maintain his dignity and reserve and could be only a distant, though powerful, support to her.

It was during this painful confinement that Kartini discovered in herself a source of inner strength. This was the ability to express herself in writing. She started writing to her former playmate in Holland, later turned to formal essays in Dutch which her brother Kartono would correct on his rare vacations from school. Although eventually Kartini was permitted more freedom of movement, her life was always exceedingly cloistered, and the volume of letters she wrote (only a portion of which are published here) attests to their meaning for her. She wrote once "Letters are truly important in my life; . . . if I did not have this exchange of letters, I would not have the courage to abandon our age-old traditional customs. How many beautiful, sweet and valuable things have come in the mail, pearls, diamonds, and precious stones for my mind and heart." (Letter to E. C. Abendanon, 8 Aug. 1902, not included in the present volume. Armijn Pane, p. 29. My translation.)

Kartini's father made one exception in his daughter's immurement, an exception which was perhaps to prove the undoing of all his efforts to make her into a pliable, socially acceptable maiden. When she was fifteen, a new Dutch Assistant Resident was stationed in Japara, a man representing an increasingly frequent, different type of colonial officer, more cultivated in outlook than his predecessors. Dutch colonial society at that time was changing rapidly. It was no longer a strictly male outpost of rough soldiers, civil servants and planters, but a swiftly growing, domesticated community with wives and children and all of the social amenities that middle class women require. One of the first of these women was the wife of the new Assistant Resident, Mevrouw Ovink-Soer. On their arrival, the Ovinks paid a formal call on the Regent, and were introduced to his three daughters. Mevrouw Ovink-Soer invited the girls to her house for lessons in drawing and embroidery and to their delight their father consented. Each day thereafter for five years, Kartini and her sisters rode the few hundred yards to the Ovink house by covered carriage.

But Mevrouw Ovink-Soer was no ordinary woman. She was highly cultured, had published a number of magazine articles, and was later to write a book "Women's Life in the (Javanese) Village." She was also a fervent socialist and feminist, and while ostensibly she was tutoring Kartini in feminine handicrafts, she must also have communicated many of her political opinions and attitudes as well.

Through Mevrouw Ovink-Soer, Kartini was inducted into a very specific aspect of Western culture, one which contrasts highly with those aspects with which she might have come in contact had her friend been, for instance, a Christian missionary—or if she had continued her education in Dutch schools. Much of the emphasis that Kartini placed on the injustices of the Javanese women's portion, and especially the inequities of the Javanese marriage, may very well derive from Mevrouw Ovink-Soer and the other Dutch women with whom Kartini came to correspond through her. While Kartini's own familial situation as the daughter of a secondary wife, and her own marital prospects, confined, monotonous and hopeless as they seemed, must have given her the impetus, it was her perception of her life as she saw it through the eyes of a progressive Western woman, that focused her rejection of it. This was a period of intensely militant feminism in Holland, in which even the institution of marriage was being attacked. For Mevrouw Ovink-Soer, the Javanese custom of arranging marriage without the prior acquaintance or consent of the young couple, and the custom of polygyny must have been abhorrent. Kartini's extreme statement that she was determined to remain a spinster in order to keep her individuality and autonomy, probably came out of her conversations with Mevrouw Ovink-Soer. The articles that Mevrouw Ovink-Soer was writing were being published in a Dutch women's magazine, *De Hollandsche Lelie*, which was carrying on a crusade for socialism and women's rights. Kartini herself took a subscription and was soon corresponding with its editor, a modern woman who had been divorced (a daring act at that time) and who had decided opinions on marriage.

It was through the pages of *De Hollandsche Lelie* that Kartini met Stella Zeehandelaar, another radical feminist. Kartini had entered a small classified advertisement in the magazine inviting someone to correspond with her, and Stella answered her. Their letters were frequent and warm, with Stella supporting all of Kartini's boldest plans. Although the two young women never actually met each other, Stella came to play the role of Kartini's ideological conscience, and each time that Kartini gave in to her father's wishes, she felt compelled to justify her actions to Stella. When, in the end, Kartini broke her resolutions and married, Stella felt it to be a complete surrender of all her ideals. It was probably Stella who introduced Kartini to a sensational popular feminist novel, *Hilda van Suylenburg*, a story of a woman who tries to support herself alone in the face of social criticism. In it there is a quotation from Richard Wagner, which Kartini took to heart, "If you marry without love, you make a liaison against God's will, and when you consummate such a marriage you sin against God."

Kartini became more convinced that she must have a vocation as a realistic alternative to marriage.

This collection of letters opens with her first letters to Stella and to Mevrouw Ovink-Soer, who was transferred with her husband to another part of Java in October of 1899. It may have been the departure of the Ovinks from Japara that brought Kartini to recognize the extent of her intellectual and moral isolation there, and it was at this time that she began to speak of her wish to join her brother in Holland for study. But she saw no practical means for doing so.

In August of 1900 the way was opened for her by a new Dutch friend, J. H. Abendanon, a man who was much more capable of effective action on her behalf than any of her earlier acquaintances. One of the earliest and most sincere proponents of the Ethical Policy, Abendanon was already taking concrete steps in its implementation in his capacity as Director of the Department of [Native] Education, Religion and Industry. One of his most earnest projects was women's education, for he felt that progressive mothers would have a deeper impact on their children than any other later influences could. He had been told about Kartini by his friend, Snouck-Hurgronje, one of the most eminent Ethici, a man of profound insight into the character of the Indonesian people.

The visit to Japara by Abendanon and his sympathetic wife had a number of significant consequences. It buoyed up Kartini's failing spirits, and set her with renewed enthusiasm to study again. But it brought to a head her talk of going to Holland to study, with the result that her father explicitly opposed it, on the grounds that she would forget she was a Javanese. He did however consent to the Abendanons' suggestion that she study for a year in Batavia, the colonial capital, with the aim of becoming a teacher in a school for the daughters of Regents to be set up by Abendanon.

Another result of Abendanon's interest in Kartini was the sudden expansion of her web of intellectual friendships. A visit to the Abendanons' lively house in Batavia by the Regent and his three daughters was an exciting eye-opener for Kartini. There she made a number of new intellectual Dutch friends with whom she continued to correspond in the next years, and even some Indonesian ones. There she may have met the Sumatran, Abdoel Moeis, who was to become twenty years later a prominent Indonesian nationalist. It seems also likely she met there, or at least heard of, the young

Agus Salim, who as Hadji Agus Salim was to become a powerful and revered nationalist political leader and one of the first Ministers of Foreign Affairs of the Republic of Indonesia. Three years later when Kartini was finally granted a scholarship by the colonial government and turned it down in order to marry, she attempted unsuccessfully to transfer the grant to Agus Salim.

Soon after this exhilarating trip the news came that Abendanon's plan to open a school for Regents' daughters with Kartini as head had been completely foiled by the refusal of the various Javanese Regents to permit their daughters to attend such a school. Kartini was plunged into despair. She had never accurately estimated, until then, the strength of the conservative Javanese opposition to reform, especially to change in the restrictions on noble girls.

The next years after this disappointment were very low ones for her. Her father had a series of illnesses, which upset Kartini immeasurably. Her great fear for his death was augmented by a deep feeling of guilt, for Javanese believe strongly that mental upset, such as that caused by an unruly daughter, will bring about serious disease. Her two younger sisters, who were to accompany her in any further schooling, both had bouts of dangerous sickness. Kartini wrote in the depths of this time that she was feeling "dull, weary and uneasy." Then in January 1902 one of the younger sisters married. This was a devastating blow, for it was not only a betrayal of their ideals, but her absence left a lonely gap in Kartini's life. The pressures from friends and relatives on Kartini to get married increased in volume. Desperately she sought some way out, and wrote again and again to Stella of her desire to go to Holland to study.

Then in April 1902 came the turning point in her life. A new and much more powerful Dutch supporter came to see her in Japara, the head of the Dutch Social Democratic Party, and member of the Dutch parliament, H. H. van Kol. Stella, who was a Social Democrat, had written van Kol telling him of Kartini's plight. Van Kol was in the midst of a continuing onslaught against the entrenched conservative majority in Parliament, on behalf of the new Ethical Policy. On meeting Kartini, he resolved to make a political issue of her, to attempt on the floor of Parliament to get a governmental grant for her education in Holland. He was to be successful by November, 1902, but meanwhile, events set into motion by his visit to Kartini were to have some unintended consequences which made it, in the end, impossible for her to accept the grant.

The first indirect result of his visit was notoriety. Van Kol had been accompanied by the editor of the newspaper, *De Locomotief*, who published an account of the trip to Japara. This was the first time Kartini's name had appeared in print, an event which her father had successfully prevented till then. The forces of reaction, both in Javanese and in Dutch circles, were mobilized against her, and a whispering campaign began. She was accused of being a coquette, of wanting a Dutch husband, even of wanting to be sexually promiscuous, and the pressures on her family to marry her off intensified. Her father became very cool to her, and soon after that became ill again. Her distress and bitterness were very great, but still she kept her resolve to follow her ideals and go to Holland for schooling.

The other unintended, but profoundly important, effect of van Kol's visit was that Kartini became newly engrossed in religion, in her own Javanese beliefs. Van Kol was a believer in occultism, and was deeply attracted to the mystical elements in Javanese religion. He described to Kartini a spiritualistic seance of the Western sort in which the spirit writes messages to the living on the wall, and Kartini was highly intrigued by it. Within a week after his visit she and a young Dutch friend, Annie Glaser, experimented. She wrote to van Kol:

Sunday evening, after we had had the immense pleasure and privilege of your presence among us, and you had taught us about the spirit world, we tried to call up the spirits. We succeeded so well that I can't neglect to tell you all about it. We had, following your advice, a pencil attached to a very light stick of bamboo. Juf. Glaser and I held the reed firmly, and suddenly it moved by itself. It was none other than my guardian spirit. We asked him a question, whereupon the stick moved aimlessly here and there for a considerable time, then suddenly it shot forward rapidly and wrote the alphabet three times on the wall, followed by the letters "good," the answer to our question. I asked my guardian spirit to give me advice, and I turned my face away. Annie Glaser also did not follow the movements of the stick. How astonished we were, when we, after a pause, looked up, and saw written on the wall the words: 'Let her finish her studies, if she is to be given gold later, that she might mint it.' [in Dutch]

The peculiarly written "d" in all the words where it appeared drew our attention, and we asked ourselves where we had seen it before. The thought gave us no rest, we kept thinking about it. The day brought us light, and the name of the person came to us, whose 'd' was like that on the wall. (Letter to H. H. van Kol, 30 April 1902; Bouman p. 46–47, my translation.)

Kartini and her friend decided that the spirit writer was a Dutch girl who had died about six months earlier, with whom Kartini had exchanged letters, and who was an acquaintance of van Kol. The dead girl had written to Kartini about her ardent interest in theosophy and spiritualism.

Kartini also began to write to Mevrouw van Kol, who did not accompany her husband on his trip through Java. In response to Mevrouw van Kol's caution about the dangers of experimenting in seances, Kartini wrote:

Above all, be assured, my dear friend, we will *not* be reckless with the spiritualism and the holding of seances. This last we have already not done for a long time, yesterday evening being the first after a long time. . . . We did it and we received a warning. . . . Oh, we will never forget, how deeply we were punished, when the stick wrote on the wall in Arabic letters. It was my grandfather on my mother's side. A little later the stick wrote in Javanese, just as before, only one line. It was grandfather on father's side. The first message said that we should trust in God, the second that we must not be afraid no matter what happens— "trust in God" was the meaning. (Neither of us can write in Arabic.) Can you imagine our amazement, our emotions, when the following evening something unpleasant happened, of which we had not the least suspicion? . . . Mother came to sit with us, she wanted very much to learn some news of our older sister, who for the last few months had felt extremely miserable, but neither she, nor her doctor, knew what was the matter. We asked the familiar spirit, and two days later a letter came from our brother-in-law, telling our mother that he and his wife had just been to the doctor again, and word for word his message was the same as that from our familiar spirit: 'Your sister carries a new life under her heart and all the illness has come from that.' Now you should know that my sister is the mother of three children and her doctor has strongly warned her that more are out of the question. (Letter to Mevr. van Kol, no date; Bouman,

p. 48, my translation.)

While such seances, that is, direct contacts with specifically identified dead souls, are not customary in Java, the basic beliefs underlying them are completely in harmony with the Javanese view of the supernatural world. Theirs is a highly complex religion, one with many facets from profound philosophical mysticism to simple faith in the placation of evil spirits by offering them good food, sweet-smelling incense and flowers, and betel nut to chew. It is open to and tolerant of all sorts of beliefs, and has absorbed, in the course of Java's long history, elements from nearly every doctrine that reached its shores, notably Hinduism and Buddhism from India, and Islam from the Middle East. Islam, coming later, had less impact on Javanese thought than Hinduism and Buddhism, especially among the gentry class to which Kartini belonged, the cultural descendants of the royal families of Java who ruled as sacred deputies of God, according to Hindu tenets. Although all Javanese are nominally Moslems, the remarks that Kartini makes indicating that she knows nothing of Islam are not surprising from someone of her social status.

Speaking now only of those facets of Javanese religion which were dominant in Kartini's circles, one of the central ideas is that spiritual beings—good and evil, all ultimately aspects of God— swarm unseen around the living, perceived only by certain gifted humans. The gift of spiritual insight can be gained only through long psychic training, through abstinence and meditation, and through the aesthetic intuition that comes from deep understanding of the Javanese gamelan music, the serious formal dance, the intricate allusive classic poetry, and the highly symbolic shadow play. All of these arts have strong significance for the Javanese, and with her turn to religion, Kartini found a renewed interest in the arts.

Some of the ethical precepts of Javanese religion appear in her letters of 1902. God is thought to be the same for all men, whatever His name or form, whatever dogma is held, and there are felt to be many different roads to reach Him. Religion thus for the Javanese is a binding force between all men as brothers under God, as equally holy vehicles for God. For Kartini this provided an emotionally powerful credo which could supplement her earlier intellectual conviction that Dutch and Javanese could be friends, working side by side to the same ends.

It is interesting to speculate just why Kartini turned to religion, and why at this particular period. Certainly the possibility was always there for her, for it was all around her. Her foster-mother was apparently very devout, as indicated by her changed attitude toward Kartini after that time. Her brother, Kartono, was to go even further in this direction some years later. After study in Delft and Leiden in languages and literature, he traveled over Europe, moving in brilliant intellectual circles, making friendships with such writers as Arthur Schnitzler; then abruptly he returned to Java, and threw himself into an entirely different calling. He became a traditional spiritual curer, a mystic who could heal the sick through meditation and prayer, and he continued as a renowned healer until his death in 1951. For a Javanese, even for an educated Javanese, this is not so surprising a *volte-face*, for even today, in the highest levels of the educated Javanese elite, persons of Kartono's temper are found.

Yet, for Kartini, it seems as though she needed direct encouragement from a respected Westerner before she could fully accept this part of her heritage. The eagerness with which she seized it, and the emotional support that this newly-refound faith noticeably gave her during the ensuing year of profound personal distress, show that she was psychologically ready for it, and needed only the final impetus given by the interest of van Kol, his wife, and her friend Annie Glaser. It gave meaning to all aspects of her life, increased her delight in Javanese poetry and music and in the beauties of the natural world, and deepened her understanding of her family. One of the central themes of Javanese religion is the idea that spiritual insight and power come to one whose inner life is orderly and controlled, and that one way to achieve inner discipline is through bringing order into one's external life, above all to one's relationships with other people. The practice of the confining rules of Javanese etiquette which accentuate the awareness of differences in social status among all persons, even within a family, against which Kartini chafed so hard, becomes in this broader view a kind of religious act, for etiquette simplifies and orders relationships by formalizing them. Kartini makes no mention of this aspect of her religion, but it seems reasonable to infer that she accepted it too. In any case, her family's attitudes toward her began to be more sympathetic after this time.

What apparently brought about a full reconciliation, with her father especially, was her final decision not to go to Holland. In this action, too, Kartini seemed to need the support of a Westerner. This time it was Abendanon. As soon as he heard of van Kol's success in The Hague in obtaining Kartini's scholarship, Abendanon rushed to Japara to dissuade her from accepting it. The argument he made which impressed Kartini the most was that such an extremely unconventional act of leaving the country would turn public opinion entirely against her, and sabotage her long-range goal of setting an example for her people. There was, apparently, considerable disagreement among Kartini's Dutch friends as to what course would be best for her. Abendanon's cautious realism stood in contrast to van Kol's more radically idealistic attitude of sharply cutting through Kartini's traditional bonds. Abendanon may have felt as one of his friends, the linguist Adriani, did, who wrote at that time directly to Mevr. van Kol, attempting to persuade her that Kartini was too tense, excitable, and eager to learn to withstand the high stimulation of a year in Holland. He wrote ". . . her inner life, which is still restless, and her thought and studies, would be put to a hard test. The danger of mental indigestion is not inconceivable."

In any case, it was with obvious relief that Kartini gave up her youthful dream of going to Holland. That was in January 1903. Within six months she had taken a much greater step toward Javanese conventionality: she had agreed to marry and to give up all plans for further education. What led her to this total reversal?

Once again we can only speculate, for Kartini gave no complete explanation of her feelings. It seems clear, however, that the decision not to go to Holland was only one of a series of steps reversing her original attitude toward herself and the course of her life. She probably did not "fall in love," but rather gave in to her father's urgent desire that she marry. The engagement was arranged in the traditional manner by her father, with the suitor sending him a written proposal by a go-between, and it is quite possible that Kartini never had more than a brief acquaintance with her husband before the day of her wedding. Despite that, the match was not a bad one, and she did not need to go into the completely passive servitude that she had imagined marriage to be. Kartini's father had always been deeply sympathetic toward her aims to educate and modernize herself and her people, and must have chosen his son-in-law carefully with her happiness in mind. The Regent of Rembang,

Kartini's husband, had had some education, had even visited Holland, and was a strong proponent of progressive social policies. Kartini now had apparently concluded, as countless people had been telling her for years, that a Javanese woman could act unconventionally only if she were married, all the more so if she had the support of a husband of both advanced ideas and high status. It is likely that the same appeal to her highest ideals for doing some practical good for the Javanese people that had convinced her not to go to Holland, was now being made to persuade her to marry.

The aim of elevating herself intellectually to the highest level possible was now being set aside for a more socially conscious goal of immediate action in giving limited education to other Javanese girls. Abendanon had suggested from the first day he met Kartini three years before that she needed no further schooling to start teaching, but she was deaf to him. Then, in June, 1903, either just before or just after the arrival of the marriage proposal, she finally decided to go ahead with a school in Japara without delaying any further. Her marriage offered her then an even better opportunity, as the woman of highest prestige in the whole region of Rembang, to open up such a school there.

These decisions were not based simply on rational calculation, but on a slow shift in her sentiments as well. The strong love for her father gradually came to overshadow her other emotional commitments, bolstered by her guilt over his constant illnesses, one of which had just left him at the time she refused the Dutch scholarship, and over his obvious distress following her notoriety and the concurrent gossip. Perhaps more fundamentally, however, she had not surrendered to her father's wishes so much as come over onto his side. Where she had fought for so long against his determination that she "remain Javanese," now she wanted wholeheartedly to be a Javanese, and especially to be a Javanese woman. Her hungry acceptance of her religion had been the first unmistakable sign that she was gaining a deeper understanding of her own culture and losing her feelings of alienation from it. For her father, to be a Javanese did not mean either returning to medieval feudalism, nor remaining colonial inferiors, but holding fast to a vital central core of Javanese values while striving to modernize the more peripheral elements.

For Kartini, this meant, concretely, accepting her prescribed role as a highborn woman and using it as a lever in her continuing efforts for social progress. It also meant a shift away from a technological view of progress to a moral view, a move from the battlefield of external social and economic reforms to the internal battlefield of men's minds and hearts. For Javanese culture, more than Western, stresses the overwhelming priority of personal spiritual growth as a prerequisite for public social advances. The school that she planned to open in Rembang was to be one which aimed above all at the character development of young women, while at the same time providing them with practical vocational tuition and general education in art, literature and science. It was to be a school which was both Western and Indonesian.

The last year of her life was given over almost entirely to domestic affairs. The sicknesses of her husband and her foster children occupied most of her energies, but she was enthusiastically making plans for the school and for various projects in the promotion of Javanese arts and handicrafts, plans which were shattered by her sudden death in childbirth. Within a few months, Kartini's father, her closest ally and most stubborn antagonist, died also.

This might have marked the end of an uneventful little life, but the historical forces which were quietly at work in this provincial sector of Java continued to gather momentum. Kartini's scattered personal letters, expressive as they are, might easily have had the same submerged fate she had had. It was Abendanon who started them on their own career, for he recognized in them a vigorous weapon in his campaign for bringing education to the Indonesians. He retired from the civil service in 1905 and spent the next twenty years in Holland actively promoting the welfare of the Indonesians. He had the letters published, first in 1911, under the title "Through Darkness into Light." In the new liberal political atmosphere of Holland of the twentieth century, the book became an immediate best seller, and went through four editions before 1923. It drew immediate popular support for Abendanon's Kartini Foundation, a private organization for girls' schools in Java mainly supported by voluntary Dutch contributions. The first Kartini Schools were opened in 1916, and one of these, in Tegal, was under the direction of Kartini's younger sister Kardinah. These pioneering schools helped break down the traditional resistance to girls' education. World War II, the Revolution against the Dutch and the subsequent withdrawal of the Dutch from Indonesia meant the end of the Kartini Schools as such, but girls' vocational schools are still in existence. Of much greater importance in the light of Kartini's ideals was the tremendous expansion in the last 40 years of Indonesian education as a whole, for boys as well as girls, and the concurrent popular acceptance of co-education. Today, nearly all Javanese children go to elementary school and the schools are completely co-educational. Nearly one-third of all secondary school pupils are girls. And with the opening up of chances for professional training, the women of Indonesia have proved to be even more enterprising, persistent and successful than those of many western countries. For instance, in a recent medical school graduating class in the University of Djakarta, out of 97 new doctors there were 21 women, a proportion which compares favorably to U.S. medical school products.

Although the struggle for women's rights was an important one for Kartini, it was actually only a minor aspect of her more general concern for the rights of Indonesians as human beings against the twin enemies of paternalistic colonial exploitation and traditional Indonesian resistance to change. The letters were translated into Indonesian in 1922 and saw numerous editions after that. As early as 1911 a society of young Indonesian nationalist students in Dutch universities took up Kartini's words as guides in their own thinking about themselves and the future of their country. Although, as the nationalist movement gained forces, Kartini's specific social ideas were increasingly viewed as reactionary and out-of-date, nevertheless she remains a popular symbol as one of the earliest fighters for freedom. Today her picture is on many schoolroom walls, and her birthday is a national holiday.

In the years after Kartini's death, with the increased educational and occupational opportunities, the whole situation of the Indonesian intellectuals changed. Had Kartini lived she would not have remained long isolated and impotent, fighting a lonely battle with herself, but would soon have found herself part of a group of men and women which was rapidly growing in both numbers and power. It was a much more diverse group too, for Western education was no longer limited to the Javanese aristocracy but was being extended to members of the merchant, and ultimately, peasant classes, and to other Indonesian cultural groups than the Javanese.

Nevertheless, despite the fact that the educated Indonesian

today is no longer alone, he must still resolve for himself many of the same psychic and moral dilemmas that beset Kartini. The political aspects of her fight for human dignity are radically different since the achievement of Indonesian independence, yet every thoughtful Indonesian still faces, and must reconcile, the contradictions between the Western view of life and his own. This dilemma is urgent and it has deep personal implications along with its public, ideological or philosophical implications. For each individual who steps into the cultural no-man's-land between the secure, but constricted and often unsatisfying traditions of his ancestors, and the intoxicating, but perhaps indigestible promises of modern Western culture, must find his own way out again. At stake is his self-esteem, which in turn rests on his reaching a stable solution to the problem of his cultural identity.

The confrontation between Western and Eastern cultures is a continuous, unending process of great difficulty and momentous significance. It is all the more painful because neither the Western nor the Oriental outlooks are single, consistent philosophies—both comprise within themselves conflicting, even warring, points of view. Within both Dutch and Javanese cultures there are numerous alternative moral doctrines. Kartini repeatedly swung back and forth between identifying herself with the Dutch liberal humanistic ethic as represented by Abendanon, with the radical socialistic ideas of van Kol and Stella, with the cultivated noblesse oblige of her father as a Javanese aristocrat, and with the mystical spiritualism of her mother. At the same time that she felt attracted to each one, she also felt revulsion—at the derogation she received from the Dutch who saw her as "only a Javanese," at the crassness and uncouthness of so many Dutch people she met which jarred against the highly cultivated courtesy of the Javanese, at the willful ignorance of her tradition-bound oldest brother, who in turn saw her as "only a woman," and at the poverty and illness of the Javanese peasants who depended on prayer and spirit-offerings to improve their conditions of life.

Few young people, of any period or place, escape a time of uncertain groping for guidelines to their life, a time of choice between conflicting moral purposes, a time of progressive compromise between abstract ideals and pragmatic realities. For each individual is usually poignantly aware that the choices he makes at the outset of adulthood will determine the course of the rest of his

life. The personal conflict is all the more intense when there is
a meeting between a traditional culture and that highly peculiar
brand of Western culture, the commitment to liberal social en-
gineering that reached its fullest bloom at the end of the nineteenth
century but continues in many forms today. Its energetic and
optimistic promises, that the entire social world is evolving toward
a higher level of civilization, and that every rational and ethical
individual is capable of knowing and fighting for this nearly inevitable and certainly good historical movement, leave an indelible
imprint on all who are touched by them—but an imprint that
takes many shapes. Every encounter with this ethic has its own
unique characteristics according to the personality, social position
and cultural constitution of the one undergoing it. Complete
capitulation, the adoption of a fully Western identity is difficult
and usually unsatisfactory, as is also total rejection of the proffered
philosophy. Kartini, as do most of those who dare this hazardous
trip, tried to find a middle road, one which was the most valid
for herself. Her letters provide—for modern Javanese, Indonesians,
non-Westerners and Westerners alike—a moving human account
of one person's courageous search for her self, for a viable, pur-
poseful life.

HILDRED GEERTZ

Chicago, Illinois
July 1, 1963

BIBLIOGRAPHICAL NOTE

Much of the detail on Kartini's life comes from H. Bouman, *Meer Licht Over Kartini* (More Light on Kartini), H. J. Paris: Amsterdam, 1954. In attempting to assess Kartini's role in the Indonesian nationalist movement, Bouman collected a good deal of significant and hitherto unpublished material about her. Another source is Armijn Pane, "Kata Pembimbing" (Preface) to *Habis Gelap Terbitlah Terang* (After Darkness Comes the Light), the Indonesian translation of Kartini's letters, Balai Pustaka: Djakarta, 1951. Pane's essay, despite its inaccuracies, gives a graceful and honest picture of Kartini and her background, and a penetrating interpretation of the meaning of her life for Indonesians. Another indispensible reference is the *Encyclopaedie van Nederlandsch-Indie,* especially the articles on "Kartini," "Abendanon," and "Japara," Martinus Nijhoff and E. J. Brill: The Hague and Leiden, 1917–1939. Further information on women's movements in Indonesia can be had from Cora Vreede-de Stuers, *The Indonesian Woman: Struggles and Achievements,* Mouton and Co.: The Hague, 1960.

Letters of a Javanese Princess

1 · TO STELLA ZEEHANDELAAR

Japara, May 25, 1899

I have been longing to make the acquaintance of a "modern girl," that proud, independent girl who has all my sympathy! She who, happy and self-reliant, lightly and alertly steps on her way through life, full of enthusiasm and warm feeling; working not only for her own well-being and happiness, but for the greater good of humanity as a whole.

I glow with enthusiasm toward the new time which has come, and can truly say that in my thoughts and sympathies I do not belong to the Indian [1] world, but to that of my pale sisters who are struggling forward in the distant West.

If the laws of my land permitted it, there is nothing that I had rather do than give myself wholly to the working and striving of the new woman in Europe; but age-long traditions that cannot be broken hold us fast cloistered in their unyielding arms. Some day those arms will loosen and let us go, but that time lies as yet far from us, infinitely far. It will come, that I know; it may be three, four generations after us. Oh, you do not know what it is to love this young, this new age with heart and soul, and yet to be bound hand and foot, chained by all the laws, customs, and conventions of one's land. All our institutions are directly opposed to the progress for which I so long for the sake of our people. Day and night I wonder by what means our ancient traditions could be overcome. For myself, I could find a way to shake them off, to break them, were it not that another bond, stronger than any age-old tradition could ever be, binds me to my world; and that is the love which I bear for those to whom I owe my life, and whom I must thank for everything. Have I the right to break the hearts of those who have given me nothing but love and kindness my whole life long, and who have surrounded me with the tenderest care?

But it was not the voices alone which reached me from that

1. Until 1949, at the time of independence from the Dutch, Indonesia was known as the Netherlands East Indies, Dutch India, Netherlands India, and often simply India; there were many variations and Kartini's references to India, the Indian world and Indian people refer to the multi-island nation and people of Indonesia.

distant, that bright, that newborn Europe, which made me long for a change in existing conditions. Even in my childhood, the word "emancipation" enchanted my ears; it had a significance that nothing else had, a meaning that was far beyond my comprehension, and awakened in me an ever growing longing for freedom and independence—a longing to stand alone. Conditions both in my own surroundings and in those of others around me broke my heart, and made me long with a nameless sorrow for the awakening of my country.

Then the voices which penetrated from distant lands grew clearer and clearer, till they reached me, and to the satisfaction of some who loved me, but to the deep grief of others, brought seed which entered my heart, took root, and grew strong and vigorous.

And now I must tell you something of myself so that you can make my acquaintance.

I am the eldest of the three unmarried daughters of the Regent of Japara, and have six brothers and sisters. What a world, eh? My grandfather, Pangeran Ario Tjondronegoro of Demak, was a great leader in the progressive movement of his day, and the first regent of middle Java to unlatch his door to that guest from over the Sea—Western civilization. All of his children had European educations; all of them have, or had (several of them are now dead), a love of progress inherited from their father; and these gave to their children the same upbringing which they themselves had received. Many of my cousins and all my older brothers have gone through the Hoogere-Burger School—the highest institution of learning that we have here in India; and the youngest of my three older brothers has been studying for three years in the Netherlands, and two others are in the service of that country. We girls, so far as education goes, fettered by our ancient traditions and conventions, have profited but little by these advantages. It was a great crime against the customs of our land that we should be taught at all, and especially that we should leave the house every day to go to school. For the custom of our country forbade girls in the strongest manner ever to go outside of the house. We were never allowed to go anywhere, however, save to the school, and the only place of instruction of which our city could boast, which was open to us, was a free grammar school for Europeans.

When I reached the age of twelve, I was kept at home—I had to go into the "box." I was locked up, and cut off from all communication with the outside world, toward which I might never turn again save at the side of a bridegroom, a stranger, an unknown man whom my parents would choose for me, and to whom I should be betrothed without my own knowledge. European friends —this I heard later—had tried in every possible way to dissuade my parents from this cruel course toward me, a young and life-loving child; but they were able to do nothing. My parents were inexorable; I went into my prison. Four long years I spent between thick walls, without once seeing the outside world.

How I passed through that time, I do not know. I only know that it was terrible. But there was one great happiness left me: the reading of Dutch books and correspondence with Dutch friends was not forbidden. This—the only gleam of light in that empty, somber time, was my all, without which, I should have fallen, perhaps, into a still more pitiable state. My life, my soul even, would have been starved. But then came my friend and my deliverer—the Spirit of the Age; his footsteps echoed everywhere. Proud, solid ancient structures tottered to their foundation at his approach. Strongly barricaded doors sprang open, some as of themselves, others only painfully half way, but nevertheless they opened, and let in the unwelcome guest.

At last in my sixteenth year, I saw the outside world again. Thank God! Thank God! I could leave my prison as a free human being and not chained to an unwelcome bridegroom. Then events followed quickly that gave back to us girls more and more of our lost freedom.

In the following year, at the time of the investiture of our young Princess,[2] our parents presented us "officially" with our freedom. For the first time in our lives we were allowed to leave our native town, and to go to the city where the festivities were held in honor of the occasion. What a great and priceless victory it was! That young girls of our position should show themselves in public was here an unheard-of occurrence. The "world" stood aghast; tongues were set wagging at the unprecedented crime. Our European friends rejoiced, and as for ourselves, no queen was so rich as we. But I am far from satisfied. I would go still further, always further. I do not desire to go out to feasts, and little frivolous amusements. That has never been the cause of my longing for freedom. I long to be free, to be able to stand alone, to study, not

2. Queen Wilhelmina of the Netherlands.

to be subject to any one, and, above all, *never, never* to be obliged to marry.

But we *must* marry, must, must. Not to marry is the greatest sin which the Moslem woman can commit; it is the greatest disgrace which a native girl can bring to her family.

And marriage among us—miserable is too feeble an expression for it. How can it be otherwise, when the laws have made everything for the man and nothing for the woman? When law and convention both are for the man; when everything is allowed to him?

Love! what do we know here of love? How can we love a man whom we have never known? And how could he love us? That in itself would not be possible. Young girls and men must be kept rigidly apart, and are never allowed to meet.

.   .   .   .

I am anxious to know of your occupations. It is all very interesting to me. I wish to know about your studies, I would know something of your Toynbee evenings, and of the society for total abstinence of which you are so zealous a member.

Among our Indian people, we have not the drink demon to fight, thank God!—but I fear, I fear that when once—forgive me—your Western civilization shall have obtained a foothold among us, we shall have that evil to contend with too. Civilization is a blessing, but it has its dark side as well. The tendency to imitate is inborn, I believe. The masses imitate the upper classes, who in turn imitate those of higher rank, and these again follow the Europeans.

Among us there is no marriage feast without drinking. And at the festivals of the natives, where they are not of strong religious convictions, (and usually they are Moslem only because their fathers, grandfathers and remote ancestors were Moslem—in reality, they are little better than heathen), large square bottles are always kept standing, and they are not sparing in the use of these.

But an evil greater than alcohol is here and that is opium. Oh! the misery, the inexpressible horror it has brought to my country! Opium is the pest of Java. Yes, opium is far worse than the pest. The pest does not remain for ever; sooner or later, it goes away, but the evil of opium, once established, grows. It spreads more and more, and will never leave us, never grow less—for to speak plainly—it is protected by the Government! The more general the use of opium in Java, the fuller the treasury.[3]

The opium tax is one of the richest sources of income of the Government—what matter if it go well or ill with the people?—the Government prospers. This curse of the people fills the treasury of the Dutch East Indian Government with thousands—nay, with millions. Many say that the use of opium is no evil, but those who say that have never known India, or else they are blind.

What are our daily murders, incendiary fires, robberies, but the direct result of the use of opium? True, the desire for opium is not so great an evil as long as one can get it—when one has money to buy the poison; but when one cannot obtain it—when one has no money with which to buy it, and is a confirmed user of it? Then one is dangerous, then one is lost. Hunger will make a man a thief, but the hunger for opium will make him a murderer. There is a saying here—"At first you eat opium, but in the end it will devour you."

It is terrible to see so much evil and to be powerless to fight against it.

That splendid book by Mevrouw Goekoop I know. I have read it three times. I could never grow tired of it. What would I not give to be able to live in Hilda's environment. Oh, that we in India had gone so far, that a book could cause such violent controversy among us, as *Hilda van Suylenburg* has in your country. I shall never rest till *H. v. S.* appears in my own language to do good as well as harm to our Indian world. It is a matter of indifference whether good or harm, if it but makes an impression, for that shows that one is no longer sleeping, and Java is still in deep slumber. And how will her people ever be awakened, when those who should serve as examples, themselves love sleep so much. The greater number of European women in India care little or nothing for the work of their sisters in the fatherland.

Will you not tell me something of the labors, the struggles, the sentiments, of the woman of today in the Netherlands? We take deep interest in all that concerns the Woman's Movement.

I do not know the modern languages. Alas! We girls are not allowed by our law to learn languages; it was a great innovation for us to learn Dutch. I long to know languages, not so much to be able to speak them, as for the far greater joy of being able

3. Opium addiction has been almost entirely eradicated in Indonesia today.

to read the many beautiful works of foreign authors in their own tongue. Is it not true that never mind how good a translation may be, it is never so fine as the original? That is always stronger—more charming.

We have much time for reading, and reading is our greatest pleasure—we, that is, the younger sisters and I. We three have had the same bringing up, and are much with one another. We differ in age, each from the other, by but one year. Among us three there is the greatest harmony. Naturally we sometimes have little differences of opinion, but that does not weaken the tie that binds us together. Our little quarrels are splendid, I find them so: I love the reconciliations which follow. It is the greatest of all lies—do you not think so too?—that any two human beings can think alike in everything. That cannot be; people who say that must be hypocrites.

I have not yet told you how old I am. I was just twenty last month. Strange, that when I was sixteen I felt so frightfully old, and had so many melancholy moods! Now that I can put two crosses behind me, I feel young and full of the joy of life, and the struggle of life, too.

Call me simply Kartini; that is my name. We Javanese have no family names. Kartini is my given name and my family name, both at the same time. As far as "Raden Adjeng" is concerned, those two words are the title. I told Mevrouw van Wermeskerken, when I gave her my address, not to put Kartini alone—that would hardly reach me from Holland, and as for writing *Mejuffrouw,*[4] or something of that kind, I have no right to it; I am only a Javanese.

Now, for the present, you know enough about me—is it not so? Another time I shall tell you of our Indian life.

If there is any light that you would like thrown upon any of our Indian affairs, please ask me. I am ready to tell you all that I know about my country and my people.

4. *Mejuffrouw* is the Dutch equivalent of "Miss."

August 18, 1899

Sincere thanks for your long letter, your cordial words warmed my heart. Shall I not disappoint you upon a closer acquaintance? I have already told you that I am very ignorant, that I know nothing. Compared to you I feel myself sink into nothingness.

You are well informed about the Javanese titles. Before you mentioned it, I had never given the matter a thought, that I am, as you say, "highly born." Am I a princess? No more than you yourself are one. The last prince of our house, from whom I am directly descended in the male line, was, I believe, twenty-five generations back, but Mamma is closely related to the princely house of Madura. Her great-grandfather was a reigning prince, and her grandmother a princess. But we do not give a two-pence for all that. To my mind there are only two kinds of aristocracy, the aristocracy of the mind, and the aristocracy of the soul—of those who are noble in spirit. I think there is nothing more commonplace than those people who allow themselves to depend upon their so called "high birth." What worth is there in simply being a count or baron? I cannot see it with my little understanding.

Adel and *Edel*,[1] twin words with almost the same sound and which should have the same meaning. Poor twins! How cruel life has been to you—it has ruthlessly torn you asunder and holds you now so far apart. Once noble meant what the word signifies. Yes, then indeed it would have been an honor to be "highly born." But now?—

I remember how embarrassed we were last year, when the ladies of the Exposition for Woman's Work called us the "Princesses of Java."

In Holland they seem to think that everything which comes out of India which is not a *babu* or a *spada*[2] must be a prince or

1. Dutch words meaning noble in the sense of "royal descent" and noble in the sense of "moral excellence."

2. *Babu* means maid or servant in Malay; *spada* is apparently a derogatory term for a native. A rough rule for the pronunciation of Javanese and Indonesian words is to give equal stress to all syllables, pronounce all vowels as in Italian or Spanish, and all consonants as in English, with

a princess. Europeans here in India seldom call us "Raden Adjeng," they address us usually as "freule." [3] I despair of its ever being different. I do not know how many times I have said that we were not "freules" and still less princesses, but they have grown accustomed to the glamour and still obstinately call us "freule."

Not long ago a European who had heard much of us, came here and asked our parents to be allowed the privilege of making the acquaintance of the "princesses"; we were brought out and shown to him as though we had been dolls; how stupid we felt!

"Regent," said he to our father, but quite distinctly before us—there was much disappointment in his voice—"at the word—princess, I thought of glittering garments, fantastic Oriental splendour, and your daughters look so simple."

We could hardly suppress a smile when we heard him. Good heavens! In his innocence he had paid us the greatest possible compliment; you do not know what a pleasure it was to us to find that our clothes were simple; we had so often taken pains to put on nothing that would look conspicuous or bizarre.

Dear Stella, I am heartily glad that I seem to you like your Dutch friends, and that you find me congenial.

I have always been an enemy of formality. I am happy only when I can throw the burden of Javanese etiquette from my shoulders. The ceremonies, the little rules, that are instilled into our people are an abomination to me. You could hardly imagine how heavily the burden of etiquette presses upon a Javanese aristocratic household. But in our household, we do not take all the formalities so literally.

We often dispense with ceremony and speak our own sentiments freely. Javanese etiquette is both silly and terrible. Europeans who live years in India, and who come in close contact with our native dignitaries, cannot at all understand it unless they have made a special study of it.

In order to give you a faint idea of the oppressiveness of our etiquette, I shall mention a few examples. A younger brother or sister of mine may not pass me without bowing down to the

the following exceptions: "oe" is pronounced "oo" as in "soon"; "j" is pronounced as "y" except in certain proper nouns such as "Java" and "Japara" where it is pronounced "j" as in "jar"; "dj" is pronounced "j" as in "jar"; "tj" is pronounced "ch" as in "chair."

3. *Freule* is the honorary title given to daughters of Dutch noblemen.

ground and creeping upon hands and knees. If a little sister is sitting on a chair, she must instantly slip to the ground and remain with head bowed until I have passed from her sight. If a younger brother or sister wishes to speak to me, it must only be in high Javanese; [4] and after each sentence that comes from their lips, they must make a *sembah*; that is, to put both hands together, and bring the thumbs under the nose.

If my brothers and sisters speak to other people about me, they must always use high Javanese in every sentence concerning me, my clothes, my seat at the table, my hands and my feet, and everything that is mine. They are forbidden to touch my honorable head without my high permission, and they may not do it even then without first making a sembah.

If food stands on the table, they must not touch the tiniest morsel till it has pleased me to partake of that which I would (as much as I desire). Should you speak against your superiors, do it softly, so that only those who are near may hear. Oh, yes; one even trembles by rule in a noble Javanese household. When a young lady laughs, she must not open her mouth. (For heaven's sake! I hear you exclaim). Yes, dear Stella, you shall hear stranger things than these, if you wish to know everything about us Javanese.

If a girl runs, she must do it decorously, with little mincing steps and oh, so slowly, like a snail. To run just a little fast is to be a hoyden.

Toward my older brothers and sisters I show every respect, and observe all forms scrupulously. I do not wish to deny the good

4. The Javanese language consists of several distinct "levels," that is, sets of vocabulary which are quite different from one another. The level spoken depends on the social status of the person addressed, i.e., whether he is of nobler blood, higher education, older, or of higher office than the speaker. Much the same principles apply as those for the use of "Du" and "Sie" in German or "Tu" and "Vous" in French, but the number of words that change with each level is so great that they sound like different languages. "High" Javanese is used to address one's superiors, and "low" Javanese is spoken by them in return. There are a number of "middle" levels of Javanese, for various intermediate social situations, as well as one "middle" Javanese spoken mainly by peasants and traders in polite contexts. There is also a "very-high" level of the language which is heard only in the royal court. It is impossible to speak Javanese correctly without knowing exactly how much higher or lower in status than the speaker is the person being addressed.

right of any one, but the younger ones, beginning with me, are doing away with all ceremony. Freedom, equality, and fraternity! For my little brothers and sisters, toward me, and toward each other, are like free, equal comrades. Between us, there is no stiffness—there is only friendship and hearty affection. The sisters say "thee" and "thou" to me, and we speak the same language. At first people smiled in amazement at the free, untrammeled relationship between us brothers and sisters of unequal ages. We were called children without any bringing up, and I was a "*kuda koré*" [5] because I seldom walked sedately but went skipping along. And they were further horrified because I often laughed aloud! and allowed my teeth to show. But now that they see how affectionate and sweet the relationship is between us, and that only the burdensome etiquette has taken flight before our freedom, they admire the harmonious union which binds us so closely together.

Thank you, dear Stella, for your charming compliment: I am as pleased as a child. There is no danger of spoiling me by praise, or I should long ago have been spoiled to death, both at home and by my friends and acquaintances.

I thank you so much for the friendly thoughts which you have for us Javanese. From you I did not expect anything else, but knew that you would have the same feeling for all people, white or brown. From those who are truly civilized and enlightened we have never experienced anything but kindness. Even if a Javanese were ever so stupid, unlettered, uncivilized, the power which governs him should see in him a fellow man, one whom God has created too, one who has a heart in his body and a soul full of sensitive feeling, although his countenance may remain immovable, and not a glance betray his inward emotion.

At home, we speak Javanese with one another; Dutch only with Hollanders, although now and then we use a little Dutch expression which has a shade of meaning that cannot be translated, often to express some little humorous point.

5. Wild colt.

3 · TO STELLA ZEEHANDELAAR

November 6, 1899

Certainly, Stella, I cannot thank my parents enough for the free bringing up which they have given me. I had rather have my whole life one of strife and sorrow than be without the knowledge which I owe to my European education. I know that many, many difficulties await me, but I am not afraid of the future. I cannot remain content in my old condition; yet to further the new progress I can do nothing: a dozen strong chains bind me fast to my world. What will be the outcome? All my European friends ask themselves this question. If I knew myself, dear people, I should tell you with pleasure. All can see that the situation is critical for us; and then they say that it was a mistake for my father to give me the little education which I have had. No! No! Not on my dearest father lies the blame. No, and again no! Father could not foresee that the same bringing up which he gave to all of his children would have had such an effect upon one of them. Many other regents had given to their families the same advantages that we have had, and it has never resulted in anything but in native young ladies with European manners, who speak Dutch.

There is no help for it. Some day or other it will come to pass, must come to pass, that I shall have to follow an unknown bridegroom. Love is a will o' the wisp in our Javanese world! How can a man and woman love each other when they see each other for the first time in their lives after they are already fast bound in the chains of wedlock?

I shall never, never fall in love. To love, there must first be respect, according to my thinking; and I can have no respect for the Javanese young man. How can I respect one who is married and a father, and who, when he has had enough of the mother of his children, brings another woman into his house, and is, according to the Moslem law, legally married to her? And who does not do this? And why not? It is no sin, and still less a scandal. The Moslem law allows a man to have four wives at the same time. And though it be a thousand times over no sin according to the Moslem law and doctrine, I shall forever call it a sin. I call all things sin which bring misery to a fellow creature. Sin is to cause pain to another, whether man or beast. And can you imagine what hell-pain a woman must suffer when her husband comes home with another—a rival—whom she must recognize as his legal wife? He can torture her to death, mistreat her as he will; if he does not choose to give her back her freedom, then she can whistle to the moon for her rights. Everything for the man, and nothing for the woman, is our law and custom.

Do you understand now the deep aversion I have for marriage? I would do the humblest work, thankfully and joyfully, if by it I could be independent.

But I can do nothing, less than nothing, on account of Father's position among our people. If I choose to work, it would have to be at something fitting! It is only work for pleasure which would not be a disgrace to my noble and highly placed family— a chain of regents from Java's eastern coast to the middle. Why did God give us talents and not the opportunity to make use of them? My two sisters have studied drawing and painting, and without any instruction, have made fair progress, according to those who know. They would gladly go on with their studies. But here in Java, there is no opportunity, and we cannot go to Europe. To go there we should have to have the consent of his Excellency, the Minister of Finance, and that we have not. We must depend entirely upon ourselves, if we wish to go forward.

O Stella, do you know what it is to long for something intensely and yet to feel powerless to obtain it? Could Father have done so, I do not doubt he would have sent us without hesitation to your cold and distant land.

I draw and paint too, but take much more pleasure in the pen than in the pencil. Do you understand now why I am so anxious to obtain the mastery of your beautiful language? Nay, do not contradict me. I construct it after a fashion, but I understand my limitations all too well. If I could learn the Dutch language thoroughly, my future would be assured. A rich field of labor would then lie open to me, and I should be a true child of humanity. For, you see, I, as a born Javanese, know all about the Indian world. A European, no matter how long he may have lived in Java and studied existing conditions, can still know nothing of the inner native life. Much that is obscure now and a riddle to Europeans, I could make clear with a few words.

I feel my powerlessness all too well, Stella. You would burst out laughing if you could look over my shoulder and read this little sheet of paper. What a crazy idea of mine, is it not? That I who know nothing, have learned nothing, should wish to venture upon a literary career? Still though every one else should laugh at me, I know that you will not—I will not think that for a moment. It is indeed a desperate undertaking, but "he who does not dare, does not win," is my motto. Forward! Dare mightily and with strength. Three-fourths of the world belongs to the strong.

You ask me how I came to be placed between four thick walls. You certainly thought of a cell or something of that kind. No, Stella, my prison was a large house, with grounds around it. But around those grounds there was a high wall and that held me a prisoner. Never mind how splendid a house and garden may be if one may never go beyond them, it is stifling. I remember how often in dumb despair, I would press my body against the fast closed gate and the cold stones. Whatever direction I took, at the end of every walk there was always a stone wall, or a locked door.

Of late Mevrouw Ovink often says to me, "Child, child, have we done well to let you come forth from the high walls of the *kabupaten?* [1] Would it not have been better if we had let you remain there? What will come of it now? What of the future?"

And when she sees us drawing and painting she cries full of distress: "Dear children, is there nothing else for you but this?" No, the only fortunate thing, the best thing that could have happened to us, is that we three were thrust out into the light. Luckily, I am optimistic by nature, and do not quickly let my head hang. If I cannot become what I so much desire to be, then I would rather be something, if only a kitchen maid. You will think now, that I am a "genius" in cooking. My family and friends need not worry about my future, do you not agree with me? For a good kitchen maid is always in demand, and can always get along.

The official salaries in Holland seem small compared with those in India. Yet they are always complaining here, about the small salaries. In India too one is entitled to a pension after twenty years' service, and the clergy after only ten years. India is an El Dorado for the officials, and yet many Hollanders speak of it as a "horrible ape-land." I get so infernally mad when I hear them

1. *Kabupaten,* a Regent's residence.

speak of "horrible India." They forget all too often that this "horrible ape-land" fills many empty pockets with gold.

A change will come in our whole native world—the turning point is foreordained; it is coming. But when will it be? That is the great question. We cannot hasten the hour of revolution. For it is only we who have rebellious thoughts in this wilderness, this dark distant land, beyond which there is no land. My friends here say that we shall act wisely if we do nothing but sleep for a hundred years. When we awakened, Java would be more as we would have her.

Work among the People of India I know. Mevrouw Van Zuylen-Tromp sent Father the book, hoping to arouse his interest. But he would rather interest himself in a book about the native woman; I had thought of that myself. I have much to tell about Javanese women, but I am still too young, and have had so little, so pitifully little, experience with life. The cause for which I would speak is to me too earnest and too sacred to be approached lightly. I cannot write now as I wish, but I know that when I have suffered more it will be different. After a few years I shall have had a more comprehending insight into much that I would know and many thoughts that now run darkly through my brain will have grown clear.

I cannot tell you anything of the Islamic law, Stella. Its followers are forbidden to speak of it with those of another faith. And, in truth, I am a Moslem only because my ancestors were. How can I love a doctrine which I do not know—may never know? The Koran is too holy to be translated into any language whatever. Here no one speaks Arabic. It is customary to read from the Koran; but what is read no one understands! To me it is a silly thing to be obliged to read something without being able to understand it. It is as though I were compelled to read an English book, and the whole thing should go through my head without my being able to comprehend the meaning of a single word. If I wished to know and understand our religion, I should have to go to Arabia to learn the language. Nevertheless, one can be good without being pious. Is that not true, Stella?

Religion is intended as a blessing to mankind—a bond between all the creatures of God. They should be as brothers and sisters, not because they have the same human parents, but because they are all children of one Father, of Him who is enthroned in the heavens above. Brothers and sisters must love one another, help, strengthen and support one another. O God! sometimes I wish that there had never been a religion, because that which should unite mankind into one common brotherhood has been through all the ages a cause of strife, of discord, and of bloodshed. Members of the same family have persecuted one another because of the different manner in which they worshipped one and the same God. Those who ought to have been bound together by the tenderest love have turned with hatred from one another. Differences of Church, albeit in each the same word, God, is spoken, have built a dividing wall between two throbbing hearts. I often ask myself uneasily: is religion indeed a blessing to mankind? Religion, which is meant to save us from our sins, how many sins are committed in thy name?

I have read *Max Havelaar*,[2] though I do not know "Wijs mij de plaats waar ik gezaaid heb!" [3] I shall look for it for I think much, very much, of Multatuli.

I will tell you another time of the position of the people, and of the ruling classes among us. I have written too much already, and that is a subject which demands no small space.

What do we speak at home? What a question, Stella, dear. Naturally, our language is Javanese. We speak Malay with strange people who are Easterners, either Malays, Moors, Arabs, or Chinese, and Dutch with Europeans.

O Stella, how I laughed when I read your question: "Would your parents disapprove if you should embrace them heartily?" Why, I have yet to give my parents, or my brothers and sisters, the first kiss! Kissing is not customary among the Javanese. Only children of from one to three, four, five, or six are kissed. We never kiss one another. You are astonished at that! But it is true. Only our young Holland friends kiss us, and we kiss them back; that has only been recently.

At first we loved to have them kiss us, but never kissed them in return. We have only learned to kiss since we have been such friends with Mevrouw Ovink. When she would embrace us, she would ask us to kiss her. At first we found it queer, and acquitted

2. *Max Havelaar*, by Multatuli (pseudonym for E. Douwes-Dekker), a novel, first published in Amsterdam in 1860, which protested against Dutch commercial exploitation of the Indonesians.
3. "Show me the place where I have sown."

ourselves awkwardly. Does this seem strange to you? No matter how much I should love one of my Dutch friends, it would never come into my head to kiss her without being asked. You ask why? Because I do not know whether she would like it. It is pleasant for us to press a soft white cheek with our lips, but whether the possessor of that pretty cheek also finds it pleasant to feel a dark face against hers, is another question. We had rather let people think us heartless, for of our own accord we would never embrace.

If as you say I am in no way behind many Dutch girls, it is principally the work of Mevrouw Ovink, who used to talk to us as though we were her own sisters. Intercourse with this cultured, well-bred Dutch lady had a great influence upon the little brown girls. And now *Moesje*[4] knows very well that though time and distance separate them, the hearts of her daughters will always belong to her. Father had promised us—in reality, Mevrouw Ovink made him give his word of honor—to let us go to Djombang. Mijnheer Ovink will take us there by and by. We love them so much, have so much love for our "Father" and "Mother." We miss them sadly. I cannot even now realize that they are actually gone from us. There was so little restraint between us. We lived all the time so cordially together.

4 · TO MEVROUW M. C. E. OVINK-SOER

November, 1899

O dearest, dearest Mevrouwtje, what a delightful Sunday we had yesterday!

Father went out with my little brother, and after awhile they came back home. Brother, with great excitement, ran to me and said, "O sister, there is a man-of-war in the harbor; all the streets are filled with sailors, and two of them have come home with us, they are with Father now."

At the word "warship," we sprang up as though we had been shot, and before brother had finished speaking, we flew to our

4. *Moesje:* Dutch affectionate term for mother, "mommy." Javanese address all persons, regardless of kinship or closeness of acquaintance by the terms for mother, father, brother, sister, and so on, so that it was natural for Kartini to address Mevrouw Ovink as "Moesje."

room to make ready. We saw two gentlemen dressed in white, come hesitating—through the grounds. After a little while, we saw them sitting with Papa in the middle gallery. Later, a boy came to us, saying that we must go to Father, which we did with the greatest willingness. One, two, three, and we had slipped on our best *kebajas*,[1] and a second later we were sitting in rocking-chairs talking to two officers from the *Edie*. I do not know how it came about, but we were immediately at our ease and spoke to the gentlemen as though we had known them for years. But how did these people happen to come to the kabupaten? I will explain that to you. Papa went, as I have said, for a little drive; he met five gentlemen walking, three of them turned another way, but these two had followed Papa's carriage in to the kabupaten. They thought (the gentlemen were new to Java) that the way the carriage took was a public road, and our house a fortress or something of the kind.

Papa sent a servant to ask the gentlemen if they wished to see him. They were embarrassed naturally, because they had made such a mistake and followed someone to his own house. What would they do now? They did not find it pleasant by any means, because they did not understand our language, and spoke only very bad, broken Malay. Papa put an end to this awkward situation by going to meet them himself, and addressing them in Dutch. Embarrassment was at an end. They would come with pleasure into the house.

It turned out that one of them was a relative of someone whom Papa knew well. I do not remember ever having felt so much at my ease with an utter stranger. I did not think once of the fact that I had never seen these people before, and had not known of their existence five minutes ago. It is strange how with sailors one feels at home right away.

Our hearts have always been set upon the sea; everything that concerns it interests us. You know well what a delight it is to us to be taken out even in a little row boat. We love the sea; you remember the time when I lay half-dead in the bow of the opium skiff, even then I found it pleasant to be upon such a bed? If I were a boy, I should not think twice, but would become a sailor at once.

Imagine to yourself Father saying to the gentlemen, "My daugh-

1. *Kebaja*: the Javanese women's blouse.

ters would be so pleased if they could be permitted to go on board."

Father knows everything that goes on in our hearts. Father does not tell us so, yet I am certain of it. Now and then Papa tells one or the other of us precisely what we have been thinking; something that we had kept to ourselves and never told to any one. It is without doubt, because Father loves us so much, and we so love him. Every now and then he discovers something, and lays it bare, that had been in the bottom of my heart, and of which I had thought no one except myself had the slightest idea. Does not that show true kinship of soul?

If I were more superstitious, I should certainly think that Papa could read thoughts.

But I am telling you now of the pleasant Sunday morning, and not of the secret telephone-cable that runs from our hearts to that of our dearest father.

The officers regretted so much that the *Edie* would not remain longer in our harbor. It would have been such a pleasure to them to have had us on board. The *Edie* must go to look for reefs on Karimun Djawa, though the commander thought Japara interesting. Both gentlemen were going to do everything in their power to persuade the Commandant to come back; for if the *Edie* set out from Surabaja on Monday, either Saturday or Sunday she could be back at Japara. If fortune should bring the *Edie* here on Saturday, then they will let us know of their presence by letting loose their fire-mouths (cannon). I have no idea that they will, but still it would be above all things pleasant if the boat should come again.

I told the gentlemen that if they passed Japara again, they must break a screw or something, near our coast, so that the ship would be obliged to lay up in our harbor for repairs.

When the officers had gone, and we were back in our room, we thought it had been a dream. And truly it was as though we had dreamed. So suddenly, so unexpectedly, had they appeared to us, and again as suddenly had they vanished. A very pleasant happening—do you not think so too? I still have to laugh whenever I think of that funny adventure.

O little Mother, dearest Mevrouwtje, I wish that you were back with us. Your daughters miss you so much. We long for the pleasant days that we spent with you to come again: the splendid times that we used to have in your dear little sitting-room, where you would read to us from great books, and where we spoke of so much, the memory of which shall always remain with us. I miss the intimate talks with you, when I used to tell my dear little mother all the rebellious thoughts that came into my head, and laid bare the feelings of my restless heart. When I was in a rebellious mood, I had but to see the love light in your face, and I was again the happy, careless child, that, in overflowing good spirits, could sing: "Whatever heaven to me shall send, I'll set my shoulders bravely under."

Mevrouwtje, you gave us too much care; spoiled us too much. Now we do nothing but wish for those happy days to come back. And although we long for you, yet we hope that the journey to Djombang will be put off as long as possible. Why? We know—we feel, that at Djombang, we shall see each other for the last time. Seeing you again will mean farewell for good. You will not come to Japara again, and we shall never be able to go to you. For that reason, let the journey be put off as long as possible. It is splendid to have a pleasure to look forward to; so we should like to prolong the feeling of anticipation. Once more the joy of meeting again, and then—all the prettiness will be over. No, it will not be over even then, the memory will be with us.

We shall still be happy as long as you think of us and love us. You know very well, dear little Mother, that love is nothing but egoism. I think there is nothing finer than to be able to call a happy smile to a loved mouth—to see the sunshine break over another's face. Nothing is more splendid than to have a pair of dear eyes look at one full of love and happiness; then it is that one feels guilty for the very joy.

How pleasant that Koki also remembers us.

5 · TO STELLA ZEEHANDELAAR

January 12, 1900

To go to Europe! Till my last breath that shall always be my ideal. If I could only make myself small enough to slip into an envelope then I would go with this letter to you, Stella, and to my dearest best brother, and near—Hush, not another word! It is not my fault, Stella, if now and then I write nonsense. The *gamelan* [1] in the *pendopo* [2] could speak to you better than I. Now it is playing a lovely air. It is like no other song—no melody, each note is so soft, so tender, so vaguely thrilling, so changing—but ah! how compelling, how bitterly beautiful: that is no tinkling of glass, of copper, of wood; it is the voices of men's souls that speak to me; now they are complaining, now sighing, and now merrily laughing. And my soul soars with the murmuring pure silver tones on high, on high, to the isles of blue light, to the fleecy clouds, and towards the shining stars—deep low tones are rising now and the music leads me through dark dales, down steep ravines, through somber woods on into dense wildernesses, and my soul shivers and trembles within me with anguish and pain and sorrow.

I have heard "Ginondjing" a dozen times, still now that the gamelan is silent I cannot recall a single note, everything is driven from my memory, the sad and lovely air is gone that made me so inexpressibly happy, and so deeply melancholy at the same time. I can never hear "Ginondjing" without deep emotion, the first chords of the splendid prelude, and I am lost. Sometimes I do not wish to listen, it is too sorrowful, yet I must hearken to the murmuring voices, which tell me of the past, and of the future. The breath of its thrilling silver strains blows away the veil which covers the secrets of what is to be, and clear as though it were today visions of the future rise to my mind. A shivering goes through me, for I see dark somber figures. I try to close my eyes, but they remain wide open, and at my feet there yawns a dizzy abyss. But I look up, and a blue heaven arches above me, and

1. The *gamelan* is the Javanese orchestra, which consists primarily of percussion instruments, bronze and wood xylophones, bronze gongs of various sizes, brass cymbals, drums, plus a stringed instrument called a *rebab*. The music is highly developed, complex and subtle. The best introduction to this sophisticated and attractive music is the record "Indonesian Music," edited by Jaap Kunst, Columbia World Library of Folk and Primitive Music, Vol. VII. See also Jaap Kunst, *The Music of Java*, Martinus Nijhoff, The Hague, 1949, and Mantle Hood, *The Nuclear Theme as a Determinant of Patet in Javanese Music*, J. B. Wolters, Groningen, 1954.

2. *Pendopo*, a large square open-sided pavilion with ornate columns supporting a high hipped roof; it is set directly in front of a traditional Javanese aristocrat's house, and serves as audience hall and as stage for orchestras, dances and shadow-plays.

golden sunbeams play with the fleecy white clouds, and in my heart it is again light.

There! Have I not convinced you what a foolish, mad creature I am? What silly thoughts, but we will not excuse ourselves to each other, Stella. Enough of that! I will now try to talk sensibly like a rational human being.

My sunny land which you so long to see, has been of late anything but sunny. There have been terrible rainstorms every day, and Sunday the Japara river rose from its banks, villages were flooded, and even the city itself was inundated by the rushing waters.

Ever since morning it has rained in torrents, and the wind has shaken our house frightfully. Outside several trees have blown down, the thick branches were broken off as though they had been match stems, and nothing remains now of the splendid *koolblanda* trees, but two cold, bare trunks. How terribly the *kampongs* [3] around must have suffered, whole roofs have been torn from the houses. Today Papa has gone out on a tour of inspection, and to succor an outlying district where many villages are under water. Papa is sore pressed in these days. First it was storm, then an earthquake, now again storm. A colossal *randu* tree was blown across a public highway, striking two passersby; they were taken from under it ground to pieces. A whole day, and a whole night we listened to the raging and the roaring of the wind. Poor Klein Scheveningen, the storm has wrought frightful havoc there. The way to the bath house is entirely covered with seething water, and the beach has disappeared, the insatiable sea has covered it. This afternoon, if it is not raining hard, I shall ask Father's permission to go and see it.

A week ago we were on Klein Scheveningen; we stood on a great rock to watch the surging of the waves. We were so intent upon the imposing spectacle that we did not see how the onrushing waters were covering our rock. Not until the children on the shore called to us affrighted did we realize that we were surrounded by a raging surf. We waded back to the children through water up to our knees.

Some time ago you asked me about the position of the "little man" [4] among us, but I had already written you so much that I

3. *Kampong*, village or neighborhood where peasants live.
4. The Javanese peasant, called in Javanese *"wong tjilik"* or "little man."

put the question aside because it could not be answered in a few words. I wished, however, to come back to it another time, and so I come to it now; I shall then have answered the whole of your last letter.

I thank God that I can answer "No" to your question as to whether the condition of our people is as sad as Multatuli has described it. No, the history of Saïdjah and Adinda [5] belongs to the past. There may be hunger sometimes among the people, but that is not the fault of their rulers. The rulers cannot be held responsible for the long droughts when the "little man" needs rain so much for his fields, nor can they be blamed for the floods that the clouds send to destroy the harvest. And when the rice harvest fails, whether it be through a plague of insects, or through floods, or through the misfortunes which the long continued "east wind" brings, then all the people who suffer from these calamities have their taxes remitted by the Government, and in time of famine, money and food are doled out to them. If the fields are over-run by a plague of mice, the Government offers rewards for the destruction of the pest. If the "west wind," as now, causes the rising of the waters in the rivers, and the dikes break, the rulers do all that is possible to mitigate the distress. [6]

Last year a fishing village lay for a whole week under water; day and night Father remained at the scene of the disaster. Out of special funds that were at the disposal of the Government, the breaks in the dikes were restored for some kilometers. But who was to give back to the people what the water had taken away from them? And what of the fish in the rivers destroyed by the floods?

Then you have Demak in my uncle's jurisdiction; that country could never be brought to a condition of prosperity, whatever one might do. From one remote valley to the other the east wind dries up the rivers, and then the west wind drowns the land with water. The Government has spent tons of gold to give water to the land in the dry season, and also in building heavy barriers against floods

5. Characters in *Max Havelaar* by Multatuli.
6. The climate in Java is tropical and monsoonal. The temperature hovers constantly around 80° F., and the only seasonal variation is the amount of rainfall. From October to May the prevailing wind or monsoon is from the west, bringing with it heavy rainfall. From about May to September the prevailing wind is from the east and there is little or no rainfall. For a study of the cultural geography of modern Java see E. H. G. Dobby, *Southeast Asia*, University of London Press, London, 1950.

in the wet season, but so far without result. Splendid canals have been dug, which have provided work for thousands, it is true, but they appear to be of little practical value. During the east winds the land perishes with thirst, and during the west winds everything floats upon the water. The Government cares much for the well-being of the people of Java, but alas it allows them to be burdened by heavy taxes, under the load of which they can move but slowly.

No, Stella, the people are no longer willfully plundered by their rulers. And if this should happen but a single time, the guilty one would be deprived of his office, be degraded. But an evil that does exist, is the taking of bribes, that even I think as wrong and shameful as the forcible taking of goods belonging to the "little man" as in *Max Havelaar*. But perhaps I would not judge this so harshly, if I considered the circumstances. At first the natives thought that the offering of gifts to their superiors was a mark of respect—a declaration of homage. The taking of presents is forbidden to the officials by the government, but many native officials are so ill-paid that it is a wonder how they can get along at all on their meagre salaries. A district clerk who all day long writes his back crooked, earns at the end of the month, the incredibly large sum of 25 florins. On that he and his family must live, and pay house rent; he must dress himself neatly, and also keep up his prestige over the lesser officials. Do not judge them harshly, but rather pity these grown-up children, for that is what my fellow-countrymen are for the most part. If a district clerk is offered something, perhaps a bunch of bananas, he may refuse it the first time, the second time he may also refuse it, but the third time he accepts it reluctantly, and the fourth time the present is taken without hesitation. What I am doing is no harm, he thinks, I have never asked for it, and yet it was given me; I should be an idiot to hesitate when it is the custom. The giving of presents is not only a token of respect, but also a safeguard against some possible misfortune, when the "little man" might need the protection of the one in authority. If he should be called to account by the *wedono* for some little fault or other, then he can count upon the support of his friend, the district clerk.[7] The native government

7. At the end of the nineteenth century, the government of Java consisted of an appointive civil service, which had roughly parallel positions for Dutch and Indonesians. That is, for every Indonesian official of any importance there was a corresponding Dutch official to oversee his work and

officials are poorly paid. An assistant wedono of the second class earns 85 florins. Out of this he must pay a secretary (assistant wedonos are furnished no secretaries by the Government, although they have as much need of written work as wedonos, *djaksas* and others). They must keep a little carriage and a horse, and even a riding horse for journeys into the country; they must buy a house, furniture, etc. They have the expense of keeping up the house and, in addition, the entertainment of the *controleur*, the regent, and sometimes also the assistant resident when they come on tours of inspection (for the assistant wedono lives far from the capital). On these occasions the gentlemen lodge in the *pasangrahan*,[8] and to the assistant wedono falls the high honor of setting the food before their noble mouths. There must be cigars, *air blanda*,[9] wines, delicacies for the table, and these, I assure you, are for an under district chief no inconsiderable expense. It would not be meet to set before his honorable guests only the things which he has at hand; so all these table luxuries must be sent for to the city. It is not a law, but the host considers it his duty to set before the grand gentlemen the best of what he has, and has not. In Father's jurisdiction this does not occur, thank God. When Father goes upon a tour of inspection and must stay several days he always takes his own provisions with him. The controleur too does this, and also the assistant resident, and no native official is ruined by the single cup of tea which he offers them.

If there is a murder or a robbery in the under district, the assistant wedono must naturally clear up the matter; it is his duty. And make any decisions of importance to Dutch interests. At the lowest governmental level there were the villages with local men appointed from above as headmen. A set of villages were under the jurisdiction of a Javanese assistant *wedono* and, at his side, a Dutch official called an aspirant. A set of assistant wedonos were under the direction of a Javanese wedono, guided by a Dutch official called a *controleur*. A set of wedonos were in turn under the supervision of a single Javanese regent, who was advised by a Dutch assistant resident. Kartini's father was such a regent. There were no Indonesian officials in positions higher than he. Most kinds of peasant legal cases were brought for judgment before the assistant wedono or the wedono, rather than to a separate court. The term "district clerk" in the text refers to the office assistant of a wedono, and the term *djaksa* to his legal advisor. For a full description of the Dutch colonial administration and economy, see J. S. Furnivall, *Netherlands India: A Study of Plural Economy*, New York: Macmillan, 1944.

8. *Pasangrahan*, a government building for the use of traveling officials.
9. Mineral water from Holland.

to trace out the guilty one he must go deep, very deep into his own purse. It has happened many times that the native chiefs have pawned the ornaments of their wives and children to obtain the money which was necessary before some dark deed could be brought into the light. But will that money which is paid out in the service of the Government be paid back by the Government? I wish indeed that it were so. Several officials have been reduced to beggary in this way. What, in heaven's name, can the officials do, who cannot make their salaries suffice, and have no parents or other relatives upon whom they can fall back for support? And if the people come forward with gifts when they see their wives and children running around in ragged clothes—judge them not harshly, Stella.

I know the trials of the native officials. I know the misery of the people, and what is the Government going to do now? It is going to reorganize the native administration. The native personnel will be reduced to the advantage of the European officials. From this reduction there will be saved annually an expenditure of 464,800 florins, and the European officials will reap the benefit of this. It is true that there are some ill-paid officials who will be bettered financially, and will become assistant wedonos instead of Government clerks; but what does that signify in comparison with the many important posts (it has not yet been demonstrated that they are superfluous) that will be abolished.

There are all kinds of rumors about the Government regulations. The bill for this reorganization has passed both chambers of the Volksvertegenwoordiging,[10] and on July 1st of next year it will go into effect. Nearly all of the residents have protested, but his excellency the Governor General wishes it, so in spite of all protests, the reorganization will proceed. I hope that the Government will eat no bitter fruit as a result.

And now about the people, about the inhabitants of Java in general. The Javanese are grown-up children. What has the Government done to further their development? For the noble sons of the country, there are, so called, high schools, normal schools, and the Doktor-djawa [11] School; and for the people, there are vari-

10. The Parliament of the Netherlands.
11. The medical school for native Indonesians in Batavia (former Dutch name for the capital city Djakarta). Its graduates were permitted to practice medicine in Indonesia, but were not considered advanced enough to continue their education in medical schools in Holland.

ous elementary schools—one in each district; though the Government has divided these latter institutions into two classes. The first class, composed of schools which are situated in the provincial capitals, are conducted just as they were before the division, but in the schools of the second class, the children learn only Javanese, reading, writing and a little reckoning. No Malay is taught as formerly—why, it is not made clear. The Government believes, to my thinking, that if the people were educated, they would no longer be willing to work the land.

Father sent a note to the Government on the subject of education. O Stella, I wish that you could read it. You must know that many of the native rulers rejoice at the actions of the Government. The Javanese nobles are in favor with the Government here and in the Motherland, and everything possible is done to help them, and to make them blossom to perfection.

The aristocracy sees with sad eyes how sons of the people are educated, and often even elevated to their ranks by the government because of knowledge, ability and industry. Sons of the people go to European schools and compare favorably in every respect, with the high and honorable sons of the noble. The nobles wish to have rights for themselves alone; they alone wish to have authority and to make western civilization and enlightenment their own. And the Government helps and supports them in this; for it is to its own advantage to do so. As early as 1895 there was a decree, that without the special permission of his Excellency the Governor General no native child (from six to seven years old) who could not speak Dutch would be admitted to the free grammar school for Europeans. How can a native child of six or seven years learn Dutch? He would have had to have a Dutch governess, and then before he is able to learn the Netherlands language, the child must first know his own language, and necessarily know how to read and write. It is only regents who do not have to ask permission for their families to go to the European schools; most of the native officials are afraid of receiving a "No" in answer to their request and therefore do nothing. Is it presumptuous of Father to call attention to the fact that African and Ambonese children may go directly to the European schools, without understanding a word of Dutch? Stella, I remember well from my own school days that many European children went to school who knew as little

Dutch as I, and I hardly knew any.[12]

Father says in his note that the government cannot set the rice upon the table for every Javanese, and see that he partakes of it. But it can give him the means by which he can reach the place where he can find the food. That means is education. When the Government provides a means of education for the people, it is as though it placed torches in their hands which enabled them to find the good road that leads to the place where the rice is served.

I will not quote any further, Stella; perhaps another time I can send you the whole note. From it you will learn something of the present condition of the people. Father wishes to do everything that he can to help the people and needless to say, I am on his side.

Father is very proud of his ancient noble race, but right is right, and justice is justice. We wish to equal the Europeans in education and enlightenment, and the rights which we demand for ourselves, we must also give to others. This putting of stumbling blocks in the way of the education of the people, may well be compared to the acts of the Tsar, who while he is preaching peace to the world, tramples under foot the good right of his own subjects. Measure with two measures, no! The Europeans are troubled by many traits in the Javanese, by their indifference and lack of initiative. Very well, Netherlander, if you are troubled so much by these things why do you not do something to remedy the cause? Why is it that you do not stretch forth a single finger to help your brown brother? Draw back the thick veil from his understanding, open his eyes, you will see that there is in him something else besides an inclination for mischief, which springs principally from stupidity and ignorance. I should not have to seek far for examples of this; nor would you, Stella. Here before you lie the innermost thoughts of one who belongs to that despised brown race. They are not able to judge us, and the things that we do, and leave undone. Do they know us?

No, even as little as we know them.

---

12. The Dutch East Indian government considered as "Europeans" the large numbers of persons whose father or grandfather was Dutch, but whose mother was Indonesian, Chinese, Indian, or other. These people, the "Indo-Europeans" grew up in Indonesia and frequently did not speak Dutch at home.

If you are interested in this subject, get the October number of *Neerlandia*. It contains an address delivered by my brother in the Dutch language at the literary congress at Ghent. Professor Kern took him there and asked him to speak. The sentiments to which he gives utterance are also mine; they are ours.

"Has your father much power?" you ask. What is power? Father has great influence, but the Governor alone has power. My brother pleaded for the use of the Dutch language officially. Read what he says, Stella, if not for your own satisfaction, then because I wish it.

The Hollanders laugh and make fun of our stupidity, but if we strive for enlightenment, then they assume a defiant attitude toward us. What have I not suffered as a child at school through the ill will of the teachers and of many of my fellow pupils? Not all of the teachers and pupils hated us. Many loved us quite as much as the other children. But it was hard for the teachers to give a native the highest mark, never mind how well it may have been deserved.

I shall relate to you the history of a gifted and educated Javanese. The boy had passed his examinations, and was number one in one of the three principal high schools of Java. Both at Semarang, where he went to school, and at Batavia, where he took his examinations, the doors of the best houses were open to the amiable schoolboy, with his agreeable and cultivated manners and great modesty.

Every one spoke Dutch to him, and he could express himself in that language with distinction. Fresh from this environment, he went back to the house of his parents. He thought it would be proper to pay his respects to the authorities of the place and he found himself in the presence of the Resident who had heard of him, and here it was that my friend made a mistake. He dared to address the great man in Dutch.

The following morning notice of an appointment as clerk to a controleur in the mountains was sent to him. There the young man must remain to think over his "misdeeds" and forget all that he had learned at the schools. After some years a new controleur or possibly assistant controleur came; then the measure of his misfortunes was made to overflow. The new chief was a former schoolfellow, one who had never shone through his abilities. The young man who had led his classes in everything must now creep upon the ground before the one-time dunce, and speak always high Javanese to him, while he himself was answered in bad Malay. Can you understand the misery of a proud and independent spirit so humbled? And how much strength of character it must have taken to endure that petty and annoying oppression?

But at last he could stand it no longer, he betook himself to Batavia and asked his excellency the Governor General for an audience; it was granted him. The result was that he was sent to Preanger, with a commission to make a study of the rice cultivation there. He made himself of service through the translation of a pamphlet on the cultivation of water crops from Dutch to Javanese and Sundanese. The government presented him in acknowledgment with several hundred guilders. In the controleur's school at Batavia, a teacher's place was vacant—a teacher of the Javanese language be it understood—and his friends (among the Javanese) did all in their power to secure this position for him, but without result. It was an absurd idea for a native to have European pupils who later might become ruling government officials, perish the thought! I should like to ask who could teach Javanese better than a born Javanese?

The young man went back to his dwelling place; in the meantime another resident had come, and the talented son of the brown race might at last become an assistant wedono. Not for nothing had he been banished for years to that distant place. He had learned wisdom there; namely, that one cannot serve a European official better than by creeping in the dust before him, and by never speaking a single word of Dutch in his presence. Others have now come into power, and lately when the position of translator of the Javanese language became vacant it was offered to our friend (truly opportunely) now that he does not stand in anyone's way!

Stella, I know an assistant resident, who speaks Malay with a regent, although he knows that the latter speaks good Dutch. Every one else converses confidentially with this native ruler but the assistant resident—never.

My brothers speak in high Javanese to their superiors, who answer them in Dutch or in Malay. Those who speak Dutch to them are our personal friends; several have asked my brothers to speak to them in the Dutch language, but they prefer not to do it, and Father also never does. The boys and Father know all too well why they must hold to the general usage.

There is too much idle talk about the word "prestige," through the imaginary dignity of the under officials. I do not bother about prestige. I am only amused at the manner in which they preserve their prestige over us Javanese.

Sometimes I cannot suppress a smile. It is distinctly diverting to see the great men try to inspire us with awe. I had to bite my lips to keep from laughing outright when I was on a journey not long ago, and saw an assistant resident go from his office to his house under the shade of a gold umbrella, which a servant held spread above his noble head.[13] It was such a ridiculous spectacle! Heavens! if he only knew how the humble crowds who respectfully retreated to one side before the glittering sunshade, immediately his back was turned, burst out laughing.

There are many, yes very many Government officials, who allow the native rulers to kiss their feet, and their knees. Kissing the foot is the highest token of respect that we Javanese can show to our parents, or elderly blood relatives, and to our own rulers. We do not find it pleasant to do this for strangers; no, the European makes himself ridiculous in our eyes whenever he demands from us those tokens of respect to which our own rulers alone have the right.

It is a matter of indifference when residents and assistant residents allow themselves to be called *Kandjeng*,[14] but when overseers, railroad engineers (and perhaps tomorrow, station-masters too) allow themselves to be thus addressed by their servants, it is absurdly funny. Do these people really know what Kandjeng means?

It is a title that the natives give to their hereditary rulers. I used to think that it was only natural for the stupid Javanese to love all this flim-flam, but now I see that the civilized, enlightened Westerner is not averse to it, that he is daft about it.

I never allow women older than I to show all the prescribed ceremonies to me, even though I know they would gladly, for though I am so young, I am a scion of what they consider an

---

13. The gold umbrella is a part of the formal regalia of the highest Javanese nobility, the princes and their immediate family.

14. *Kandjeng:* A Javanese title meaning, roughly, "Lord"; originally applied only to the indigenous ruling elite.

ancient, noble and honored house; for which in the past, they have poured out both blood and gold in large measure. It is strange how attached inferiors are to those above them. But to me, it goes against the grain when people older than I creep in the dust before me.

With heavy hearts, many Europeans here see how the Javanese, whom they regard as their inferiors, are slowly awakening, and at every turn a brown man comes up, who shows that he has just as good brains in his head, and a just as good heart in his body, as the white man.

But we are going forward, and they cannot hold back the current of time. I love the Hollanders very, very much, and I am grateful for everything that we have gained through them. Many of them are among our best friends, but there are also others who dislike us, for no other reason than we are bold enough to emulate them in education and culture.

In many subtle ways they make us feel their dislike. "I am a European, you are a Javanese," they seem to say, or "I am the master, you the governed." Not once, but many times, they speak to us in broken Malay; although they know very well that we understand the Dutch language. It would be a matter of indifference to me in what language they addressed us, if the tone were only polite. Not long ago, a Raden Aju was talking to a gentleman, and impulsively she said, "Sir, excuse me, but may I make a friendly request, please, speak to me in your own language. I understand and speak Malay very well, but alas, only high Malay. I do not understand this *pasar* Malay." [15] How our gentleman hung his head!

Why do many Hollanders find it unpleasant to converse with us in their own language? Oh yes, now I understand; Dutch is too beautiful to be spoken by a brown mouth.

A few days ago we paid a visit to *Totoks*.[16] Their domestics were old servants of ours, and we knew that they could speak and under-

15. *Pasar* Malay, or market Malay, was the crude, highly simplified dialect spoken in the market places and in European kitchens. It contrasted sharply in richness and expressiveness with the true classical Malay which has an ancient and fine literature of its own. Both pasar and classical Malay provided the basis in the early twentieth century for Indonesian, now the official national language, used in schools, government and literature.

16. Foreigners who are newcomers in Java, as distinguished from those who were born of foreign parents in Java and spent their childhood there.

stand Dutch very well. I told the host this, and what answer did I receive from my gentleman? "No, they must not speak Dutch." "No, why?" I asked. "Because natives ought not to know Dutch." I looked at him in amazement, and a satirical smile quivered at the corners of my mouth. The gentleman grew fiery red, mumbled something into his beard, and discovered something interesting in his boots, at least he devoted all of his attention to them.

Still another little story; it happened in the Preanger. It was in the early evening and the Regent of X was receiving visitors in his kabupaten. There was an intimate friend of the Resident of the department; afterwards a little Assistant Controleur came in and joined the company. The son of the house, a schoolboy at home on his vacation, ran into the pendopo. As soon as he saw that his father was not alone, he started to turn back, but the Resident had seen him and called him. His Excellency greeted the youth cordially and had a long and friendly talk with him. When the conversation with his Excellency was over, he went up to the young official and made a polite bow. The little gentleman saw no necessity for answering the courteous greeting with more than a barely noticeable nod of the head, and while his cold eyes took in the boy disdainfully from head to foot, he said coolly the little word "*tabé*" (a Malay greeting). The young man turned pale, his lips trembled; two fists were clenched.

Afterwards he said to the intimate friend who had been present "Sir, I like the Hollanders very much; they are among my best friends, but I shall never be able to forget the "*tabé*" of that assistant; it cut me to the soul."

Oh, Stella, I have had glimpses into all sorts and conditions of Indian society; involuntarily I see behind the curtain of the official world. There are abysses so deep, that the very thought of them makes me dizzy. O God, why is the world still so full of evil deeds—of horror and of sadness? There are residents and assistant residents compared to whom Slijmering in *Max Havelaar* is a saint; but I do not wish to turn my letter into a scandal chronicle.

Oh, now I understand why they are opposed to the education of the Javanese. When the Javanese becomes educated then he will no longer say amen to everything that is suggested to him by his superiors.

In the last few days, articles written by natives have been published in the *Locomotief*, the foremost paper of Netherlands India. In these articles they lay bare the opinions, which have secretly been held for years by, not all, but by far the greater number of Indian officials. Not only the highest in the land, but also the most humble are allowing their voices to be heard. The paper calls this a good sign of the times, and rejoices. What the European officials in general think I do not know; a controleur, who is one of the organizers of the native administration, says that good will come of it, not only to the Europeans, but also to the native rulers. He is pleading for a trained corps of native officials. The proposition will come before both chambers of the States General soon. It is also urged that the Dutch language be used officially in business between European and native officials. Splendid! then my brother does not stand alone. In July, the question of the education of women will come up too. The Javanese are emancipating themselves.

Still this is only a beginning, and it is splendid that men of influence and ability are supporting our cause. The strife will be violent, the combatants will not have to fight against opposition alone, but also against the indifference of our own countrywomen, in whose behalf they would break their lances. While this agitation among the men is on the tapis, that will be the time for the women to rise up and let themselves be heard. Poor men—you will have your hands full.

Oh, it is splendid just to live in this age, the transition of the old into the new!

I read the other day, "Turn not away, you who are old of days, from everything that is new. Consider all that is now old has once been new" (I quote from memory).

I have written so much, I hope that I have not made you weary; and forgive me, if I have been carried away by my enthusiasm and have here and there written something that may cause you pain. Stella, forgive me for having forgotten so entirely to whom I was speaking. I find such great sympathy in you; you have told me that you and I were kindred spirits, and even as such have I considered you. I am no Javanese, no child of the despised brown race to you; and to me you do not belong to that white race around us that holds the Javanese up to scorn and ridicule. You are white to me in your understanding of the truth, white in heart and soul. For you I have a great admiration. I love you with my whole heart, and many of my fellow countrywomen would do likewise if they knew you. O that all Hollanders were like you and some of my other white friends.

I have ordered *Berthold Meryan*, but up to the present time I have not received it; most likely the bookseller had first to order it from Holland. I have read lately *Modern Women* translated from the French by Jeanette van Riemsdijk; disappointed, I laid the book down. I had seen so many brilliant criticisms of this problem novel, it was said to be in all respects finer than *Hilda van Suylenburg*, to be powerful and without faults.

But for myself I still think H. v. S. the Ratu (princess) of all that up to now has been written concerning woman's emancipation. I am on the lookout now for a critic (!!) to whom I may speak my mind about *Modern Women*, for to my thinking that book lacks the strength and inspiration of H. v. S.

I read H. v. S. through in one sitting. I locked myself in our room, and forgot everything; I could not lay it down, it held me so.

It is a pity that my notebook is lost. I would ask you to read what I had written there. It is an outline of a translation from the English and called "The Aim of the Woman's Movement." I know of nothing better than that having been in the *Gids* or even in the *Wetenschappelijke Bladen*, and then what you must read, if you do not already know it is "De Wajang Orang" by Martine Tonnet; it is in the *Gids*, November number. It is about the Javanese and their art, and the court of Djokjakarta, very interesting; you would enjoy it. I have just read for the second time *Minnebrieven* by Multatuli. What a brilliant man he is. I am glad that soon a cheap edition of all his works will appear. I shall be very affectionate to Father.

The father of our Assistant Resident is a good friend of Multatuli's; and through him, we hear strange stories from the life history of that genius.

Couperus is still in India. When he is back in the fatherland, I believe that a brilliant book about my country will appear. Is not his style singularly clear and beautiful?

6 · TO MEVROUW M. C. E. OVINK-SOER

1900

We want to ask the Indian Government to send us to Europe at the country's expense. Roekmini wishes to study art, and later to work for the revival of our native art. Kleintje wants to go to the school of domestic science, so that she may learn to teach frugality, good housekeeping and the care of money to our future mothers and housewives. For these virtues, the careless, idle, luxurious and splendor loving Javanese people have much need of schooling. And I, as a teacher, am to instruct the future mothers in practical knowledge—to teach them to understand love and justice and right conduct, as we have learned them from the Europeans.

The Government wishes to bring prosperity to Java and to teach the people frugality; it is beginning with the officials. But what good will it do, if the men are compelled to lay aside money, when the women in whose hands the housekeeping rests do not understand the worth of that money?

The Government wishes to educate and civilize the Javanese people and must needs begin by teaching the smallest and highest class, which is the aristocracy, the Dutch language.

But is an intellectual education everything? To be truly civilized, intellectual and moral education must go hand in hand.

And who can do most for the elevation of the moral standard of mankind? The woman, the mother; it is at the breast of woman, that man receives his earliest nourishment. The child learns there first, to feel, to think, and to speak. And the earliest education of all foreshadows the whole after life.

The most serious fault of our people is idleness. It is a great drawback to the prosperity of Java.

So many latent powers lie undeveloped through indolence. The high born Javanese would rather suffer bitter want and misery than have plenty if he must work; nothing less than a gold-colored *pajung* [1] thinks the high born head. The noble makes light of

1. A pajung or parasol is the symbol of rank in Java. They are of many colors and variations of stripes denoting the degree of the personage above whom they are held. The pajung of a prince is gold with an orange stripe, that of a regent gold, of a princess and her children white; below those are

everything except that most desirable article—a golden parasol!

Our people are not rich in ideals, but an example which speaks, would impress them. They would be impelled to follow it. My sisters and I wish to go before and lighten the way; for that reason we want more than anything else to go to Holland to study. It will be well with us if we can go. Little Mother, help us!

When we come back to Java, we shall open a school for girls of the nobility; if we cannot get the means through our Government, then we will work for it in some other way, ask our friends to subscribe, start a lottery or something. The means will be found when we are ready to do the work—but I am running ahead, because we have the hardest struggle here at home; with Father's consent we should be richer than queens. If we could only have that.

It is frightful to be a Javanese girl and to have a sensitive heart; poor, poor parents, what a fate was yours to have such daughters! We hope and pray fervently that they may be blessed with a long life, and that later they will be proud of us even though we do not walk abroad under glittering golden sunshades.

I will work hard over the Dutch language so that I can have it completely under my thumb and do with it as I will—and then I shall seek, through means of my pen, to arouse the sympathy of those who are able to help us in our work to improve the lot of the Javanese woman.

"Poor fool," I hear you say, "if you push with all your might against the gigantic structure of ignorance, will you be able to overturn it?" But we will push, little Mother, with all our strength, and if only one stone of it falls out, we shall not have worked in vain. But first we are going to seek the cooperation of the best and most enlightened men in Java (even one of them could help us). We wish to form an alliance with our enlightened progressive men, to seek their friendship, and after that their cooperation with us. We are not giving battle to men, but to old moss-grown edicts and conventions that are not worthy of the Javanese of the future. That future, of which we (and a few others) are the forerunners. Throughout all ages the pioneers in the struggle against tradition, have suffered, we know that. Call us mad, foolish, what you will,

various combinations of red, blue, black and yellow the use of which is strictly prescribed by the laws of heraldry. A pajung is borne above the head of a Javanese dignitary whenever he travels about.

we can not help it, it is in our blood.

Grandfather was a pioneer half a century ago; he gave his sons and daughters a European education. We have no right to be passive, to do nothing. *"Adeldom verplicht."* [2] Excelsior! We wish that we could make common cause now with the men of the younger generation, but if we did we should be distrusted at once; friendship between unmarried women and men whether married or not, would not be understood. Later when we shall have gained our independence, it will be different. My brother knows many progressive young men personally and through correspondence. We know that there are men who appreciate a thinking, educated woman. I heard a man say once (he was a highly placed native official) that the companionship of a woman who was educated and enlightened was a great comfort and support to a man.

7 · TO MEVROUW ABENDANON-MANDRI

August, 1900

"What language, however powerful, can express every emotion of the soul. It cannot be done, it is impossible."

I believe with you that it is impossible, at least as far as writing and speaking go, but there is a silent secret language which never expresses itself in words, or written signs, and yet is understood and comprehended by everyone who has faith, because in its whole vocabulary the little word "lie" is unknown.

It is the pure chaste language of the eyes, the clear mirrors of the soul, and if you could have seen me this morning as five delicate, scented leaves quivered in my trembling hands, and warm tears coursed down my cheeks, you could, without hearing a single sound from my lips, have understood what I felt. Neither the mouth nor the pen can express it, but the eyes drowned in a flood of tears were raised on high as though to seek among the angels of God the ones who with tender wings came down to us, who were sad and wept bitterly upon earth, to comfort, and fill us with heavenly joy.

Every heartbeat, every pulsebeat, and each indrawing of the

2. Nobility involves obligation.

breath was a prayer of thanksgiving.

We are only ordinary human beings, a mixture of evil and of good like millions of others. Can it be that at first glance there is more of good than evil in us? One doesn't have to seek far for the cause of this; when one lives among innocent surroundings, it is not hard to be good, one does that of oneself. And, it is certainly no credit to do no evil when one has had no opportunity. Later when we have flown from the warm parental nest and are in the midst of ordinary human life, where no faithful parent's arm is thrown protectively around us, when the storms of life rage and rave above our heads, and no loving hands support us, and hold us fast as our feet waver—then for the first time, you will see what we are. Oh! I pray so fervently that we may never add to the mountain of disappointment which life has already brought to you; another just as fervent prayer, do not think us beautiful; it cannot be otherwise, some day you will be disappointed, and that would cause us bitter grief.

Now slowly by bits and pieces I shall tell you truthfully nearly all that I can about ourselves, so that you can have some insight into our true characters, and will not in your great goodness endow us with fine attributes, which we have not. Still a whole lifetime lies before us; let us see what can be made of it.

.   .   .   .

"I feel so much for the cause of woman, I am touched by her fate; she is still unappreciated and misunderstood in many lands even in this our age of light. I would help her so earnestly, and so willingly." Thank you for these splendid sympathetic words. In them, your great compassion speaks, your deep pity for the suffering of woman who through the ages has endured wrong from her fellow creature—man. I thank God that there are some who are noble in heart and spirit, and feel for the sad fate of our native women, and wish to send light into their poor, dark world.

White sister, with your warm deep-feeling heart, your pure eyes, your rich spirit, reach your hand to us; help us out of this pool of grief and misery into which the selfishness of men has plunged us, and holds us fast. Help us to overcome the relentless egoism of man—that demon which for centuries has held the woman lashed, imprisoned, so that accustomed as she is to ill treatment she sees no injustice but submits with stoicism to what seems the "good right" of the man, and an inheritance of sorrow to every woman.

I am still young, but I am not deaf nor blind and I have heard and seen much, too much, it may be, so that my heart is drawn with pain and I am swept violently forward in opposition to those customs and conventions which are the curse of women and children!

Helpless in bitter grief, I wring my hands and feel myself powerless to fight against an evil so gigantic! and which, O cruelty! is under the protection of the Islamic Law, and is fed by the ignorance of the women themselves, the victims of the sacrifice. Fate allows that cruel wrong which is called polygamy to stalk abroad in the land—"I will not have it," cries the mouth vehemently and the heart echoes the cry a thousandfold, but alas—to will! Have we human beings a will? It is always, we must, *must* do everything, from our first infant cry till our last breath.

Life is full of dark riddles and of secrets. We think that we know so much, and all the time we know nothing! We think that we have a will, an iron will, and picture ourselves strong enough to move mountains—then a burning tear, a sorrowful look from eyes that we love, and our strength is gone.

Let me tell you a story that is neither amusing nor interesting, but dull, monotonous and long drawn out, and which will demand much patience. First I ask your forgiveness, humbly, for the weary hour I am going to cause you.

It is the history of three brown girls, children of the sunny East; born blind, but whose eyes have been opened so that they can see the beautiful, noble things in life. And now that their eyes have grown accustomed to the light, now that they have learned to love the sun and everything that is in the brilliant world, they are about to have the blinders pressed back against their eyes, and to be plunged into the darkness from which they had come and in which each and every one of their grandmothers back through the ages had lived.

It is said that books full of "nonsense" came from the distant West and penetrated the heart of the *"Binnenland,"* [1] that quiet peaceful place on Java's ever green coast, where the sisters dwelt, that these rebellious ones were unwilling to bear the yoke which had been borne meekly and patiently by all women before them, and which now hangs suspended above them, so that any second

1. The Dutch term for "interior," meaning those regions of the East Indies which had had little contact with the West.

it may be dropped upon their unwilling shoulders.

People are wrong. It is not only the books that have made them rebellious, conditions have done that, conditions that have existed from time immemorial, and which are a curse, a curse—to every one who happens to be born a woman or a girl.

Already in her earliest youth when emancipation was for her an unknown word, and when books and other writings which spoke of it, were far beyond her reach, in one of the three sisters was born the desire to open the door of life.

It was recreation hour at the European school at Japara. Under the yellow blossoming *waru* trees in the schoolyard, big and little girls were grouped in happy disorder. It was so warm that no one cared to play.

"Shut your book, Letsy, I have something to tell you," pleaded a brown girl, whose costume and headdress betrayed the Javanese.

A great blonde girl, who leaned against the trunk of a tree reading eagerly in a book, turned around and said, "No, I have to study my French lesson."

"You can do that at home, for it is not school work."

"Yes, but if I do not learn my French lessons well, I shall not be allowed to go to Holland year after next; and I am so anxious to go there to study at the Normal School. When I come back later as a teacher, perhaps I shall be placed here; and then I shall sit on the platform before the class as our teacher does now. But tell me, Ni,[2] you have never yet said what you were going to be when you grew up."

Two large eyes were turned toward the speaker in astonishment. "Only tell me."

The Javanese shook her head and said laconically, "I do not know."

No, truly she did not know, she had never thought of it, she was still so young, still so full of joyous young life. But the question of her little white friend made a deep impression upon her; it would not let her rest, incessantly—she seemed to hear sounding in her ears the words "What are you going to be when you grow up?" That day she did much task work in school, she was so absent-minded, gave the most foolish answers when she was asked a question, and made the silliest mistakes in her work. It could not have been otherwise, for her thoughts were not on her lessons, she

2. "Ni," from the last syllable of "Kartini," is Kartini's nickname.

was thinking of what she had heard in the recreation hour.

The first thing that she did when she got home was to run to her father and lay the problem before him.

"What am I going to be when I grow up?"

He said nothing, but smiled and pinched her cheek. But she would not allow herself to be put off, and waited, teasing him for an answer. At last an older brother came in, and answered the question. Her greedy listening ears heard these words:

"What should a girl become? Why a Raden Aju, [a Javanese married woman of high rank], naturally."

The little girl was satisfied with the answer, and went quickly and happily away.

"A Raden Aju," she repeated several times to herself. "What is a Raden Aju?" The idea was with her always; she thought constantly of the two words, "Raden Aju." She must later become such a one. She looked around her, saw and came in contact with many Raden Aju's, regarded them attentively, studied them, and what she learned (as much as a child could understand) of the lives of these women, caused the spirit of opposition to awaken in her heart against this being a Raden Aju—the ancient iron-bound rule, that girls must marry, must belong to a man, without being asked when, who, or how.

This little girl reached the age of twelve and a half, and it was time that she should say farewell to her merry childish life, and take leave of the school benches upon which she had been so glad to sit; and of the little European companions among whom she had studied so willingly. She was old enough to come home according to the custom of her country. It demands that a young girl remain in the house, and be rigidly secluded from the outside world until that time when the man for whom God has created her shall come and take her to his dwelling.

She knew all too well that with the school door much that was unutterably dear would be closed to her for ever. The parting from the dear teacher, who bade her farewell with such sympathetic, cordial words, counseling resignation, and from little companions, who with tears in their eyes pressed her hand.

It was hard, but it was as nothing in comparison with the giving up of her lessons, the ending of her studies. She was so bent upon learning, and she knew that there was much more yet to be studied before one can even go through the lower school. She was ambitious, and she did not wish to stand below her little white friends, most of whom were going to Europe later, or her brothers who went to the high school.

She implored her father to allow her to go to the high school at Semarang with the boys; she would do her best; her parents would never have to complain of her. She crouched on her knees before him, her pleading hands resting upon his lap, her great child's eyes were raised up to him full of longing, and in breathless suspense and anguish she waited for his answer.

Caressingly he stroked the dark little head, his fingers pushed back tenderly the rebellious locks from her forehead, and softly and yet firmly, the word "No" came from his lips.

She sprang up, she knew what "No" from him meant. She went away and crept under the bed to hide herself; she wished to be alone with her grief.

Once her teacher had asked her if she could not go to Holland to study with Letsy, his daughter, who was her friend. She listened eagerly and with shining eyes.

"Would you not like to go?"

"Do not ask me if I would like to go; ask me if I may," came hoarsely from her trembling lips.

Good man, he had meant to be so kind to her. Stranger that he was to native customs, he did not know how cruel his question was. It was putting dainties before the eyes of one starving for bread.

Foolish girl, it was never the intention of your good parents to send you to school to raise rebellious thoughts in your heart. You were to learn Dutch, and Dutch manners, nothing more. Stupid little thing, if that had been all you had learned so much misery in the future would have been spared you. But the stupid little thing had not made herself, she couldn't help it if God had given her a sensitive soul, and a heart which readily absorbed all that the Dutch language had helped her to think beautiful.

Poor little one. In her heart, Western thoughts found a joyous entrance, yet she saw herself fettered hand and foot by Eastern tradition. And her muscles were still too weak, too soft to enable her to break the chains which bound her. And later when she found herself strong, so that with a single jerk they could be wrenched sunder—did she do it? But we will not run ahead with the story, we have not gone very far as yet.

The school door lay behind her, and the house of her parents welcomed her to herself. Great was that house, and spacious were the grounds, but high and thick were the walls that surrounded them and the closed in four cornered space was henceforth to be her world, her all. Never mind, how spacious and handsome, even comfortable a cage may be it is still a cage to the little bird that is imprisoned there.

Gone, gone was her merry childhood; gone everything that made her young life happy. She still felt herself such a child, and she was that in fact too, but the law placed her inexorably among the full grown. And she to whom no ditch was too broad to be leapt, no tree too high to be climbed, who loved nothing so much as to run like a wild colt in the meadows, must now be calm, composed and grave, as beseemed a Javanese young lady of a high and noble house. The ideal Javanese girl is silent and expressionless as a wooden doll, speaking only when it is necessary, and then with a little whispering voice which can hardly be heard by an ant; she must walk foot before foot and slowly like a snail, laugh silently without opening her lips; it is unseemly for the teeth to show, that is to be like a clown.

Ni sinned every second.

A dull, monotonous, slow mode of life began for her. Day after day passed wearily away amid the same occupations, and the same people. Sometimes there would be a bright spot in those first dark days, a visit from Letsy. It was like a holiday when Letsy was with her; she became as of old the merry child and forgot that she was a prisoner, but she suffered doubly for the temporary forgetfulness after the little white friend had gone.

The slow moving life went on, more stupid, more monotonous—

She watched her younger sisters with hungry longing every time that they went out of the door, armed with their schoolbooks, to go to the temple of wisdom where knowledge was to be found.

For a time she tried to study her lessons by herself; but it seemed useless—a pupil alone without a master soon grows discouraged. With a deep sigh she hid her books away.

If pillows and cushions could but speak what would they not be able to tell! They could tell of the misery of a little human soul that with scalding tears cried herself to sleep on their bosom night after night.

Young people cannot learn to be resigned. In their silly little heads and hearts dwell a hundred wild, restless and rebellious thoughts. They feel themselves so alone, and draw back timidly from those with whom they live day in and day out.

It is very easy to live for years with one's brothers and sisters and to remain always as strangers. Ni had an older sister who shared her imprisonment. She was fond of her but there was no confidence between them. They differed too much both in character and point of view. The older sister was quiet, conventional, calm and composed, and the younger one was just the opposite; all life and fire by nature. Her ideas were wrong in the eyes of the other, who believed firmly in all the old traditions and customs.

Often the younger sister had gone with shining eyes to tell of something which filled her brimful with enthusiasm; and when she had finished, the older sister would answer coldly. "Go your own way; as for me I am a Javanese."

Ni's heart would stand still within her, as though touched by a rough hand, she would grow icy cold. The younger sisters too were estranged from her; the older one was not pleased when they were with Ni—Ni who had such strange ideas. And sister was very strong; the little sisters were afraid of her.

Ni found it hard, but not so hard as to feel that her own mother was opposed to her. She too closed her heart to her, because her child's ideas were diametrically opposed to her own. Poor little Ni—her small soul was longing for tenderness and she found only coldness; where on her side she gave love, she received at best tolerance. Why was she always so strange, so peculiar, so different? Ah, she had tried so often to be like others, to think like others, yet always when she was almost happy, something would happen, that would make the slumbering thoughts burst forth tumultuously, and reproach her for her seeming forgetfulness, so that she would hold to them all the more firmly.

Still her life was not so wholly colorless and dull. There were two who held to her, who loved her just as she was; she felt their love warming her inmost being, and clung to them with all the tenderness of her thirsting heart. They were her father and her third brother—the youngest of her older brothers. It is true that they could not satisfy her most intimate and dearest wish to be free; could never gratify her longing to study. But her dear father was always so good to his little daughter, his own silly girl; she knew that he loved her, she felt it. He would look at her tenderly, his gentle hands would stroke her cheeks, her hair, and his strong arms would go so protectingly around her.

And she knew that her brother loved her too, although he had never told her so, had never spoken a loving word to her, had never caressed her. But a thousand little delicate attentions of which only a loving heart could think spoke constantly of his warm affection for her. He never laughed at her when she told him her thoughts, never made her shiver with a cold, "Go your own way; as for me I am a Javanese." And although he never told her that he sympathized with her ideals, she knew in her heart that he was as one with her, she knew that he was only silent because he did not wish to make her more rebellious. The books which he placed in her hands showed her that. Ni felt so rich with the love of her two dear ones, and with the sympathy of her brother.

But her father was not always with her; he had his work to do, and where he worked she might not go. She must never go out of the fast-closed place which was her dwelling. And her brother was at home only once in the year, for he went to school in Semarang.

Her oldest brother came home. He had obtained an appointment in the neighborhood and lived with his parents. If Ni had suffered before his coming, from the coolness of nearly all those who lived in the house with her, from their indifference to all that interested her, from her imprisonment, there now began a series of teasings and tormentings which added a thousand times to her distress. Ni was wild; she could not dance to the piping of her brother. "Young people should be submissive and obey their elders," was constantly preached to her; and above all, "Girls must be submissive to their older brothers."

But headstrong Ni could not see why this should be. She could not help it, that she should have been born later than her brother; that was no reason why she should be submissive to him. She was not answerable to any one, only to her own conscience and her own heart. She would never give in to her brother except when she was convinced that he was right.

At first he was astonished, and later he grew angry, when he saw that a little girl who was half a dozen years younger than he dared to defy his will. She must be forcibly suppressed. Everything was wrong that Ni did. She was severely reprimanded for each little fault. No day passed that brother and sister did not stand facing each other in anger. He with a dark countenance and stern words that made her heart bleed, and she with quivering lips tremblingly defending her good right to do something which he wished to forbid.

She was entirely alone in her fight against the despotism of her brother—her future protector, whenever she should have the misfortune to lose her parents, until she should leave his roof under the protection of the man for whom God had created her! He took very good care not to torment her when her father was there; father would never have allowed it, and he knew well that she was too proud to tell.

But the others who lived in the house were silent too, although they knew that she was within her rights. It would not do to allow impertinence, and the girl was impertinent; young as she was, she dared to say "No" to the "Yes" of her so much older brother. A girl had no right to do anything which would even partially detract from the importance of a man. It was not right for this girl to oppose her ideas to those of her self-willed brother.

In later years, when Ni remembered all this, she could understand very well why the man was so egotistical. Always, by every one in the house, he was taught as a child to be selfish, by his mother most of all. From childhood he was taught to regard the girl, the woman, as a creature of a lower order than himself. Had she not often heard his mother, his aunts, and all the women of his acquaintance say to him in scornful, disdainful tones, "A girl is only a girl"? It is through woman herself that man first learns to scorn woman. Ni's blood boiled whenever she heard deprecating words about girls spoken by a woman.

"Women are nothing—women are created for men, for their pleasure; they can do with them as they will," sounded brutally in her ears, and irritating as the laugh of Satan. Her eyes shot fire, but her fists clenched, and she pressed her lips tightly in impotent distress. "No, No," cried her fast beating little heart, "We are human just as much as men. Oh, let me learn. Loose my bonds! Only give me the chance, and I will show that I am a human being, a woman just as good as a man." She writhed and twisted, but the chains were strong and locked tightly around her tender wrists and ankles. She wounded herself, but she did not break them.

Too early ripened child, at an age when a young head should only be filled with dreams of merry play, she was busy with somber dark thoughts about the sad things in life. It could not have been otherwise; she was not deaf nor blind and lived in the midst of a civilization which took no account of youth and sensitive feelings. Roughly the young tender eyes were opened to the realities of life, in all their coarseness, ugliness and cruelty. From her parents themselves she never heard a harsh word that would have shocked her pure mind or wounded her sensitive heart, but she did not live only with her parents.

O Death! why are you called terrible, you who release mankind from this cruel life? Ni would have followed you thankfully and with joy. She had no one to show her what was lofty and beautiful in life, and that everything was not low and vile. Ni loved her father with her whole soul, and although she lived constantly with her parents she could never lay her inmost thoughts before them. Coldly the strong Javanese etiquette stood between them.

Ni avoided, as much as she could, those people who with their cynicism had withered her; and while the manners and customs of her country did not allow her stricken little soul to seek refuge in her parents' arms and on her parents' hearts, she found comfort in those quiet, silent friends "books."

She had always been fond of reading, but now her love for reading became a passion; as soon as she had time, when all her little duties were done, she would seize a book or a paper. She read everything that came into her hands; she greedily devoured both the green and the ripe. Once she threw a book away which was full of horrors. She did not have to look into books when she wished to know of loathsome, nauseating things; real life was full of them; it was to escape from them that she buried her soul in realms which the genius of man has fashioned out of the spirit of fantasy.

There were so many beautiful books which gave her unspeakable pleasure, and which she will never be able to forget; stories of strong characters nobly laying hold on life, of great souls and spirits, which would make her heart glow with enthusiasm and delight. She lived in everything that she read, while she was reading there was nothing more for which she wished, she was lost! Her father took great pleasure in her love of reading and showered her with presents of books. She did not understand everything that she read, but she did not allow herself to be discouraged by that. What she could not understand in the first reading became in the second less obscure, and at the third or fourth, it would be quite clear. Every unknown word that she found she noted down; and later, when her dearest brother came home, she would ask him its meaning. And he helped his little sister so willingly, and lovingly.

If she had not had her loving father, her dear brother and her books, she could not have lived through the sorrowful years. Father and brother stilled the yearning for love and affection, and the books gave to her hungry spirit food.

A little brother was born, and this helpless baby held Ni back from misfortune; he brought her again into the good path from which she had begun to wander. She was fast becoming a bad child toward her mother. She had closed her heart more and more toward her, and the little brother made the doors of that heart spring wide open again. Little brother taught her what a mother is, and what a child owes to its mother.

Mother had dark rings under her eyes, and looked weak and worn out, and little brother had done that; little brother who would not let her rest, but called her every night again and again. Never mind how wearisome the heavy burden might be, there was never a single expression of impatience on Mother's face; whenever little brother cried for her, in a second she was by him. She would take him up and never lay him out of her arms till he was in a sweet sleep. Had Mother held her, too, and never put her down, till she was sound asleep? The ice-crust around Ni's heart melted, and it beat warmly once more toward the woman who had given her life.

Brother was a healthy child during his first year, but when he was weaned, and for three years after that the little one was sick, as though he kept wrestling with death. And by his sick bed, Ni the young child, learned to understand her mother.

She saw her own shortcomings; she was too selfish, she was always thinking of her own troubles, and never thought that others could have troubles and that she could have a share in causing them. She had once been always with Mother as little brother was now, she could do nothing without Mother. Mother must have suffered and perhaps did even now; well, she could not help it if she thought differently from her mother, but she could be very careful to do nothing that would cause her pain.

Little brother taught her consideration; how to see the other side of things; he taught her submission, and gratitude, and to give without asking anything in return.

Four years went by, calm and quiet on the surface, but to those who could see below it, full of strife for Ni. She learned much in those years; self-mastery, submission, not always to think first of herself; but peace and acquiescence she had not learned, could never learn; her head was haunted by turbulent thoughts. Voices too still came to her from the distant West in books, newspapers, and magazines, and in letters from Dutch friends.

For a year her sisters and she had every day an hour's lesson in handiwork from a Dutch lady. These were pleasant hours for Ni because then she could speak Dutch, the language which she loved so much.

Her oldest brother, meanwhile, was given a position at a distance, and Ni was ashamed that she should be so very glad. He was still her brother, although he had not loved her.

Time and separation work wonders; they took away all resentment from Ni's heart, and she grew to love her brother. She felt sorry for the great boy who had allowed himself to be deceived by the silly flattery of fawning, favor-seeking men. It comforted her to think that toward the last she had noticed a change in his conduct toward her. He said nothing in words, but his actions spoke of his sorrow for his former injustice; and Ni thanked God with tears in her eyes that her brother was beginning to be fond of her. She who had been formerly disliked and hated was now first. She was always with him, and he would do more for her than for any one else.

A half year before a younger sister had come to share the imprisonment. Bemi was fortunate, at an age when Ni had already been for a long time safely immured behind high thick walls, she could run freely around, go on little journeys and do many other things that were forbidden to Ni. Bemi was fourteen and a half years of age when she came home to stay.

Ni was now sixteen. The oldest sister married, and with the wedding celebration changes came into her life. Ni learned to know her sisters, who up to this time had lived near her, but as strangers. There could never have been very much confidence between her older sister and herself; she was only an older sister.

And Ni did not wish to be so regarded by the younger ones: she wished to be loved, and not feared. Freedom and equality were what she asked for herself; ought she not to begin by giving them to others? The intercourse between the younger sisters and herself must be free and unrestrained. Away with everything that would hinder it. With Bemi and Wi, a little sister who had meanwhile come to the house, Ni took sister's room. And the three lives that had hitherto been strange to one another met, flowed together and became as one.

8 · TO MEVROUW ABENDANON-MANDRI

August, 1900

O, the inward pain of caring for nothing. We must have something; work, that will take entire possession of us, and leave no time for torturing thoughts. That is the only thing that can awaken our slumbering souls, and give us back our strength of spirit. Work, that is just it. The longing for work that we will love is what presses upon us so heavily. It is frightful to feel the power to work, and the will to work, and yet be condemned to idleness.

We will not believe that our whole lives to the very end will be monotonous, dull and commonplace. And yet we see no chance for a single one of all our beautiful dreams to ever become a reality. We do not know clearly what we shall do, but we are determined to follow only the voices of our own hearts.

"If we had been boys, our father could have brought us up to be fine fellows," we hear till we are weary. When it is certainly true that if the same material is in us out of which fine boys could be made, the same trouble could just as easily make fine women of us. Is it only fine men that have been of use hitherto? And are fine women of no value to civilization?

But we Javanese women must first of all be gentle and submissive; we must be as clay which one can mold into any form that he wishes. But why speak of this now? It is as though men on a sinking ship complained because they had not remained at home, investigated the cause of the misfortune, and punished those responsible for it. That would not prevent the ship from going down; they would be drowned just the same, and only the courage of the hand at the rudder, and pumping at the leak, could have saved them from destruction.

9 · TO STELLA ZEEHANDELAAR

August 23, 1900

Your encouragement is a support—it strengthens me. I will, I shall obtain my freedom. I will, Stella, I will! Do you understand that? But how shall I be able to win it, if I do not strive? How shall I be able to find it, if I do not seek? Without strife there can be no victory. I shall strive, and I shall win. I am not afraid of the burdens and difficulties; I feel strong enough to overcome them, but there is one thing I am afraid to face squarely.

Stella, I have often told you that I love Father dearly. I do not know whether I shall have the courage to carry my will through, if it would break his heart, which is full of love for us.

I love him unspeakably, my old gray father—old and gray through care for us—for me. And if one of us should be condemned to unhappiness, let me be the one. Here lurks egoism, for I could never be happy, even if I had freedom, even if I gained my independence, if in attaining them, I had made Father miserable.

In thinking over Javanese and European conditions and comparing them with one another, one can easily see that it is hardly better there than here in so far as the morality of the men is concerned, and that women are unfortunate there as here, with this difference, however, that the great majority there, of their own free will follow the man in the marriage bond; while here the women have no say at all in the matter, but are simply married out of hand, according to the will of their parents, to whomsoever those powerful ones shall find good.

In the Islamic world the approval, yes, even the presence of the woman is not necessary at a marriage. Father can come home any day at all and say to me, "You are married to so and so." I must then follow my husband. It is true I can refuse, but that gives the man the right to chain me to him for my whole life, without ever having come near. I am his wife although I will not follow him, and if he will not allow me to be divorced, then I am bound to him all my life, while he is free to do as he pleases. He may marry as many women as he chooses without being concerned in the least about me. If Father should marry me off in this manner then I should find a way out at the beginning, one way or another. But then Father would never do that.

God has created woman as the companion of man and the calling of woman is marriage. Good! it is not to be denied, and I gladly acknowledge that the highest happiness for a woman is, and shall be centuries after us, a harmonious union with the man of her choice.

But how can one speak of a harmonious union as our marriage laws are now? I have tried to picture them to you. Must I not for myself, hate the idea of marriage, scorn it, when by it the woman is so cruelly wronged? No, fortunately every Moslem has not four wives or more, but every married woman in our world knows that she is not the only one, and that any day the man's fancy can bring a companion home, who will have just as much right to him as she. According to the Islamic law she is also his wife. In the directly ruled regions, the women have not such a hard time as their sisters in those ruled by the princes, as in Surakarta and Djokjakarta.[1] Here the women are fortunate with only one, two, three or four co-wives. There, in the principalities, the women would call that child's play. One finds there hardly a single man with but one wife. Among the nobility, especially in the circle surrounding the sultan, the men have usually twenty-six women. Shall these conditions endure, Stella?

Our people have grown so accustomed to them, and moreover they see no other way in which every woman would be provided for. But in her heart almost every woman that I know curses this right of the man. But curses never help; something must be done. Come, women, girls, stand up; let us reach our hands to one

1. At the time of these letters, the Dutch governed in a fairly direct manner most of the island of Java, with the exception of four small regions, of which the main ones were Surakarta (Solo) and Djokjakarta. These sections, usually called "the Principalities," were ruled by their traditional hereditary princes, and although the Dutch were in fact in control, they did not greatly interfere with the customary mores. For this reason, the Principalities were more conservative culturally, in some ways, than elsewhere in Java.

another, and let us work together to change this unbearable situation.

Yes, Stella, I know it; in Europe, too, the state of morality among men is tragic. I say with you, teach the young men to turn their backs upon temptation and deplorable, half-acknowledged customs, and to feel disgraced at the existence of those short-sighted girls who follow men not ignorantly into the places where life is sordid. Yes, certainly the young mothers could do most there, I have already maintained that to my sisters.

I should so love to have children, boys and girls to nourish and to form after my own heart. But above all things I should never follow the unhappy custom of putting boys before girls. We have no right to be surprised at the egoism of men when we consider how as children they are placed above the girls, their sisters. Even as a child a man is taught to despise girls. Have I not many times heard mothers say to their boys when they would fall and cry: "Fie, a boy cry just like a girl!"

I should teach my children, boys and girls, to regard one another as equal human beings and give them always the same education; of course following the natural disposition of each.

I should not allow my girl, although I wished to make a new woman of her, to study as though she had no other desire in life; nor would I cut her off in anything so that her brother could have more. Never!

And then I should let down the bars which have been so foolishly erected between the two sexes. I am convinced that when this is done much good will come of it, especially to the men. I shall never believe that educated and cultivated men designedly avoid the society of women who are their equals in education and enlightenment, to throw themselves deliberately into the arms of disreputable women. While many men seek the society where cultivated ladies are to be found, there is a vast army who cannot take the slightest interest in a girl without thinking of sex. Now all this will disappear when men and women can mingle freely together from childhood.

You say, "We girls could do much toward bringing young men upon the good path, but we know so little of their lives." Everything will change with time, but here in Java we stand only on the threshold of the new age. Must we not go through all the corresponding stages of development, through which you have already passed in Europe?

Among my new treasures I have *Het Jongetje* by Borel.[2] A delightful book. Many here think it sickly and overdrawn. But to me; it is sickly not at all, and overdrawn even less. There may not be many like Borel's little boy, but I know at least one. The child of the assistant-resident is Borel's boy personified. Once he said to Kardinah, "Tante, I like girls so much. Girls smile so indolently. They are quite, quite different from boys; they are so sweet, so soft." A little fellow of five said this. He bit Kardinah's arm once, saying, "Tante, why are women so soft?" Then he bit his own arm and said, "Though I am so little, yet I am a man, that is the reason I am hard."

He is such a lovely child, with great dreamy eyes and brown curling hair. Before he came here he made our acquaintance at Surabaja through our portraits.

His mother told him that they were going to the place where his dear aunts lived. The child thought that he must marry and asked "Maatje, must I marry all three or only one of them?"

When he came here and saw us, his mother said to him, "Well, little brother, have you chosen which one of the aunts you will marry?"

"Maatje, I cannot choose, for I love all three just the same."

The dear little angel then turned to each one of us and said, "I love you, I love you, I love you. Yes, I love the whole world for everything is good, everything is beautiful."

If this had been told me by some one else, I should not have believed it, but I saw and heard it with my own eyes and ears.

The subject which Mevrouw van Suylen-Tromp wishes to have treated is the "The life of the native woman." On that I had rather not write just yet. I have far too much to say, and could not possibly make an orderly whole of it now. In a few years perhaps, when I shall have learned more, I shall undertake it.

Now the thoughts blow and whirl through my brain like falling leaves that are driven by the wind. What a comparison, eh?

.   .   .   .

The mornings are magnificent now and so are the evenings, but in the middle of the day I should like to do nothing but lie in

2. Henri Borel, novelist and journalist born in 1869. Also noted as an authority on Chinese art and literature. The author of *Kwan Yin De Laatse Incarnatie, Het Jongetje*, etc.

the water, if that were not so warm. We enjoy the mornings so much, nature is then splendidly fresh and beautiful. We wander around the garden where everything is blooming and fragrant. It is truly a pleasure to be out of doors in the morning. If you could only wander around with us; or do you not care for flowers and plants? Mother has her vegetable garden, and we our flower and rose garden; this last is next to our room, and when there is a full moon it is so idyllic out there. The sisters bring their guitars and sit under the flowering shrubs and make music. After the concert, we sit idly, sometimes chattering and laughing.

. . . .

Your indignation over the treatment which my two educated and enlightened fellow countrymen had to endure, did me good. But believe me, they are not all stupid men who conduct themselves so scornfully toward the Javanese. I have met persons who are far from stupid, who even belong to the aristocracy of the mind, but are so haughty and overbearing that they do not like to be in the same house with me.

Too often we are made to feel that we Javanese are not really human beings at all. How do the Netherlanders expect to be loved by us when they treat us so? Love begets love, but scorn never yet aroused affection. We have many friends among the Hollanders whom we love dearly, even more than we do friends of our own race. They have taken the trouble to try and understand us, and they have won our love. We shall never forget that we have to thank the Hollanders for the awakening of our minds, for our civilization. They may wrong us, but we will like them because we owe them so much.

People may say of the Javanese what they will, but they can never say with truth that they have not hearts. They have them manifestly and they know how to be grateful for benefits, whether they are of a material or of an intellectual kind, although their unmovable countenances change not one jot to betray their inward emotion. But I shall never have to tell you, I am sure, that all creatures of whatever color, are human beings, just as much as you yourself.

I am happy because I have been able to know you. I shall not let you go, Stella. I love you so much that I do not know what would become of my life, if, as God forbid, we should ever become separated. As though the wide ocean were not already between us!

But spirits among whom there is great sympathy know no distance; they bridge the widest seas and most faraway lands to commune with one another. Letters too are splendid. Blessed be he who first invented them!

A week ago we had a visit from the Director of Education, Religion, and Industry, and his wife from Batavia—and Stella, rejoice with me, the Director came here especially to see Father and to ask his advice personally about the erection of the native school for girls which the Government is planning.[3]

I was sick and miserable, not only from bodily pain, but misery of soul. But Stella, I believed that my dream of freedom was on the point of realization when Father gave me the Director's letter. That letter cured me entirely. It did me such infinite good to know that in Batavia one of the highest officials of the Government had a heart for the Javanese, and for the Javanese woman.

Soon afterwards Mama came to look for me, and she found her daughter in tears; I was so happy, so thankful.

Before he came I had the greatest desire to see him alone, if only for a moment, just to express something of what I felt.

And he came—but not alone—his wife was with him. O Stella, never in our lives have we made such a charming acquaintance! I had already great sympathy for him, because I knew why he was coming; and the sympathy grew, when I saw him ride into our grounds on the front seat of the carriage with his wife on the back seat, and next to her, Father, who had met them at the station.

I knew that Father would never have sat there without being pressed. You would have seen nothing remarkable in this, and you will laugh at me when I say that it impressed me very much, because it spoke of the modesty of the Director, and told me that he was a stranger to all the self-important airs and painful respect which so many officials here demand. I was accustomed to seeing Father on the left side of Resident or Assistant Resident, never mind how much younger the latter might be.

But not only I, Europeans even are seriously annoyed by the silly regulations of rank here. The newly arrived European officials and the regents take their places upon chairs while the cold ground covered (and sometimes uncovered) with a bamboo mat is good enough for a native wedono, who has grown gray in the service.

3. This was Mr. J. H. Abendanon.

The most petty European sits upon a chair, while native officials of any age, who are below the rank of regent, though they are often of distinguished ancestry, must sit upon the floor in their presence.

It certainly does not please the heart to see a gray wedono creep upon the ground before a young aspirant,[4] a youth who may have just left the school benches. But enough of that, it was only to explain why the courtesy of the Director, a man of such high authority, struck me so forcibly.

We heard the Director say to Father, "I have been all over Java and have talked with many officials, Regent. You have set the example by sending your girls to school. I have asked girls who were going to the grammar schools if they would like to go on with their studies, and they have all answered enthusiastically, "Yes."

He asked Father where he thought the girls' school ought to be erected, whether in West, Middle or East Java.

O Stella, how my ears and eyes tingled and my heart beat with joy to hear that. At last we are to have light in our poor dark woman's world.

While Mijnheer talked to Father, Mevrouw talked to us. We drew near to her with such pleasure. She told me of the plan of her husband, and asked what I thought of it.

"A splendid idea, Mevrouw, which will be a blessing to the native women, but it would be a still greater blessing, if the girls were also given an opportunity to learn a vocation, that would place them in a position to make their own way in life, if after receiving an education, they should feel reluctant to go back into their old environment. And the woman whose spirit has been awakened, whose outlook has been broadened might not be able to live again in the world of her ancestors. She will have been taught what freedom means, and then shut up in a dungeon; taught to fly and then imprisoned in a cage. No, no, the truly enlightened woman could not possibly feel happy in our native environment, not as long as it remains as it is. There is only one road in life open for the native girl, and that is 'marriage.' And what marriage means among our people cannot be unknown to you, who have been so long in Java. Oh, we think it is splendid that your husband wishes to give girls advantages and education,

4. An "aspirant" is the lowest in rank among the Dutch officials in Java.

but let that last be also a vocational education, and then your husband will truly have showered blessings upon our native world."

"Do you hear that?" she said enthusiastically to her husband. "This young lady asks vocational training for native girls."

Astonished, he turned to me and said, "Really, do you ask vocational training for girls? How would you arrange it? But tell us what you would like to be yourself?"

I felt all eyes fastened upon me; those of my parents burned into my face. I cast down my own eyes. There was a buzzing and roaring in my ears, but above it I seemed to hear the words "Kartini be brave, do not waver."

"But tell me what do you wish to be?

"I know you wish to become a writer; but you do not have to be educated especially for that, you can become that by yourself."

Alas, for study I am too late; but at least I may "Raise my eyes on high and go humbly and quietly forward."

Mevrouw spoke to me for a long time about what you and I have discussed so often—"woman." When we bade each other "Goodnight," and were going to bed, she took my hands in both of hers, pressed them warmly and said "Little friend, we shall discuss this again some time; meanwhile I shall write to you often; will you do the same to me?"

The following morning we went with her part of the way, and during the three hours that we sat with her in the carriage she and I told each other so much. Although it was twelve o'clock when we separated the evening before, she had told her husband everything that she had learned from us.

"O Regent," she cried again and again, "Give me one of your daughters, let her come to Batavia with me. Do let this young lady come to visit me; I shall come and fetch her myself."

Father told her that he thought of going to Batavia this year, "But they must remain at home with Mama, Mevrouw!" With that she appeared overcome with distress; was it earnest or a jest?

They wish us to come to Batavia to plead our cause, and the cause of the native woman, in person before the high authorities. Oh, Stella, pray that if it should come to pass I shall be able to plead well.

At parting she said to me, "Be brave, have faith and courage, this cannot last for ever, some way will be found, be brave!"

Stella, am I dreaming or waking? Is there a happy future for us?

Is it possible to hope that our dream is coming true? She has told me more but I dare not tell you now. It is still so far away, but it shines and beams before me like a star of hope. Later, Stella dear, when I have it in my arms and hold it tight, so that it cannot slip away, you shall know what it is. I have asked my sisters if I were really alive; I felt so unspeakably happy. Pray for me, dearest, that this may be no illusion, no empty mirage, that would be terrible.

When the Director saw our work, painting, embossing, etc., he asked if it would not be possible in a year's time for us to have an exhibition. He was sorry that we had not sent more to the French exposition.

The next morning he said that he would speak to influential people at Batavia and see if an exposition of native work could not be arranged there for next year. "You must send a great deal of what you have shown us."

O Stella, I could not speak; I turned to him and to her with tears in my eyes.

We felt as though we were in a dream, there was no yesterday—no tomorrow for us; only the joyous, splendid day existed. It made me dizzy, made me afraid! What if these dreams and illusions should vanish like smoke!

When I came home, I took up my pen at once to write to our friend Mevrouw Ovink. A few days ago I sent her a cry of despair, and my dear Moedertje must know that her daughter is happy again. I have told her nothing of what I have written here for you alone, I have only told her that I felt happy and full of the joy of life.

But I have told you everything, with just one exception, although you have a right to that too. For you have comforted me when I was in despair; your enthusiasm has given me strength, when I was weak. Stella, if I can ever do anything for my sisters in Java, it will be solely and only because of you.

I told you that Mevrouw Ter Horst invited me to write for her paper on the condition of the native woman; she believed that I was too reserved and suggested a form herself under which I could treat the subject: "A Talk between Two Regents' Daughters." She on her part will do everything to further the good cause.

I have Father's permission, Stella. So much lies under my hand; God grant that I can bring it to maturity.

All too often I write sketchy, commonplace things taken from our own lives. One of them appeared in *The Echo*. As pseudonym I chose "Tiga Soedara" (The Three Sisters), although we three are one. Soon the identity of "Tiga Soedara" was discovered, and there was a notice about my work in the *Locomotief* (a daily paper here in India).

I found it tiresome; I should gladly have kept my writing secret; I do not like to be discussed. It may sound ungracious, but truly I did not deserve so many compliments. Still that notice in the paper had its good side too, and a very good one at that, for the next month two numbers of a new newspaper for natives were sent to Father, with the request that they be given to us, and also a letter came asking for the cooperation of "Tiga Soedara."

This is the first Dutch language newspaper that has been founded for natives, and I expect many blessings for my people through the Dutch language. It is like our lilies! Dutch flowers which bloom in added fragrance and beauty when they are transplanted to distant India! *The Echo* is now the *Nederlandsche Taal*.

You can easily imagine that I wrote an enthusiastic letter to its editor and founder (director of the high school at Probolingo), placing my services at his disposal.

And soon a letter came from him with a list of subjects which he would like to have treated by me: the first was "Native Education for Girls"; after that "A Native Institute" and "Javanese Art." Kartini, never say I cannot—but I will. I will, Stella, I will. I hope fervently that you have not over-estimated my strength. I shall do my best.

Now I shall tell you something else. We three have begun to study French out of the little books of Servaas de Bruijn. We have wrestled through most of the four volumes and we now want you to recommend to us some simple, easy French books (not school books).

Father has also given us a German grammar. When we get through with our French studies, and have German under our thumbs, we hope to begin English, if we live long enough.

We try now to read French illustrated papers, but reading and understanding are two different things; is it not true?

In the beginning we made the stupidest mistakes, but we have improved slowly and we feel in fine good humor. Roekmini declared once that she had dreamed in French, she was with Chateaubriand and in Louisiana, the beautiful country of which he wrote.

The French language has many resemblances to ours, and the "h" is exactly like ours. Our new friend said to her husband, "They are anxious to learn languages, how glad I should be to teach them myself."

Yesterday I received a letter from her; it was twenty pages long. She wrote so affectionately and said that she felt that she would see us again. "Trust to the future," she wrote. And I will trust, so long as I know that I have you and her on my side. Her letter made me ashamed just as yours do; you and she think too well of me.

And yet, Stella, life is so full of riddles and of secrets. Human beings are subject to change and it is not always from feeble character. Circumstances can come into life, which in the twinkling of an eye will turn a hero into a coward. Do not judge any deed, never mind how base it may appear, till you know all the causes which lead to it.

I have experienced much in these last days, many different emotions. First I was almost in despair because my dream of freedom seemed to lie deeply buried in the ground.

Then the friends from Batavia came and such happiness came over me that it overwhelmed me; I was as though intoxicated! and then I was frightened and awakened by a pain so heavy that I thought I should not be able to breathe; that was not on account of myself, but of another whom I love with my whole soul.

Why must happiness and misery follow one another so quickly?

Poor dear Father, he has suffered so much, and life still brings him new disappointments. Stella, my father has no one but his children. We are his joy, his consolation, his all. I love my freedom, the idea is always with me and the fate of my sisters goes to my heart; I would be ready for any sacrifice by which good could come to them. I should only look on it as happiness—the greatest happiness that could ever come to me in life. But my father is dearer to me than all these put together.

Stella, call me a coward, call me weak, for I cannot be anything else; if Father is set against this dedication of myself, never mind how my heart may cry out, I shall hold it still.

I have not the courage to wound that true heart that beats so warmly for me, and to make it bleed again; for it has bled all too much already and I myself have not been altogether without guilt.

You say that you cannot understand why every one must marry. You say to oppose that "must" with "will"; as for me I should certainly say it in so far as others are concerned, but never in opposition to Father; especially now, that I know what heavy grief oppresses him. Whatever I shall have to do will not be looked upon as compulsory because of a "must" but as something which I freely take upon myself for his sake.

I write, paint and do everything because Father takes pleasure in it. I shall work hard and try my best to do something good so that he may be proud of me. You may call me foolish, morbid, but I cannot help it. I should be miserable if Father should set himself against my plan of freedom, but I should be still more miserable if my dearest wishes should be fulfilled and at the same time, I should lose Father's love.

But I shall never lose that; I will not believe it possible, though I could break his heart. From any one he could endure disappointment better than from me. Because perhaps he loves me a little more than the others, and I love him so dearly.

10 · TO MEVROUW OVINK-SOER

August, 1900

"If we do not go to Holland, may I not go to Batavia and study medicine?"

Father's answer to this was easy enough to comprehend: "I must never forget that I am a Javanese"; that it would not be possible for me to take such a step now, after twenty years it will be different—now it would never do. There would be too many trials and difficulties to be overcome because, "I should be the first." Father could not contain himself any longer, but sprang up and put an end to the conversation. Father said that he must first think about this earnestly and speak with others and ask their advice.

At least Father did not wholly reject my idea, for Father knows that I wish to become at any price, free, independent and unshackled, and that I could never be happy in a married life as marriages are now, and have always been.

Then I asked, "If the native girls' school of Mr. Abendanon

should materialize, may I not become a teacher?" and I told him what Mevrouw Abendanon had proposed to me.

Moedertje, it was as though the doors of heaven had sprung open and an eternal splendor blazed before my eyes when I heard Father say: "That is good; that is a splendid idea, you could do that very well."

"But first I should have to be trained for the position; I should have to go to school for a year or so and study, to be able to pass the examination, because I would not undertake the work unless I were fitted for it."

And Father thought I was right and agreed with me.

I was unspeakably happy, I had never thought that it would be so easy, not a single bitter sharp word had been spoken; I felt as though a great weight had been lifted from my heart. Father had been so tender, so loving. Then I had not been mistaken in my faith in his love for me, in my belief in his sympathy for his child: I knew that Father would suffer more than I, if he should cause me misery and that he hoped even as fervently as I, that a way might be found for me.

It was because of him that I felt so miserable for months; that I was so vacillating, weak and cowardly; because I could not bear to hurt him, and I felt that I must; for I could not debase myself or allow my woman's heart, my dignity as a woman, as a human being, to be trampled upon. I would have set myself against my parents. I was morally bound by my own pride and self-respect, my duty to myself not to submit in silence. The inward strife has been terrible.

And now I have won Father over to my side. With that the greatest difficulty is overcome, the greatest stumbling block cleared from the way. I can go forward now to meet the enemy unafraid, gay and self-confident, with a smile on my face.

Now everything depends upon myself alone. It will be the fault of my own will if by any chance I shall fail to reach my goal, but I am full of hope and courage. I have already asked Father if I may tell the good news to Mevrouw Abendanon, and I may; this very evening I am writing to you and to her.

It is still doubtful whether the native girls' school will come into existence, but I never despair. It will be accomplished one way or another, for there are some, though not many, it is true, who are striving to help our native world and to bring light to the native woman.

At Djokja we went to see Mevrouw Ter Horst, as I have already written you. She was very cordial to us and went to the station to meet us, where however she missed us, for we got off a station further on. She had a table already spread for us when we arrived. We went to see her because she had something to talk about with me.

She told me that the plans of Resident de B., of which we had known nothing, differed from those of Mr. Abendanon. His idea was to build a domestic school for daughters of native officials, with the Government's help, if possible. If not, by some other means.

The Resident had asked her to sketch out a plan, the details of which he would fill in; she now asked for my ideas, and what I thought the native girls, daughters of officials, high and low, should be taught.

If the endeavor of Mr. Abendanon to found a native girls' school, should fail, which heaven forbid, and I should not become a teacher after all, then you will not desert me Moedertje, will you? But you will try to help me to obtain Father's permission to study medicine. May I not have that assurance from you and your husband too? You could do so much because you have great influence with Father.

Since that memorable noonday talk, Father has been so affectionate to me; he takes my hand between his two hands tenderly, and puts his arm around me so lovingly, as though he would protect me from some impending danger. Through everything I feel his immeasurable love, and it makes me very happy.

Since we have come back from Batavia, we have a queer feeling as though we had only come home to rest until evening, to say "Good day" and then to fly away again. Whither? I shall enjoy being at home now to the utmost for nowhere in the whole world will it be as pleasant to me as in my own parents' house, and I am so thankful because whenever—be it today or tomorrow —I shall leave that house, it will be with their blessing; and I hope also from my heart, with the blessing of its other inmates too.

As a child I could learn with a fair amount of ease, I was never backward, but between then and now lies a whole lifetime. Everything that I learned at the grammar school I have forgotten. I was twelve and a half years of age when I left it. But one can almost always accomplish what one wishes to very hard. Is it not true, Moedertje?

I have written this confession with the full conviction, the firm trust that no one can take a warmer interest in my plans than you and Mijnheer, and what I have just related concerns my whole future. I know that I can go to you at any time when I need advice, support and comfort; in the time to come I shall certainly go to you many times.

11 · TO MEVROUW ABENDANON-MANDRI

October 7, 1900

I calmly bide my time. When it comes then men shall see that I am no soulless creature, but a human being with a head and a heart, who can think and feel. It is frightfully egotistical of me to make you a sharer in everything that concerns me. It brings light to me, but to you, it must be vexation! Everything for myself, nothing for you. I long to tell you everything simply because I love you so much. Draw back from me, thrust me from your thoughts, from your heart, forget me, let me struggle alone, for O God, you do not know into what a wasps' nest you stick your hand, when you reach it out to me!

Let me alone, I shall only be thankful for your sympathy and because you have crossed the path of my life and caused sunshine and flowers to fall across it. Let our meeting be as that of ships on the wide ocean that pass in the dark night. A meeting—a blithe greeting—a foamy track through the smooth water and then—no more! But I fear—I know that you could never go by like that—even though you might wish it. Let us never speak of it again.

.   .   .   .

A little while ago in talking to Mama, about something of interest to women, I told her what I had said so many times before, that nothing attracted me more, that nothing was more longed for by me than to be able to fly alone upon my own wings. Mama said, "But there is no one now, not among us, who does that!"

"Then it is time that someone should do it."

"But you know very well that every beginning is difficult. That

the fate of every innovator is hard. That misunderstanding, disappointment on top of disappointment, ridicule, all await you; do
you realize that?"

"I know it. But it is not today nor yesterday that these ideas
have come to me; they have lived in me for years."

"But what will come of it for yourself? Will it bring you con-
tentment, make you happy?"

"I know that the way I wish to go is difficult, full of thorns,
thistles, pitfalls; it is stormy, rough, slippery and it is—free! And
even though I shall not be happy after I have reached my goal,
though I may give way before it is half reached, I shall die gladly,
for the path will then have been broken, and I shall have helped
to clear the way which leads to freedom and independence for the
native woman. I shall feel a great content because the parents of
other girls who wished to become independent would never be
able to say 'There is no one, not among us, who does that.' "

Strange, but I am not uneasy or disturbed; I am calm and full
of courage; only my stupid, foolish heart feels sick.

12 · TO MEVROUW OVINK-SOER

October, 1900

I wish to prepare myself to teach the two grades, lower and higher;
and also to take courses in hygiene, bandaging and the care of
the sick.

Later I should like to take a language course. First to learn
thoroughly my own mother tongue. I want to go on with my studies in Holland, because Holland seems to me in all respects a
more suitable place of preparation for the great task which I
would undertake.

How shall we great each other when we meet at last? I know
exactly what you will say to me at first: "But child how stout
you have grown!"

And I shall whisper between two hugs, "I have grown old, both
outwardly and inwardly, but that little spot in my heart where
love is written in golden letters remains the same, forever young."

13 · TO STELLA ZEEHANDELAAR

New conditions will come into the Javanese world, if not through us, through others who will come after us. Emancipation is in the air; it has been foreordained. And she whose destiny it is to be the spiritual mother of the new age must suffer. It is the eternal law of nature: those who bear, must feel the pain of bearing; but the child has all our love, though its very existence, above that of all others living, has harassed us. Though it has been received through suffering, it is eternally precious to us.

. . . .

Nothing is more miserable than to feel the power to work within one, and yet to be condemned to idleness. Thank God, this curse has been taken from me.

A short while ago, a professor from Jena, Dr. Anton, with his wife, was here with us; he was traveling in pursuance of his studies. They came here to make our acquaintance.

I am afraid that people see too much in me. I am certain that they allow themselves to be misled through the charm of novelty and perhaps also through sympathy. We are a novelty to many people, especially to those from a distance, to whom everything that is new is more or less attractive. The professor expected us to be half savage, and found us quite like ordinary people. The strangeness was all in our headdress, clothes and surroundings, and these merely gave to the commonplace a stamp of individuality.

Is it not pleasant to find one's own thoughts reflected in another? And when the other is a stranger, someone of another race, from another part of the world, of different blood, manners and customs, it but adds to the charm of kinship of soul.

Still I am convinced that not a quarter so much notice would have been taken of us, if we had worn petticoats instead of sarong and kebaja, had Dutch manners, and if European instead of Javanese blood had flowed through our veins.

Our friends made us a present of several books; among them that spendid work by Baroness von Suttner, *De Wapens Neer Gelegd* ("Lay Down Your Arms").

I have read several other books, among which *Moderne Maag-*

97

den [1] impressed me most, because I had found in it much that I myself had thought and experienced. Marcel Prevost has spoken the truth, and knows how to express his ideas, I think his book very beautiful. Nowhere have I seen the aim of the "woman's movement" expressed with so much truth and power. Still I am just as far from the solution of that great problem as I was before making the acquaintance of *M. M.*

I do not take it amiss that the writer—and this not in a spirit of childish mockery—represents all opponents of the woman's movement with the exception of Fedi and Lea, as absolutely base and detestable. What splendid words he puts into the mouth of the lovable and deformed apostle of feminism—Piruet—at the end of the book—words which express clearly the whole aim of the woman's movement. I have taken a double pleasure in this book because a man thought of it and wrote it.

Just before I read *Moderne Maagden,* I wrote long letters to my two best friends here. Now I want to write to them again while I am still under its influence. I want to point out the analogies between much that is in the book and both the intimate letters.

I wish that I had someone here to talk to me about *M. M.* There is so much in it that I should like to discuss with someone of experience and understanding.

I have a great deal to tell you about the establishment of schools for native girls. It is now generally discussed but I must be brief today. The plan of Mr. Abendanon was looked upon with interest by everyone. Many influential European officials gave it their warm support, and it is upon them its success depends.

We have many friends among the high European officials and these are striving with Mr. Abendanon to lift our native women out of their age-long misery. There are also many unknown to us personally who are deeply interested in the cause. I shall send you a circular by Mr. Abendanon addressed to the heads of the provincial Government, concerning the establishment of these schools. "In all ages the progress of woman has been an important factor in the civilization of a people." "The intellectual education of the Javanese people can never progress if the woman is to be left behind."

"The woman as the carrier of civilization." Stella, does not your

1. Dutch version of *Les vierges fortes* by Marcel Prevost.

heart beat warmly for our friend?

For the last year there has been great progress among the natives. They are growing more earnest and are interested in the study of your beautiful language. Many Europeans see this with regretful eyes. Although there are others who are noble-minded and rejoice.

In many cities small Dutch schools have sprung up like mushrooms, and they are filled with little children as well as with grown men, who have been for years in the service of the state.

Influential men in the Government, with the Governor General at their head, are strongly in favor of spreading the Dutch language among the natives, not only for enlightenment but as a means of bringing the Javanese nearer to the Hollanders; so that these last may seem, not as strangers, but as loved protectors.

14 : TO MEVROUW ABENDANON-MANDRI

January 21, 1901

We went at midday to the shore with Mevrouw Conggrijp to bathe. It was splendidly calm, and the sea was all one color. I sat on a rock with my feet in the water, and my eyes on the distant horizon. Oh! the world is so beautiful! Thanksgiving and peace were in my heart. If we go to mother nature for consolation she will not allow us to go away uncomforted.

.   .   .   .   .   .

I have thought so long and so much about education, especially of late, and I think it such a high, holy task that I feel that it would be a sin to dedicate myself to it, and not be able to fill in my account to the utmost; if I thought otherwise, I should be a teacher without worth.

Education means the forming of the mind and of the soul. I feel that with the education of the mind the task of the teacher is not complete. The duty of forming the character is his; it is not included in the letter of the law, but it is a moral duty. I ask myself if I am able to do this? I who am still so uneducated myself.

I often hear it asserted that when the mind is cultivated, the spirit grows of itself; but I have seen for a long time that that is not always the case, that education and intellect are not always a patent of morality. But one must not judge those whose spirits remain unawakened, who lack the higher education of the soul, too harshly; in most cases the fault lies not in themselves, but in their bringing up. Great care has been taken in the cultivation of the understanding, but in the cultivation of the character, none!

I subscribe warmly to Mijnheer's idea, which is set forth so clearly in his paper on the "Education of Native Girls: Woman as the Carrier of Civilization!" Not because she has always shared the fate of man, and is a partner in his destiny, but because as I too am firmly convinced, she has a great and far-reaching influence, which can be for either good or evil; and because she, most of all, can help toward the spiritual regeneration of the world.

Man receives from woman his very earliest nourishment, at her breast, the child learns to feel, to think and to speak; and I see more and more clearly that the very earliest education has an influence which extends over one's whole later life. But how can the native women teach their children when they themselves are so ignorant?

There is great interest in education in the whole world of native women, so far as we know it. Many wish that they might be children again, so that they might profit by this opportunity. And splendid! the number of native scholars at Panti, Kudus, Japara and the other districts are the first visible foreshadowings of success. Already there are some girls' schools among the people and their number is increasing.

Tomorrow my mother will send a little girl (half orphan and child of her *anak mas* [1]) to school and last month our parents sent a good studious boy to learn to read in Dutch.

15 · TO MEVROUW ABENDANON-MANDRI

January 31, 1901

I turn my face pensively to the far away, staring into the blue light, as though I expected to find there an answer to the tumultuous questions of my soul. My eyes follow the clouds as they

1. *Anak mas*, foster child.

journey through the vast heavens till they disappear behind the waving green leaves of the cocoanut trees. I see the glistening leaves painted with the gold of the sun, and suddenly the thought comes, "Men have always asked, why does the sun shine? What sends his rays? O my sun, my golden sun! I shall strive to live so that I may be worthy to be shone upon, and tended and warmed by your light."

Do not be distressed dear, if things do not go as I would have them. My life shall not have been in vain: there is always something to be done. I will have it so! Those who seek God do not live in vain—and whosoever seeketh after God will find happiness, truth and peace of soul—and these are to be found at Modjowarno [1] as well. Who knows? perhaps there sooner than somewhere else. Never be discouraged; never be dismayed! We are only thankful that in any event a beginning has been made, that the foundations of our freedom and independence are being built.

16 · TO DR. N. ADRIANI

March 19, 1901

Highly Honored Dr. Adriani:

For a long time I have wanted to write to you, but several things, among them the indisposition of almost all of my family, have prevented me.

Now that the whole kabupaten, great and small, is again rejoicing in excellent health, I shall not allow this letter to remain any longer unwritten. It has been in my thoughts so long, and doubtless you have expected it as well. Forgive me for the delay.

First of all I want to send my hearty thanks for your amiable letter to my sister Roekmini, and for your kindness in sending the books.

The three of us were made so happy by them, and are still for that matter. We think it is splendid that you should think of us.

1. In the Residency of Surabaja. The most important as well as the oldest mission station in Java. It includes schools and hospitals. A medical missionary at Modjowarno had offered to train Kartini as a midwife, if her plan of going to Holland should fail.

We also think and speak of you and of your Toradjas,[1] of your work, and of everything that we discussed that evening at the Abendanons'. The hours that we spent in your company are among the most delightful memories of our visit to Batavia.

We hope with our whole hearts that will not be our only meeting, but that we may see you often again. What a pleasure it would be to us, if some day we might bid you welcome to Japara.

We have much sympathy for the work of the Christian missionaries in Dutch India, and we admire the nobility of heart of those who have established themselves in the most remote stretches of wilderness, far from their own country and kindred, and from all congenial companions, and cut themselves off from the world in which by virtue of birth, ability and education they would have an honorable position, to bring light into the lives of fellow men called by the cultivated world "savages."

We read both your letters with deep interest and I am grateful to you for telling us so much that was interesting, and of which we were ignorant.

In 1896 we had the privilege and pleasure of witnessing a solemnity the memory of which will probably remain with us all of our lives. That was the dedication of the new church at Kedung Pendjalin. It was the first time that we had ever been in a Christian church, and at a Christian service, and what we saw and heard there made a deep impression upon us. It was long ago, but it is still fresh in my memory. The spacious building was decorated with green foliage and the singing which echoed under the high roof was beautiful. With the reverent attentive multitude we followed the words which came forth from the chancel in pure Javanese.

Besides Heer Hubert, there were three missionary students, who preached upon the occasion; and it was certainly not the least solemn moment of the whole solemn service, when an old decrepit Javanese stood up to speak of his faith to his fellow countrymen. Everything was so impressive that the occasion has always been a memorable one to me.

It was on that morning that I had seen the outside world again for the first time since my school days.

We read in the paper under the sailing news that Mevrouw was back again in India, so she will be with you very soon. We were

1. A tribe in central Celebes among whom Adriani was working.

very glad for your sake, when we read it. This letter is as though we made you and Mevrouw a visit of felicitation upon her return, to wish her, although we are still unknown to her, a hearty welcome to Mapane. Are not the Toradjas very happy to have their "Mother" among them again?

17 · TO STELLA ZEEHANDELAAR

May 20, 1901

I have been through so much in my young life, but it is all as nothing in comparison with what I have suffered in these last dreadful days of Father's illness.

There were hours when I was without will, but trembled with inward pain and the lips that had defiantly proclaimed "Come what may," now stammered "God pity me." My birthday was a double feast—a celebration also of Father's restoration to health. I let Father see your present, and told him how pleased you were with his portrait. Father lay upon a lounging chair; I sat next to him on the floor, his hand resting upon my head; it was thus that I spoke to him of you.

Father smiled when I told him of your enthusiastic expression of sympathy for him, and with that smile on his face, and certainly with a thought for the distant and loved friend of his child, my sick one slept.

See how near you are to me, Stella—to us. Do you believe now that it was not lack of affection which kept me silent for so long, and can you forgive that silence now?

Let me earnestly thank you now for your friendship and your love, which have added so much to my life, and let me now press you fast to my heart in thought. If I could only see you in reality, face to face and heart to heart, so that I could open my soul to you—my soul which is so full of sadness. Stella, my Stella, I should be so glad if I could make you happy with but one rejoicing letter, cheer you with the tidings that we had succeeded, that we had reached our goal. Alas, instead this bears a complaint; I do not like to complain but the truth must be told.

An unexpected turn has come in our affairs; the question is now more difficult than ever; it is a matter of standing or falling, of blessed success or of complete undoing, and—OUR HANDS ARE BOUND.

There is a duty which is called gratitude; there is a high holy duty called filial love, and there is a detestable evil called egoism! Sometimes it is so difficult to see where the good ends, and the bad begins. One may go a certain distance, and then the boundary between the two extremes is hardly visible. Father's health is such that he is subject to severe heart attacks. Do you know what that means? We are defenseless—delivered over to the pleasure of blind fate.

We have stood so close to the fulfillment of our dearest wishes, and now we are again far away. It is a bitter awakening after we had thought that all stumbling blocks had been cleared from our way. The poor, tortured heart cries out, "What is my duty?" and no answer comes, while those who wait grope round in deepest darkness.

We can no longer seek for consolation in that splendid plan of the Government to open a school which would educate the daughters of regents to become teachers; nothing will ever come of it. For many regents whose consent had to be obtained, declared themselves against any innovation that would interfere with the custom of secluding young girls, and releasing them from their imprisonment by allowing them to go away from home to school.

It has been a hard blow for us, for we had built all our hopes upon it. Adieu illusions—adieu golden dreams of the future! You were too beautiful to be true.

I used to sit idly and take pleasure in the thought of how your eyes would shine when you heard the splendid news. And now the whole proposal has evaporated like smoke—has gone to the moon.

I do not know exactly how the matter stands; our friends at Batavia are away on a journey, but it goes very, very badly. Now if the plan for the domestic school for native girls should be in the same case, put down through the unwillingness of the parents themselves, there will be nothing left.

My fingers burn to write about the splendid plans of the Director of Education, and about the proposed education of regents' daughters to be teachers, but I remain idle. I must not express my opinions on important subjects, least of all through means of the press.

Many persons in our immediate surroundings know nothing of what is brooding and raging within us; they know nothing of our plans. One of our acquaintances who comes to the house often, read in the newspapers about the proposed school for regents' daughters, and said to my sisters, that would be just the thing for me, and that she and her husband would urge me to think seriously about it! Her husband spoke to me of the same thing, and with a blank face, as though knowing nothing, I let him speak.

Both husband and wife are enthusiastic for the work of emancipating the native woman. He is a government official, and for that reason can do much for our cause. He will soon be promoted, and then they will both be able to do much more for our people.

We have devised a plan for her, and she and her husband have listened to it with interest. When he becomes assistant resident, she is to invite the little daughters of the native officials serving under him to come to her house on certain fixed days, and give them instruction in handiwork and cooking; perhaps also in reading and writing. That would be a useful and beneficent work; the lady is delighted with the idea.

I have naturally told her much about you. She will become with pleasure a member of the Onderlinge Vrouwenbescherming.[1] She has two little daughters in Holland; one wishes to become a lawyer, and the other too will study a profession.

I told her that it was my earnest wish before I started out in life in whatever capacity, to spend first at least half a year at work in a hospital to learn something of the care of the sick because now if sickness should fall under my hands, I should not know which way to turn. She said at once that her brother-in-law who is a doctor, would help to initiate me into the secrets of sick nursing. The doctor is a newcomer, speaks no Javanese and very broken Malay. I can be of service to him in turn by acting as interpreter, for a large majority of his patients are either natives or Chinese.

I am thinking seriously of this plan of spending some time in a hospital, it would add a great deal to my education; I have sat and pondered over it long. What do you think of it? Oh it is misery on top of misery to see some one suffer frightful pain, and not to know how to alleviate that pain. Those who watch suffer even more than the patient himself. I have sat by many

1. Society for the Protection of Fallen Women.

sick beds, even as a child, and speak from experience. The idea of studying nursing came to me at the bedside of a dear one.

Later I shall speak out and say frankly what I have in my heart in regard to the education of girls. I shall plead for the importance of a knowledge of hygiene and of the structure of the human body to women. I want to see hygiene and physiology placed on the curriculum of the school, which is to be erected. Poor bunglers, eh? who after so much hodge-podge must gulp down those subjects. What an ideal school that Institute for Native Young Ladies will be! Science, cooking, housekeeping, handiwork, hygiene and vocational training; all must be there! It is only a dream, but let us dream if it makes us happy. Why not?

. . . .

What I have written thus far for the public has been but nonsense, suggested by some special happening or other. I may never mention serious subjects, alas! Later, when we shall have wholly wrested ourselves loose from the iron grip of agelong traditions, it will be different.

It would be different now, were it not for the love which we have for our dearest parents. Father would not be pleased if the name of his daughter should be rolled under the tongues of men. When I am wholly free and independent, I shall speak out and say what I think. So till that time comes, patience, Stella, for I cannot send you nonsense. When I write something in which I myself am pleased, in which my deepest convictions are expressed, I shall send it to you.

18 · TO PROFESSOR AND MRS. G. K. ANTON
OF JENA, GERMANY

June 10, 1901

We know what Borel has written on the gamelan (he calls it soul music). Do you know other things by him as well? *Het Jongetje* is charming. Many think Borel morbid and unwholesome, but we enjoy him. *De laatse incarnatie* is very fine, and his *Droom uit Tosari* is still finer, in that he writes of the wonderful natural beauty of Java's blue mountains. How much we enjoyed it! One must be an artist, or at least, have been subjected to a lively dose of artistic feeling to see and take pleasure in the beauties of mother nature, and to be able to express it in fine, clear style; such an one must be a dear privileged human child, upon whose forehead the muses have pressed a kiss.

I hope some day to have an opportunity to study your beautiful, musical language; I shall not let the chance go by without making use of it, you may be assured. To be able to read and write it would make me happy above everything. And if I should ever be so fortunate as to master the German language then I shall go and look for you. Will it not be a good idea? In the meantime flying machines will have come into use, and on some golden day you will see one of them flutter over Jena's blue horizon bringing a guest from afar!

I should indeed have been born a boy; then, perhaps, I should be able to carry out some of my high-flying plans. Now, as a girl, in our present native civilization, it is almost impossible to take a little walk down a turnpike. How can anything else be expected, when in Europe, the center of civilization, and of enlightenment, the strife should have been so long and so bitter for the good right of the woman? Could one in earnest expect that India, uncivilized, unenlightened, slumbering India, should take it well that her daughters, women who through centuries had been looked upon as beings of a lower order—yes, why should I not say it—as soulless creatures, should suddenly be regarded as human beings, who have a right to independent ideas, to freedom of thought, of feeling and of conduct?

Alas! nothing will come of that splendid plan of the Government, from which we expected so much; nothing will come of it because the majority of native officials opposed it. Adieu illusions! Ah! I have often thought and repeated aloud, that dreams and ideals were useless ballast in our native civilization, a superfluous and dangerous luxury! But the mouth alone says that, at the instigation of the cold understanding. It makes no impression upon that stupid crazy thing, the heart. For dreams of freedom have taken such deep root in our hearts, that they are never more to be uprooted without making desolate the soil from which they have sprung.

I think it is very good of you to give yourself such concern in regard to my future. I am deeply grateful. But oh, do you know nothing but sadness concerning me? We know what awaits us. We three are going hand in hand through life that for us will be full of struggle and disappointment! The way that we have chosen is certainly not strewn with roses; it is filled with thorns, but we have chosen it out of love, and with love and a joyous mind we shall follow it.

It leads to the raising of thousands and thousands of poor oppressed and downtrodden souls, our sisters; it leads toward freedom and happiness for millions. For our fellow countrymen too will inevitably be brought to a higher moral condition, and then they will work with us on that eternal work of striving for perfection. That giant's work at which through the centuries the noblest and best have toiled, trying to lead mankind upward toward the light, and in short, to bring our beautiful earth nearer to heaven. Is not that worth striving for all one's life?

It is the dream of "Tiga Soedara," the three Javanese sisters in the distant sunny land. Oh, could we but go to the land of changing seasons, the land of warmth and cold, the fatherland of learning, to prepare ourselves there for the good fight that we wish to make for the future happiness and well-being of our people. Above all the mind should be cultivated, before one can do good. Although people assert that to do good and to be intellectual are two different things; but I think that it takes the greatest wisdom to overcome the opposing forces that we human beings all feel in us, to temper them, and to regulate them so that they may work harmoniously together. I have seen so often that to try to do good ignorantly, does more harm than good.

Europe! Must you then remain always unattainable for us? We, who long for you with heart and soul.

But I do not believe in repining. Life is too beautiful—too splendid—to be wasted in complaints about things which can never be changed. Let us be thankful for the many blessings that the good God has bestowed upon us. Are we not fortunate above thousands and thousands of others, in the possession of our dear parents, good health, and in a number of little blessings, which make up the sum of our daily lives?

When we have enjoyed the music of singing birds then we are thankful that God has not created us deaf! When we are at Klein Scheveningen, that idyllic spot by the sea, where everything breathes quiet and peace, and watch the sun go down, then we know that we cannot be grateful enough that we have good eyes to enjoy the beautiful light which plays upon the golden water, and in the heaven above it! and a still prayer of thanksgiving toward the invisible Great Spirit who created everything and governs everything—a joyful thanksgiving rises from my heart, thanksgiving that I may, and am able to see so much. For there are many who cannot. Not only the poor people to whom the days and nights are as one, an impenetrable blackness, but there are many who are in full possession of their faculties, yet never see.

And we realize how privileged we are above so many of our fellow men, and gratitude for all the blessings of the good God fills our souls. But is it not a sad thought that we must be reminded of the lack in others, in order to appreciate our own advantages?

There are many educated native women; many, many cleverer and more talented than we, who have been hampered not at all in the cultivation of their minds, who could have become anything that they would, and yet they have done nothing, have attempted nothing that could lead to the uplifting of their sex, and of their race. They have either fallen back wholly into the old civilization, or gone over to that of the Europeans; in both cases being lost to their people to whom they could have been a blessing, if they had but willed it. Is it not the duty of all those who are educated and on a higher plane to stand by with their greater knowledge and seek to lighten the way for those who are less fortunate? No law commands this, but it is a moral duty.

Forgive me if I have tired you by writing at too great length. How did I come to take up so much of your valuable time with the babble? Forgive me, but you yourself are not without blame; your two letters which are lying before me are so sympathetic; when I read their cordial words, it is as though I had you before me, and that is what I have imagined all the time that I have been writing.

That one of Java's volcanoes on the eastern cape has broken out frightfully, and cost many lives, you will certainly have learned from others, so I shall not write of that. According to the papers, two other volcanoes are now active. Oh, inscrutable, beautiful blue mountains!

The eclipse of the sun on the 18th of May, for the observation of which scientists from all over the world came to Java, we could scarcely see here at all, owing to the unfortunate weather. The day was cloudy and there was, and is still rain. But what was vexation to us, was a blessing to the farmers! Father was made very happy by the good rain which refreshed the thirsty fields, and so much depends upon that. So much can depend upon a single shower of rain, woe or weal to hundreds, yes to thousands.

19 · TO MEVROUW H. G. DE BOOIJ-BOISSEVAIN
June 6, 1901

Dear Hilda:

Let me begin by sending you both, in the name of my sisters too, heartfelt wishes of happiness on the birth of your second son. We hope from our hearts that he may become just such a sweet, healthy little fellow as his brother, who will grow in time into a fine man, and make you both very proud.

How does our little friend act under his new dignity of big brother? Does he not want to play with Alfred right away? The little one is too eager, is it not true?

A May child! De Genestet [1] has written such a beautiful poem about that; the ending is sad but I fervently hope that the prayer of the poet in the last two couplets may be fulfilled for your May child. Although naturally you know the lines yourself, I cannot help repeating them again here:

"De God der lente spreide Bloei in uw vaders gaarde,
* U rozen voor den voet   Bloei aan uw moeders zij*
De God der liefde leide   Hun schoonste bloem op aarde,
* U zachtkens, trouw en goed! Gij, knaapje van den Mei! [2]*

---

1. Peter Augustus De Genestet (1829–1860), noted Dutch poet.
2. *"May the God of springtime spread, Bloom in your father's garden,*
 Roses before your feet,   Bloom at your mother's side,
 May the God of love lead and The loveliest flower on earth to
 Keep you gentle, true and good!   them,
            Thou little blossom of May!"

I hear you laugh when you have read the verses, how foolish, eh? but do not be surprised at them, all old aunts become more or less sentimental, and to that category belongs she who now writes.

20 · TO MEVROUW ABENDANON-MANDRI

August 1, 1901

We Javanese cannot live without flowers and sweet odors. The native flowers in their splendor awaken in me a world of thought and feeling whenever I breathe in their perfume. Days afterwards it lives in my memory, and I feel the strong Javanese blood coursing through my veins. Oh soul of my people, that used to be so beautiful, that was full of grace, poetry, humility and modesty—what has become of you? What have time and dull routine made of you?

It is so often said that we are more European than Javanese in our hearts. Sad thought! We know that we are impregnated with European ideas and feelings—but the blood, the Javanese blood that flows live and warm through our veins, can never die. We feel it in the smell of incense and in the perfume of flowers, in the tones of the gamelan, in the sighing of the wind through the tops of the cocoanut trees, the cooing of the turtle doves, the whistling of the fields of ripened rice, in the pounding of the *padi-blocks* [1] at the time of the rice harvest.

Not for nothing have we passed our whole lives amid surroundings where everything depends on mere form; we have seen the emptiness of those forms, and deeply, deeply felt the lack of meaning and substance. A cry of despair, a lament, overtakes our soul: "What is form without content?" The form may be perfect but the content is the main thing. Still, there is much good in the Javanese people. We are so anxious for you to admire our people. When I see something fine, some trait of character, that is peculiarly Javanese, then I think "How glad I should be if Mevrouw A.

1. In Java the rice is separated from its husk by beating it in great wooden mortars with five-foot long pestles. Usually two or three women work together pounding out the rice, and the sound produces a rhythmic cadence.

were with us. She would be pleased at this thing, would appreciate it, she who has wide open eyes for everything that is noble."

Our little Javanese wood carver artist as you call him, has made something very beautiful with the whole *wajang* history carved upon it.[2] Wajang figures on the cover, on the outside and inside both, and on all four walls. There is a case designed to protect it, which is also ornamented with wajang figures. The box is lined with orange satin, which is gathered and pleated, and it is set off by a silver rim, also of native workmanship. Indeed it ought to be very beautiful, for it is designed to hold the portraits of the regents of Java and Madura, which the queen has ordered sent to her. This mark of homage is a pretty idea. The Regent of Garut ordered the box and I was given free play. I might spend as much as I liked for both objects.

2. The *wajang* (pronounced wayang) is the classical Javanese drama. Its most ancient, most profound and perhaps most important form is that of the shadow-play, the *wajang kulit.* It is performed with the aid of large flat leather puppets which are supported from below on sticks, and which have movable arms. Their shadows are projected on a white screen by the flickering light of an oil lamp, but the audience may sit on either side of the screen. They are manipulated by a single puppeteer, the *dalang,* who recites all the lines, sings songs, and directs the gamelan orchestra which accompanies the performance. The shadow-play in its modern form dates from before the 11th century. The plays were drawn from the Hindu literature of the Mahabarata and the Ramayana, but have been considerably augmented with indigenous Javanese themes and characters. The stories and the personalities of the various heroes, clowns and villians are known by heart by every Javanese, and the performances, which last from sunset till sunrise, are always attended by large crowds of every age, who give them their full attention. Every performance is accompanied by a religious ritual, and has considerable supernatural significance. The shadow puppets have highly stylized shapes, and are intricately carved and painted. These figures are found in many other Javanese arts, in woodcarving, and textiles, for examples, and have a place in various religious ceremonies. There are also narrative dance performances, both classical and popular, which depict the same characters and plots. For a description of the *wajang* with fine illustrations see Frits A. Wagner, *Indonesia: The Art of an Island Group,* New York: Crown Publishers, Inc., 1959, pp. 119–139.

21 · TO MEVROUW H. G. DE BOOIJ-BOISSEVAIN

August 19, 1901

You must have thought it ungracious of me to remain silent for so long after your charming letter and your goodness in sending the dear snapshot, which I have enjoyed so much. The silence has not been from lack of appreciation, but because the one wholly sound Kartini had all of her time taken up with the little sick sisters. It was so warm, it was not hard to exaggerate a little indisposition, so that we could not help spoiling our invalids. Just now one of the pairs of eyes which I have seen so troubled, peeped over my shoulder and read this. Child, child, what do you gain by it? The children will never hear any praise from me, I assure you. But what am I doing now—speaking ill of my dear little sisters?

. . . .

Nothing is impossible in this world. What we look upon today as an impossibility, tomorrow may be an accomplished fact.

There is a restlessness in our native civilization, the spirit of progress is moving among us. It is strongly combated by the inherent love which the Javanese has for the ancient "laws." There will be a hard fight before these hoary ideas and customs shall be deeply buried in the ground, never again to rise.

22 · TO MEVROUW VAN KOL

August, 1901

I should be so glad, so happy, if I could be in a position to lead children's hearts, to form little characters, to awaken young minds, to help to mold the women of the future who will be able to carry forward enlightenment like a torch. There is much misery in our Javanese woman's world, there has always been so much suffering, so much bitterness.

The only road which lies open to a Javanese girl, and above all to one of noble birth, is marriage.

From far and near we know of the horrible misery of the woman caused by certain Islamic institutions that are so easy for the man, but oh, so bitterly hard and miserable for her.

"She soon grows accustomed to it, she finds that it is nothing," say the wise men, and then "We should have no more peace if we put such ideas into her head."

Let me, a child of Java, nourished at her breast, who has lived here all her life, assure you that the native women have honest, simple hearts that can feel and suffer as well as the most delicate, sensitive woman's heart in your country.

But here there is a suppressed suffering which consumes itself. For she feels herself powerless and defenseless through her ignorance and inexperience.

The old traditions speak. Fatima's bridegroom takes a new wife and she is asked by the prophet what she feels: "Nothing, Father, nothing," she declared. And while saying this she leaned against a banana tree; the leaves, formerly fresh and green, withered, and the trunk against which her body rested shrivelled into ashes.

Again the father asked her what she felt and she said, "Nothing, Father, nothing."

The father gave her a raw egg and bade her hold it against her heart; he asked her to give it back to him, he broke it open and the egg was cooked.

The Eastern woman's heart has not changed. Many think it an honor to tolerate with unmoved countenances the one or more women their husbands have brought home, but do not ask what is hidden behind that iron mask, or what the walls of their dwellings could tell when the eyes of the world are removed. There are so many burning women's hearts, with poor, innocent, suffering, childlike souls.

And it was the misery that I saw, even in my childish years, that first awakened in me the desire to fight against these time-honored customs, and substitute justice for old tradition.

Our work will have a twofold aim, first to help to enlighten all our people, and secondly to raise up our sisters, so that they may live and be treated as human beings. To all of you who have sympathy for Java, and the Javanese, we send an urgent prayer— help us to realize our ideals; they mean so much to our people and to our sex.

Raise the Javanese woman, educate her heart and her understanding, and you will have splendid workers to cooperate with you in your noble work, your giant's work, the work of civilizing and enlightening a whole nation.

Teach her a trade, so that she will no longer be powerless when her guardians command her to contract a marriage which will inevitably plunge her and whatever children she may have into misery.

The only escape from such conditions is for the girl herself to learn to be independent.

There is no one yet who does it, who dares do it.

It is a disgrace for a girl not to marry, to remain an unprotected woman.

Our idea is to open, as soon as we have the means, an institute for the daughters of native officials, where they will be fitted for practical life and will be taught as well the things which elevate the spirit, and ennoble the mind.

Would such a school succeed? We are bold enough to answer "Yes." Many of the native officials send their daughters to school now, but it is only for the accomplishments, and not because they expect it to be of any practical use; or of real benefit to the woman herself. Still that does not minimize the importance of the fact that more and more, they are educating their daughters. The many government and private schools can testify to the truth of this. Even the Sultan of Solo sends his daughters to school.

In progressive Preanger, where the education of girls is no new thing, a special school for daughters of the nobles, subsidized by the Government, has been opened. There are even regents' daughters who go to a domestic school in a strange place!

Then there are many parents who would like to send their daughters to school, yet refuse to send them where they would have to study with boys. The expense of having a governess is far beyond the means of an ordinary native magistrate, only a few are able to afford it. No wedono who has not an independent fortune can keep a governess for his little daughter.

There was a young mother who asked her husband on the last day of her life as a dying request, to carry out one of her dreams, which was, as soon as he should be in better circumstances, to send her little daughter to the European school.

We have talked over this question, and also the idea of an

independent self-supporting woman, many times with the wives of officials, and all of them have strengthened us in our belief that someone is only needed to take the first step; to set the example, and then the path will have been opened and others will follow it. There are many girls who think and feel as we and who would be glad to break the bonds in which the Islamic law holds them cloistered. But they remain quiescent before that "There is no one now who does it."

There must be some one to be first.

There is a native official who sought permission from the Director of Education for his daughter to enter the medical school. Thrice blessed father—thrice blessed daughter! she will be of great service to her country. I hope that she will be able to carry out her intentions.

A younger sister of mine, Roekmini, has a great love for painting and it is her wish to be able to study at the Art Academy, so that later she may work for the development of our native art. Does not a people's art go hand in hand with a people's civilization? And if she found that the Art Academy was not the place for her, that she had not sufficient talent, then she could go to the Household School and later teach the future women the worth of money, which would be a very useful thing for our people.

My sister and I should then be able to work together. And what we are most anxious to have taught in our future schools is hygiene, and a knowledge of sanitation and nursing. Hygiene and nursing should be part of one's education. So many misfortunes could have been averted or at least reduced to a minimum, if everyone, men, as well as women, had been taught something of this useful study.

It is not in the least our intention to try to make European-Javanese of the Javanese by giving them liberal educations; our idea is to develop the fine qualities that are peculiar to their race; to help them to gain by contact with another civilization, not to the detraction of their own, but to its enoblement.

. . . . . .

I enjoyed your introduction so much to "The Land and People of Java." It warmed my heart to read the charming manner in which the beauty of my country was pictured and its wonderful places described.

Often an overpowering feeling of happiness comes over us,

when we are out in God's free nature. Far from the doings of little souled men, alone with nature; above our heads the blue heavens and at our feet the unfathomable sea, behind us waving cocoanut palms. Oh! who would not be happy amid such surroundings?

Sometimes I am betrayed into an egotistical thought, "Oh, let me live alone in this pure atmosphere, far from the noise of the market place, from worldly cares, alone with nature, and with my own soul!" That is pure egoism! it is not the voice of life, we are meant to live with and for humanity. But I have kept you too long already; you have other and more useful things to do than to read all this prattle from a "sentimental" Javanese girl.

23 · TO MEVROUW ABENDANON-MANDRI

September 4, 1901

We will not, we cannot believe that our lives will be only commonplace and monotonous like the lives of thousands of others before us, and as will be those of thousands of those who come after us! and yet any other destiny seems so improbable. Only once the fulfilment of our nearest and dearest wishes seemed near; now it is unattainably far away.

There are hours when the tortured human heart, torn with doubt, cries, "My God, what is my duty?"—seeing two duties which directly oppose and antagonize one another. Yet how can two things that are diametrically opposed be called by the same name?

"Stay," says a voice behind me, "surrender your own wishes and longings to the will of him who is dear to you, and to whom you are dear; the struggle has been good, for it has served to strengthen and ennoble your own spirit. Stay!" And then again, I hear another voice ever loud and clear, which says: "Go, work for the realization of your ideals; work for the future; work for the good of thousands who are bent beneath the yoke of unjust laws, who have a false conception of good and evil. Go suffer and fight. Your work will be for all time!" Which is the higher duty, the first or the last?

There are not many people in the world, never mind how closely they may be bound together by ties of blood, who love and understand one another as do my father and I. There is much resemblance in our characters. We sympathize in everything with each other; there is only one point where we differ. Oh, why that one, why? Is it true, what is told us, that in the whole of wide, wide nature no two things are absolutely alike?

Father has borne so patiently with all my caprices; I have never heard a harsh or bitter word from his lips. He is always loving, always gentle. Through everything I feel his great love. Sometime ago when I pressed him for a decision, he looked at me so sorrowfully, it was as if his sad eyes asked, "Are you in such haste to leave me, child?"

I turned away my head; I did not wish to see the dear true eyes; I wanted to be strong and not weak.

My heart almost broke once, when, as we stood opposed to each other, Father clasped me in his arms, and in a voice trembling with emotion said, "Must it be so, child? Is there no other way? Must it be?" And we stayed there, heart pressed to heart, looking into each other's eyes.

That was a heavy time, as heavy as a time can well be on this earth. It was shortly before Father's illness. Later, when Father was recovering, Mother said to me, "Ah, child, give in to him."

"I cannot," I answered in a choking voice.

Since then Mother has never spoken about it to me. But when Father gives his consent, she will not withhold hers. She is all love and tenderness towards us, but that only makes the struggle the harder.

Pain, nothing but pain, is all that we have brought to those true loving hearts.

24 · TO MEVROUW ABENDANON-MANDRI

September 30, 1901

In Preanger there are a great many women and girls who have been to school, and who speak Dutch. Most of those whose acquaintance we made talked Dutch with us because we do not know each other's language.[1] Strange! that we should make an agreeable acquaintance with people of our own country, and of kindred race by means of a foreign tongue. Our intercourse was cordial, free and unrestrained. They are a cheerful people, full of jest and merriment.

.   .   .   .

I have many things in my mind. Sometimes my fingers itch so to write down my thoughts, to be able to throw them in the faces of the multitude.

But what good would that do? People would shrug their shoulders, some of them would laugh, and most of them would take no notice whatever. One might as well be an idiot or a simpleton.

Perhaps it is better so, for who knows what harm a pen might do in the hands of an inexperienced, uncomprehending hothead.

Now after that tirade, something that you will think pleasant. A short while ago the Quarteros, with another controleur, were at our house. The gentlemen were speaking of a regent whom the strange controleur knew well. "A fine man," we heard him say, and then, "No, he is not married, except to a woman whom he cannot present, just an ordinary woman of the people by whom he has several children. He does not intend to marry; he will marry no Raden-Aju because then he would have to send the woman away, or relegate her to a second place, in either case making her miserable, and he will not do that."

My heart leapt when I heard that. Then there is indeed such a one! Splendid!

Mevrouw Quartero told us afterwards that both she and her husband glanced quickly at us, thinking at the same time, "Should the girls have heard that, how he will rise in their esteem?" So it is, too. We hope fervently that the regent will always remain of the same mind, and that he will never be turned aside from his good resolution.

It would be a great pleasure to us to make his acquaintance; we hope that we may some day.

The young guard, regardless of sex, should band themselves together. We can each of us do something unaided, towards the uplifting and civilizing of our people, but if we were united our

1. In the Preanger region in the western part of the island of Java, Sundanese is the language spoken. It is quite different from Javanese, although related to it.

strength would be multiplied many times. By working together we could gather a goodly store of fruit.

In union there is strength, and power.

25 · TO STELLA ZEEHANDELAAR

October 11, 1901

And now dear friend, I am going to speak of myself and give you in strictest confidence some idea of our plans. As doctors, mid-wives, writers, teachers or artists, we could gain our own inde-pendence and at the same time work for the good of our fellow countrymen. All these ways now stand open to us and there are others too in which we could be independent. But we do not desire them, because we would only be working for ourselves, and not for our people.

What could we do for them if we were pharmacists' assistants, bookkeepers, telegraph operators, clerks in an office or something of that kind? Those spheres of activity do not attract us. We want to lead full rich lives. You know the Government, through the Director of Education, is planning to erect schools for native girls; and by way of example a domestic school for the daughters of the nobles.

When we heard of this plan last year from the Director himself, his wife asked me if I would teach in this last school. I answered that I took much interest in the plan, but that the undertaking would be too great for me, because I had no training and would not be capable of filling such a position.

Mevrouw said that her husband wanted me just as I was; to help to lead the young hearts and to form the young characters, I must go among the children as an elder sister, and be an exam-ple to them. I felt highly honored at the suggestion, but unfitted for the task as I was; I had no right to undertake it. Mevrouw said that if I really must have some preparation, then I could go for a little while to the normal school at Batavia, there would be no difficulty about that, it was only a question of my own wishes.

That my father approved of this suggestion, you know already. When I went to Batavia I saw the Directress of the Girls' High

School and she said that she would do everything in her power to help me. This cordiality from one who was almost a stranger, was very encouraging. Unsought and unexpected, this offer of assistance was simply thrown into my lap. I was in the clouds and thought that my departure for Batavia was only a question of weeks, or at most, of months.

I have already told you that we are not rich; though Father has a large income, at the same time, his expenditures are great, so that we have only enough to live quietly and to give our boys (boys must be helped before everything) good educations.

I had also thought of the financial difficulties, and had made a plan so that the expense of my studies would not be too great a burden. It would cost my father twelve hundred florins for one year, a whole month's income, and no small sum for a household as large as ours; so my thoughts turned towards the medical school at Batavia, tuition in medicine is free, at least for boys (there have never been any women medical students). One can study medicine at the expense of the country. The students receive free lodging, a monthly allowance to cover cost of food and clothing, and there is free medical attendance.

When I was in Batavia I asked the Director of Education to which department the school of medicine belonged, and if girls would be admitted to it. Mr. A. had nothing against that, but naturally girls would be special students. My idea was to ask the Government to admit me upon the same footing as the men students. For everyone with any brains at all can see how useful a woman doctor would be, especially among the women of the people, who usually would rather die than be touched by a strange man.

If the chief of the Department of Education would support my petition there is no doubt that the government would receive it favorably. I have already thought much about the medical profession, the length of time required for study alone disconcerts me. For one who is not yet twenty, seven years of study does not seem so long; but for one who has already passed that age, it is very long. And then as a full grown girl to have to sit in the beginning day after day, between boys of from thirteen to eighteen, and to be the only woman in a circle of men is not pleasant. But these are minor difficulties, which I could force myself to overcome.

There is still something else; Father and my friends are against it, though fortunately not unconditionally. Father objects because I should be the only girl among all those men and boys, such a thing would be unheard of here—and my friends object because they are afraid that I would not have the necessary nerve to go through with the studies.

Medicine is certainly a splendid calling, but not a profession for everyone; a strong will and perseverance are not enough, nerves of steel are also a necessity. That is what worries my friends, so that they give me no peace.

Father thinks that teaching would be the best profession for me, as do also my friends in Batavia. They think that would be a suitable, fine work for me, where I could spread my ideas broadcast among the younger generation, the women and mothers of the future. As a teacher, even of a little circle, there would be a direct influence exerted upon that little circle, which would in time, widen and spread out so that many would follow my example.

You know my love for literature; it is one of my dreams to be able to accomplish something there. It is true one cannot serve two masters at the same time, but I see no reason why if I were a teacher, after being busy with the children all day, I could not work at literature at night. I want to do only one thing at a time and do that well. *Entre ces deux mon coeur balance!* As a doctor or something else, perhaps I should not have the opportunity to do that other work of which I am so fond, scribbling with my pen.

But teaching, the bringing up of children, is something so earnest and sacred in itself, that I should never be at peace if I attempted it, and felt myself unable to do it well.

As a teacher of the domestic school, I should be with the children the whole day, even in the evening and at night I should not be wholly free, because the children would be under my care. Such a post would bring with it heavy responsibilities and duties. Perhaps you think I am exaggerating the difficulties and responsibilities; but I cannot look upon it in any other way. To me it would be a crime to devote myself to the bringing up of children, future carriers of civilization to the race, and not to be fitted for that great task, which is so high and holy in my eyes.

What do you desire for me, Stella? Which road would you most gladly see me started upon? Tell me honestly and frankly what you really think. You have already shown yourself a good true friend; here is another opportunity.

There is still another profession open to us. A missionary doctor, personally unknown to us, but of good name and established reputation, has heard much of us from our friends and has offered of his own accord, to train us, free of cost, to be midwives.

You will certainly have heard of the great mission station in Modjowarno in the residency of Surabaja? The name of this missionary doctor is mentioned in the book *Social Work in India,* published at the Exposition of Women's Work. You must know too that there is a crying need for midwives here in India. Every year in Java and the whole of the Netherlands Indies, about twenty thousand women die in childbirth, and there are on an average thirty thousand stillborn children; all from lack of intelligent care. In that direction there certainly stretches out before us a broad field of usefulness where we could be a blessing to our sisters.

We take a great interest in this cause, but it would be an untruth if we said that it was one of our dreams to be midwives. But it would be one thousand times better to be midwives than to be dependent, held to narrow household cares through a compulsory marriage.

We have Father's permission to go to Modjowarno and study to be midwives when all other doors to independence shall have been closed to us. He is strongly opposed to a work of personal service; he thinks that kind of work would be degrading to our aristocratic hands. Our friends, at first, deplored the idea too, but they put their objections on such a noble, such a high plane! They thought that it would be hard for us because we had other dreams and ambitions. But would our desire to lighten the way and to be examples to others be reached in this manner? Even in civilized Europe, the calling of midwife is looked down upon, more or less. Would India with all its ceremony and form be able to appreciate the beauty of the work? People here would only see its humbleness; for everything that does not shine, is looked upon as of no worth by my poor countrymen. You understand very well that we personally would be indifferent to the lowliness of our calling; but the effect which that would have, should not be a matter of indifference to us.

If we want to break the path to freedom and independence for the Javanese woman, we must set a practical example. And a calling that is looked down upon and considered degrading would not find a following, and we want others to follow in our footsteps. Our example then must be something that compels respect and inspires emulation. We have not only our own wishes to consider, we must reckon with the prejudices and the character of the people whom we wish to enlighten.

Lately in Holland, and especially at The Hague, there has been a growing movement of interest in Indian art. The Association of the East and West, an offspring of the Exposition of Women's Work of which you must know, has as one of its chief purposes the encouragement of things Indian. There is a special division for art, composed entirely of artists of reputation.

They are planning to send an artist to India to help the cause of Indian art in general, but especially in its practical application, and to protect it from the strange influences, above all those imported from Europe, which would contaminate its true character.

I have already told you that Roekmini has a great love for painting, and certainly some talent in that direction, and it is her desire to become a painter. Of course study in Europe would be necessary and that alas, is unattainable for her. Perhaps through our own efforts, we may be able to help little sister to realize her dream. Could we not get into communication with East and West and might not my sister by the help of that association be enabled to study drawing and painting at the Art Academy at The Hague? Later she could return to Java and dedicate herself wholly to the art of her own country.

If all our plans should suffer shipwreck, then Roekmini will fit herself to be a midwife. She will become either a midwife or a painter, but whichever she does she will do well. In either case she should study in Europe. In Holland she could take a full course in obstetrics and could be of great service then to the future mothers of her land.

The doctors here could only train her to be a midwife, who works under the direction of a doctor. To our indolent people with their exalted ideas, it would make a great difference whether a midwife had been trained here or in Europe. With a European diploma, she would not be looked upon as degraded so much by her work and might still serve as an example, and as a light to be followed. We are going to apply for an appropriation from the Government to pay for her education in Holland. We hope for the assistance of Prof. Hector Treub in Amsterdam, and of Dr.

Stratz in The Hague, men who have already broken their lances many times for the cause of obstetrics in India. Through ignorance of this science, thousands of lives are needlessly sacrificed every year. In the general assembly also, attention was called to this cause by Van Kol. A certain member of Parliament is coming to India; I hope to see him and to have an opportunity to speak with him; my brother knows him very well.

The Government here in India has already taken steps toward the improvement of these sad conditions, of which I have spoken. In Java all doctors who wish to charge themselves with the training of midwives receive a monthly subsidy from the Government. The prospective midwives receive an allowance during their apprenticeship to cover the cost of board and other necessities, and after they have passed their examinations they are also paid by the Government.

After she had completed her studies in Europe, sister Roekmini would open a clinic in Java. There is only one fault to be found with the teachings of the doctors that we have here; that is obscurity, because it is impossible for the teachers to make themselves clearly understood by the students, when they speak different languages. Almost without exception, the doctors here have little or no command of our language. Malay and usually very much broken Malay at that, is the language which the doctors use towards the people. Hardly a single doctor speaks Javanese, and so very few of the Javanese people understand and speak Malay. The difficulties would fall away if some one with a thorough knowledge of the native language would undertake the task of training. Roekmini's birth will be of great help to her in this, for the natives are very loyal to their nobles.

On the 24th of October, just two weeks after the interruption of this letter I come back to it again. My card, sent meanwhile, will have told you of the sad state in which we have been; happily that is now past.

As you know already, Roekmini has been dangerously ill; twice her life seemed to hang upon a single thread. Now thank God, she is on the road to recovery and grows each day a little stronger. Today she has been out of doors.

I cannot tell you how happy and thankful we are that everything has gone so well with her. Sister Kardinah, too, is on her feet again. She can now take little walks and her poor thin cheeks are beginning to fill out. We have certainly had our share of suffering.

It is now so unhealthy everywhere on account of the drought. Poor country—so much hangs over you besides sickness. Many *sawahs* (rice paddies) over the whole country have been destroyed by the great drought. The suffering is worse in the neighboring town of Grobogan and we look toward Demak with fear and anguish; there, twenty-six thousand sawahs have already been destroyed and cholera is raging. The west winds will soon come that drown the land every year. Poor country! that after the east winds, dries up and perishes from drought, and after the west winds, is drowned with floods. But I shall write no more about this misery, but only tell you what has happened during the last fourteen days.

Sister Kardinah also wishes to become a teacher, and has chosen as her specialty domestic science and cooking. Our plan is to remain together always and to work side by side for our common goal; the education of our people.

If fate is propitious we shall open a school, in which instruction will be given along broader lines than mere book education; it will include lessons in handiwork, household arts and kindred subjects, and there will also be classes in wood-carving and painting, and in midwifery. But a course in domestic science can only be taken in Holland; there is no opportunity here. Kleintje's forte is really music and her dearest dream was and still is, to become a musician, but that is absolutely impossible for her; so my little maid has resigned herself to the inevitable.

She is so eager to work for our people, and a teacher of the household arts could do a tremendous amount of good. More and more the Government realizes what a great advantage it would be to the people and their rulers, if they could learn economy.

We may appeal to the Government on behalf of Kleintje, and ask that she be placed at a school where she could be qualified to teach domestic economy. My little sister wishes to undertake the great task of teaching the women and future mothers of Java economy and frugality.

Lately the Government has shown that it wishes to place a premium upon education and enlightenment in its magistrates; this has been evinced by the latest regents' appointments. According to custom, regents have been appointed by the law of heredity, from father to son, and if there is no son available, then some near relative of the last regent is appointed. It has never happened before that the new regent was no connection at all; but the two newly appointed men are progressive and enlightened and have been educated in Europe.

It is evident that the Government is in earnest in its endeavor to civilize and educate the people of Java, and especially the classes from which the Government servants are recruited.

Heer Abendanon has said that there can be no argument against the statement that the intellectual awakening of the native people cannot progress appreciably as long as the woman is left behind in the forward march. The education of woman has always been an important factor in civilization.

In the last fifteen years, the Government of the Netherlands Indies has sent four young Javanese to Holland at its own expense, to be educated there as teachers so that they come back later to work for the good of their fellow countrymen. The Government realized that their work would have better results if they received their educations abroad. But the desire to do this did not come of itself to these men; it was suggested by those who had the awakening of India at heart.

With us it is different. In us the impulse, the longing to do something for our people was born in our own hearts, from deeply rooted conviction, and came through suffering, and through sympathy for the suffering of others.

We are only waiting for Father's permission now. Forgive a father, Stella, that he hesitates to give his children as hostages to an uncertain future. As innovators, as pioneers, we must stand alone, combat and overcome obstacles; our way will lead through much suffering and discouragement, it is certain. And what parents would wish to see their children zealous for suffering? What parents willingly see their children voluntarily dedicate themselves to lives of struggle and disappointment?

I do not know that I should go to Holland to study now, even if the opportunity were offered me, though to go has always been one of my greatest desires. Last year when it was suggested that I study at home I set myself against the proposition with all my might. If I studied at all, I wanted to study properly, and I could only do that in Holland or at Batavia. And as Holland was beyond my reach, my head was set upon Batavia.

I did not think I could study well at home, because I could not devote my whole time to my books. At my time of life there would be too many other claims upon me. Household and social duties would keep me too much from my work, it would be impossible to eliminate them if I remained at home. That was last year when Father was well and strong; now Father is that no longer alas!

Forgive a daughter, Stella, if once when she might have had the opportunity to fulfill her heart's wish, a wish upon which the future well-being of many others also depended, she held back, because she had not the heart to separate from a father who had given her love and care her whole life long and whose feeble health now demanded more than ever the care and affection which she alone could give.

Stella, I am a child, I am a daughter, not a woman alone who can give herself wholly, and dedicate herself to a great and beautiful work. I am also a child bound by the bonds of tenderest love and gratitude to an old gray father, who has grown old and gray through care for his children. Of these children perhaps I am dearest.

Stella, you who know my great love for him, and next to that my love for what I regard as our calling, who know the strength of my affection for my sisters, will be able to understand what a hard conflict there is in store for me. I must be separated from my sisters, away from the work that I would do, or separated from Father, united with my sisters, and giving my all to our calling.

Father is weak now, needs care, and my first duty is to him. Oh Stella, I should never have a moment's peace if I carried on my own work far away from Father, knowing that he was suffering and needed me.

The work which we would do is noble. It will not be only for the present but for all time. Still I should never be able to answer to my own conscience if I should neglect my old, gray father for any cause whatever. He has the first right to me.

One of the precepts which I wish to inculcate is this: honor every living creature, respects their rights, their feelings; and even when it seems necessary, shrink from causing the least suffering to another. Should I be able to teach others what I myself neglected in practice?

I must never forsake my duty as a child, but neither must I forsake the duty which I owe to myself, for it is not my own happiness that depends upon its realization but great good to others. The problem now is to try and harmonize as far as possible these two duties which are diametrically opposed to each other. The only solution seemed to be to find some way by which I could stay with Father, and also go on with my studies.

I am going to study at home, and fit myself for the profession of teaching, just as well as one can be fitted by self-study, when it is supported by a strong will, and perseverance.

I had already thought of this plan, but Mevrouw Abendanon gave it the impetus which pushed it forward, when she suggested some time ago that, without waiting for further arbitraments of capricious fate, we three go ahead and study here at home.

We have had a governess for two months; in her we have found a charming and affectionate friend. She is still very young, a girl of strong character who has left her family in the fatherland and come here to earn her daily bread.

It is only unfortunate that this miserable sickness has come; otherwise we should be getting along famously. Naturally all this time I have not been able to look at a book. Annie Glaser, that is our teacher's name, has engagements which take her on some days, to another family here. But as soon as she can arrange it, she will give her entire time to us or to me alone most probably, for my poor sisters must not have anything in their hands, and above all in their heads, just now. They feel very miserable under the enforced idleness, but hands and heads are still weak.

What do you think about all of these high flying plans? If only you do not say, "Poor thing, you are trying to fly too high," I shall be satisfied. Do you know what I have noticed among our friends? That they have too high an opinion of us. They ascribe to us qualities and abilities which we do not possess. Sometimes we have to laugh at their enthusiasm. The saying that "love is blind" is here applicable. You should only hear some of the things of which they think us capable. We feel our own limitations deeply, whenever our friends set us so in the sun. We feel small, but we feel grateful too for the love of which it speaks. One friend would be glad to see me work with my pen, for our people. I must found a journal devoted to their needs, and must be its editor, or I must become a writer on the foremost daily newspaper of Indonesia and write articles, by which those who are now fast sleeping will be frightened wide awake! Had I no reason for my assertion that "love is blind"?

And, now I must think of parting from my sisters, the idea is frightful to them, and it is no less so to me. If they are successful in getting that for which they are asking they will be far from us in a strange land. It is fortunate that they have a brother there, who even as I, loves the sisters from his soul. This brother is full of enthusiasm and sympathy for our ideals, for in them he finds an echo of his own. We have made a compact with him, that when he has completed his studies, he will come back to us and we will work together.

It is an inspiration to us that he should share in the ideals of his sisters, it lifts us up, draws us forward, just as does the great sympathy and understanding which you have for us. There is still another young man, European, who only knows us through his mother, but who sympathizes with our cause and takes a lively interest in it. The sympathy and understanding of friends even when we do not know them personally, is a great support to us. We need this support very much. You will always give me yours, will you not, Stella?

26 · TO MEVROUW ABENDANON-MANDRI

November 20, 1901

One should never promise anything, even when it depends entirely upon oneself, because one can never tell beforehand what will happen. Never mind how honestly the promise is made, and how earnestly one desires to keep it, unforeseen circumstances may arise, which make its fulfillment impossible. There is a belief among us Javanese, that those who break a promise will be visited by a poisonous serpent. The serpent comes to remind them of their promise, if they do not quickly fulfill it, they will be visited by another more venomous serpent, whose bite is deadly. If they delay longer, misfortune will surely overtake them. The serpent only lives upon the promises of holy spirits, as the souls of the righteous who are dead are nourished by flowers, perfume and incense. The serpent is sent by the departed souls of the righteous to remind men of their forgotten promises. But why do I tell you of our Javanese beliefs? Forgive me, when there is so much besides that I want to tell you.

I deserve a fine scolding for my long delay in writing; in large measure, it was due to indolence. I am not satisfied with myself! What makes me so lazy and restless? I do not understand it. I am not definitely sick, but at the same time I am far from well. I am dull, weary and uneasy; nonsense—hypochondria—there! I must seize hold of myself; it is work that I need—work that my heart is in. And now comes my stupidity; because I cannot work at that which I would, I turn with distaste from all other forms of toil. That is weakness, I know. But I could stand a whole avalanche of work better than these unbearable trivialities with which my time is filled.

27 · TO MEVROUW ABENDANON-MANDRI
November 29, 1901

I fear that it made you both sad to read my last letter, and it will certainly please you now to learn that though there is no change in outward conditions, there is a change in us. It is no longer night in our souls; a great calm has descended upon us. And through darkness and mist we see the splendid light break, which beckons us with friendly hands. It is the light of our ideal! We know now that we shall never be able to cease from striving; it has grown to be part of our being—of our very existence. It is not only today or yesterday that we have felt and lived for our cause! We should have to be given new hearts, new brains, and new blood would have to be put into our veins before it would be possible for us to live for anything else.

I have thought and experienced all that you wrote me. Long ago, in the very beginning of our close association, I said many times to the sisters, I begged and implored them, to tear themselves loose from me, and not to allow themselves to depend so wholly upon me.

For who am I, presumptuous fool, to calmly lead and allow my little sisters to follow me? I am going on strange unknown ways, which will lead toward heaven, but must first take me down into hell. This last, much more easily than the first. Hell is near, and the way to it is lighted: but heaven is so far off and difficult to find.

"Yes," say my sisters, "But neither you nor anyone else, could sow the seeds of ideas in us, so that they would bear fruit, unless the soil were suited to them. We are going together whether it be to heaven or to hell." My beautiful faithful little souls; no, they have learned nothing from me, for I have always been their pupil. Oh, they have taught me much.

We are one in ideas and feelings, everything has combined to make us one. We have been together all our lives; though you can take away the long years that we lived together but outwardly and count only these last intimate years.

Souls that have dwelt together for only one moment in great sympathy, can never wholly forget one another. But we have dwelt together in complete harmony for years. The years have added to the bond tenfold.

We see the same things, hear the same things, day after day, and talk over everything with one another. We take delight in the same things, read books, magazines and newspapers together—discuss what we have read, and exchange opinions and ideas. Our parents see our intimacy with pleasure and encourage in every way. They are so pleased with the three-in-one idea that they are sometimes unjust to those outside, for the triple bond must come before everything else.

Our protectors as you know may marry us to whomever they will. The only circumstances in which they may not compel our obedience is when the candidate for our hand is of rank inferior to our own. Parents may not compel their daughters to marry a man who is beneath them in station. That is our only weapon against their arbitrary will.

The prospective bridegroom has only to go with the father or other male relative to the *pangulu* [1] or someone else of the kind, and the wedding is over. The girl may know nothing whatever about it at the time.

Mother knew a woman who refused to marry. She said she had rather die than marry the man her parents had chosen for her. Heaven was merciful, three months before the date set for the wedding the cholera took her away. Had she lived, no one would have been disturbed in the least by her refusal. She would have been married out of hand despite her protests.

1. *Pangulu*, mosque official who keeps a record of marriages and divorces.

There is nothing new under the sun; long ago in old times there were rebellious daughters too. It has always been preached to us that it was our duty to belong blindly to our parents. At the same time it had happened that when a young woman, submissive to their decree, was married, and afterwards unhappy, they would make sport of her and say: "Foolish one, why then did you marry? When you were married, you were willing, you wished to follow your husband; you must not complain now."

When I received your letter, we were about to go to a wedding. It is not customary for young girls to go to weddings and sit among the wedding guests, but Mama graciously gave us her consent. If the bride's mother, an old friend of ours, had not pressed us to honor her with our presence at the great feast, we would have gladly stayed away. Before we started from our house, we saw the retinue of the bridegroom going toward the mosque; there was a downpour of rain, and the carriage in which the bridegroom sat was closed, as were the other carriages which followed it. Gold-striped banners were streaming over the *alun-alun*.[2] It was a melancholy looking train; we were depressed by it. Indeed, it made us think of a funeral procession. When we came to the home of the bride, we found her sitting in front of the *kuwadé* (canopy) waiting for the bridegroom. Father went with us, too.

We sat on the ground close by the door; the eldest between the two little sisters. Incense and the perfume of flowers filled the room. Gamelan music, and the soft buzzing of voices reached us from outside. Gamelan broke into a song of welcome; the bridegroom was coming.

Two women seized the bride by the arms, lifted her up, and led her to meet the bridegroom, who was also being led toward her by two persons. After a few steps, they are opposite each other and bride and bridegroom give, each one to the other, a rolled-up *sirih*[3] leaf. A few steps nearer and both sink to the ground. The bride prostrates herself on her knees before him, as a symbol of her subjection to the man. Flat before him, she makes

2. Grounds in front of a regent's residence. Usually square in shape and surrounded by trees, sometimes with a group of trees in the center.

3. The prepared mixture for so-called "betel-nut chewing," a custom found throughout Indonesia, is rolled up inside a *sirih* or betel leaf. The mixture is made up of lime, *gambir* (a spice) and the nut of the areca palm. The small packet is used in offerings in many types of religious rituals, and as an element in the traditional Javanese marriage ceremony.

a respectful sembah, and humbly kisses his foot! Again, a submissive sembah, and both rise and go hand in hand and seat themselves under the canopy.

"Ju, Ju," [4] whispered Kleintje to me with dancing eyes and a roguish twist to her mouth. "He! I should go wild, if I could only see a bridal pair come smiling to meet each other and hand the sirih leaf with eyes sparkling with joy. Of course, that would have to be among the younger generation—a bridal pair who had known each other beforehand. Would not that be fine—eh, Ju? Will it ever happen? I should go crazy with delight, if I could ever see it."

"It will come," I said mechanically, and smiled; but in that room, I felt as though my heart were being pierced with a dagger; and there at my side, with face beaming and dancing eyes, sat my sister.

A few days ago I opened a book by chance. It happened to be Multatuli, and the first thing I read was "Thugater." I still seem to see the words before my eyes: "Father said to her that to know, and to understand, and to desire, was a sin for a girl."

Certainly the great, genial writer had little idea when he wrote that, what a deep impression it would make some day upon one of the daughters of the people whom he loved, and for whose welfare he sacrificed so much.

There was a woman of the people who became wife number two of a native official. The first wife, who was not quite right in her head, after a little went away from him, leaving behind a whole troop of children. Number two became the official wife and was a painstaking, loving mother to her step-children; she was very diligent and worked hard to save something from the income of her husband, so that later they would be able to educate his children. And it was thanks to her that the sons turned out so well. Now I come to the thanks. Once when her husband had gone to the city he came back home late at night, and called his wife outside. A guest had come with him for whom she must care, and make ready a room. The guest was a young woman, and when her husband told her that the guest was his wife and that she, his older wife, must thenceforth share everything with her, at first she was stunned, for she did not understand. She only stood and looked at him. But when the frightful truth penetrated

4. *Ju* is the affectionate form of *mbakju*, which means "older sister."

to her brain, she sank without a single word to the ground. When she came to herself again, she rose to her feet, and asked, standing, for a written notice of divorce from her husband. At first he did not wish to understand her, but she persisted till at last he yielded and gave her the requested paper.

That very night she went out of the house on foot through fields and forests, to her parents' house in the city. How she got there she did not know. When she could think again, she was with her family and they told her that she had been ill for a long time.

Later, after she had recovered, she looked at the letter which she had forced from her husband on that terrible night, and saw that she was really not divorced at all. The letter merely contained her description and the information that she had run away from him.

He had no idea in the world of giving her back her freedom. Later she became reconciled to him. The other wife left the house and went to live in another dwelling, while she resumed her old rule of the household. On that frightful night, she had sworn a solemn oath, she swallowed dust, and vowed never, never, to raise her hand to deprive another of her rights. She had done it herself ignorantly as a child; when she was fourteen years of age, her parents had married her to her husband. She did not know what she was doing, she belonged only to her parents, who often used to beat her at their pleasure. She knew now what a hell pain it was to be pushed from the side of a husband by another. She had remained true to her oath.

Not long ago her husband married a niece to someone who already had a wife; she defied the wrath of her husband and refused persistently to have anything to do with the wedding preparations, and the wedding was not held in her house.

We know her very well, and have great respect for her. She has made herself what she is by her own efforts, she has worked hard and improved herself, though she has never had an opportunity to study.

She has taught herself to read and has worked her way through several books with profit.

We are sometimes astonished at her conversation, the result of deep thinking, and also of a sound understanding. She is truly an unusual woman (it would be well if there were more like her) who has had neither education nor opportunities, but who thinks and feels as we because she has known suffering.

Her history is not unique; there are many like it. But where shall I end if I once begin to tell you of the misery of the native women? Anyone whose eyes are not blind and whose ears are not deaf, knows what goes on in our world. Pluck the hearts from our bodies and the brains from our heads if you wish to change us.

Long before you quoted from Zangwill's *Dreams of the Ghetto* to me, Kleintje said almost the same thing, though of course in different words. We were eating tarts, or something of the kind, when little sister came running up and wished to have some too. There was no clean plate for her, and Kardinah said, "Eat off Ju's plate and then you will become clever like her," whereupon Kleintje said solemnly, "No, I will not do it; I want to remain stupid; to be clever is not to be happy—not for everyone. It is a misfortune to be able to think and not to be able to act; to be able to know, to feel and to wish, and not to be free. I want to be only stupid."

Once when I was distraught with trouble, and leaned against the wall motionless, with wide open eyes that saw nothing, but only stared at the light, a cry of sorrow smote my ears and brought me back to a sense of reality. Father leaned over me, his arms were around me, though his face was turned away. "Do not give way like that, Ni. Have patience." Oh, my father, why have you not listened to the voice of your own heart; why have you heeded the voice of the world?

28 · TO MEVROUW ABENDANON-MANDRI

December 31, 1901

We do not want to sail any longer upon a weak ship, something must be done for this great, this unhappy cause. We should be satisfied if only the attention of the intelligent world were fastened upon it. Many times have I talked with women, both with those of the nobles and those of the people, about the idea of an independent, free, self-supporting girl, who could earn her own living; and from each one comes the answer, "There must be some one who sets the example."

We are convinced that if one has but the courage to begin, many will follow her. There must always be a beginning. One must go first to show the way, and the example must be good; each one waits for the other; no one dares to be first. The parents too wait for one another to see which one will have the moral courage to allow a daughter to become independent and self-supporting—to stand by herself.

We know a regent's daughter, our own age, who is also full of enthusiasm for the idea of freedom. She is crazy to study; she speaks excellent Dutch, and has read a great deal. She is the daughter of the Regent of Kutoardjo. There are two great girls, charming children; we are very fond of them. I know from a teacher, an acquaintance of ours, that the older girl is crazy to study. She has told me herself that she is very anxious to go to Europe. The second sister also is a dear, clever child. A few years ago they were at our house on a visit. When they first came, they began to draw and paint with us, and now the younger one paints very well. Their father has a great respect for an educated woman. We know another one of his daughters, who is married; she speaks no Dutch, but she has gone further than the others. She has a great admiration for the free, independent European woman; she would think it ideal if we could have the same conditions in our native world.

Another regent's daughter has been here; she is a Sundanese girl; she does not speak a word of Javanese, but she was brought up with Europeans, so we talked in Dutch.

The first question that she asked me was, "How many mothers have you?" I turned to her in pained astonishment, and she went on (do not be shocked) "You know that I have fifty-three mothers and there are eighty-three of us. I do not know the majority of my brothers and sisters. I am the youngest, and never knew my father; he died before I was born."

Is not that deeply, deeply sad? In the Preanger, girls of noble birth are free to choose their own husbands, and many of them even know the man to whom they are betrothed. The young people meet one another, and become engaged after the European manner. Blessed land—and yet—!

There is a girl, a granddauughter of a regent (her parents are dead), who has had a splendid bringing up, and if her teacher is a good judge, must be a wonder of learning. She plays the piano well, etc. She became engaged after the European manner and married someone, who had many wives, and a whole troop of children; some of them full grown. I knew one of her step-daughters, a charming little woman who speaks Dutch and is the mother of a two year old child. She was seventeen years old, a year or two younger than her stepmother. She told me that she chose her husband herself and was very happy.

.   .   .   .

The idea of publishing all that I think and feel about conditions among our Moslem women, has been with me for a long time. I thought of putting it into a book, in the form of letters between two regents' daughters—a Sundanese and a Javanese. Already I have written several letters, but I shall not go on with it at present. It will be perhaps some years before I can finish it, but I shall not give up the idea. That too was suggested by Mijnheer. The great difficulty is that Father would not allow me to publish such a book. "It is good for you to be versed in the Dutch language," says Father, "but you must not make that an excuse for telling your inmost thoughts."

We girls must have no ideas, we have but to think that everything is good as we find it, and to say "yes" and "amen" to everything.

I was asked a few years ago by a Dutch authoress of reputation, editor of a woman's journal, with whom I correspond, and whom I like very much, for permission to publish a letter in which I had touched upon these questions. The publication of private opinions such as mine would be good for the cause, she thought. She would have kept my identity a secret; name, dwelling place, everything would have been concealed. Only those places would have been mentioned wherein I allude to certain peculiar customs of my country. The letter was sent back to Java, so that it could be shown to Father. He said that it must not be published; "Later perhaps." I knew what that "later" meant. It meant that when I should have become harmless, by having the Raden Adjeng changed to Raden Aju.

Lately we had the same thing over again. Mevrouw Ter Horst, founder and editor of the Indian woman's journal, *The Echo*, sent me her paper. She knows personally much about the life of the native woman, and has great sympathy for the well-born girls in the Principalities [1] who are given away like so many presents. She wanted me to begin a series of articles, "Talks between two regent's daughters." Secrecy, should it be necessary, was absolutely assured with her. She also thinks that it would be a good idea to write sketches of the life around us. I gave the letter to father, hoping for his permission, which was again denied. I must not tell my ideas too early, always it is "later."

The Heer Boes, of Probolingo, wrote to Father and asked if I might write some articles for his paper, *De Nederlandsche Taal*, a periodical for natives.

The Heer Boes asked for a reply, and sent me a list of subjects that he would like to have treated, such as, "Native Education for Girls"— "Native Art," "Useful Native Institutions."

At that time we had gone to Batavia. So many things came up after that I could not write, I was in such trouble that my pen refused to go. And I hoped that each day would be better than the one that had gone before. But the next day would be just the same, and I would tear up what I had tried to write; that was stupid. But I was beside myself with waiting and delay. I was in despair. I was to be allowed to write only nonsense, earnest things I must not touch upon.

Then I began to think that if I did write upon serious subjects, I should have the whole native world against me; if I became a teacher, the people would not trust their children to me. I should be called crazy. The idea of serving our cause with my pen is so dear to me, and yet picture to yourself a school without children, a teacher without pupils!

But we have not gone as far as that. We must have education first. For that we must first obtain Father's permission, and then we have to present our petition to the Governor General.

We must not count too much upon the success of our suit. And if it should fail, O God, what then? There remains only one thing for us, to become midwives; we should then have to give up our hope of being examples and of lighting the way for others, for then we could be of service only to a few. But we think that would be far better than just to be bookkeepers, pharmacists' apprentices, or something of that kind. Work in which our lives should be so barren, so empty, we should be living only for ourselves, and we want to live for the good of society as a whole.

1. See note on p. 82.

I have information about the Government School of Obstetrics at Amsterdam, where one can be educated for that profession absolutely free of charge. We should have to have the help of Prof. Hector Treub.

The course lasts two years. How should we be able to get to Europe? We do not know. Some way must be found.

We will not go into that, until we have exhausted every means in our power towards the carrying out of our other plans.

Alas, if we could but get into communication with our own educated young men, men like Abdul Rivai and others, and win their sympathy for our cause. When will the time come when boys and girls, men and women shall look upon one another as equal human beings, as comrades? As it is now—bah! how we women are degraded at every turn, again and again.

29 · TO MEVROUW ABENDANON-MANDRI
January 3, 1902

When we were in Semarang, our eldest sister came over to see us. "Sister, sister," was all that she said, when she had seen me. The arms that were thrown around me trembled, and her eyes were filled with tears. We were silent; we understood each other. At last we have found our sister.

At last, after years, we have gained her understanding and respect. That gives us new courage, because at first, she was very conservative, and was opposed violently to every innovation.

.   .   .   .

Formerly it was not the custom to send children to school. Now it is an everyday occurrence; but when one has a little matter of twenty-five children, can one educate them all?

The question is never raised, that one has not the right to awaken life when one cannot maintain life. Alas, how simple I am!

.   .   .   .

I thought to myself that if I did something terrible which would call down universal scorn upon my head, if everyone passed me by, and I were showered with insults, would Father and would Mother turn away from me? No, they would not. I should still be their child, and have a place in their hearts. All the time we were sitting quietly here in our room, sewing on Kleintje's clothes. She will have nothing that a strange hand has touched. We must do everything for her ourselves. The door opened a little way and Father came from behind it to stroke the rebellious head that surged with so many unruly thoughts.

After four weeks, sister will be with us no longer. "You will all miss me very much; I know it," she said, "In everything, always, we three have been together."

30 · TO MEVROUW ABENDANON-MANDRI

February 15, 1902

When someone does something unkind to me, it makes my blood boil, I grow very angry, but afterwards something like joy comes to me. I am glad that it is the other person who has injured me and not I that have hurt him; for then it is I that should be base, and if I were troubled, it would be because I had been guilty and injured another unjustly.

Forgive me for having taken so long to write. After the departure of our darling, our heart and soul sister, I could not write.

Sister went from here to her new home on the 31st of January. God grant that our little girl may be as happy as it is possible for a young, pure and innocent creature to be in this world. You know how we three have always clung together and that she has been our darling, because she is not strong, and needed our care. Before her marriage, we thought so much about the coming separation; but when the great blow fell, we felt nothing. We were so dismally calm, we were not capable of thought. We saw her go with dry eyes.

Annie Glaser, our companion, who came on a visit, reminded us so much of sister. One evening she played on the piano the pieces that sister had loved most. And under the spell of her music the ice crust melted from our hearts. But with the warmth the pain too came back. Thank God, that we could feel again. "Thank God, thank God!" we said, in spite of the pain. For those who cannot feel pain are not capable, either, of feeling joy.

She has gone far away from us, and we cannot realize that she will be with us no more—our Kleintje, our own little girl. We see her in everything, she is with us always, only we cannot prattle aloud to her as formerly. We can only do that in our thoughts. It is still so strange to us that we must take a pen and paper to tell her something or other.

Kleintje, our little one, have you really gone away from us? Ah, dear sister, be happy in your new life and shed happiness around you there, just as you did here, when you bond all our hearts so fast to yours.

There is a young man with a very clever head, and at the same time of high position, who does not know us personally, but who has much sympathy for our struggle, and takes as much interest in it as if he were our own brother. We correspond with him and, later, he is coming himself to make the acquaintance of his sisters. He is so different from all the other men that we know. I read once that the greatest thing in the world was a noble man's heart. I understand now, truly a noble man's heart is the most priceless thing in the world; it is so rare. We are happy because we have found such a one.

Sister Roekmini thinks of you often and has such a high opinion of you. She is a fine child, so good, so faithful. You would like her I know, if you could meet her; but you do know her already through me, do you not?

When I was sick, I tried to make her write to you, but she would not because it might make you uneasy. When she was with me, and I was so very sick, I thought to myself, it was very discouraging. Here is someone who glows with enthusiasm for a noble cause; who longs to be strong and brave, to overcome mountains, and see; now she lies helpless, powerless. If someone picked her up and threw her into a well, she could make no resistance because she would be wholly defenseless.

Now for the first time we understand what De Genestet means in his "Terugblik":

What we wish and will and strive for
We pray high powers to grant.
For free man, you do not make yourself, and your own life
The eagle's flight is always fast enclosed,

The Almighty bends our will, our strength,
As the wind bends the wheat.
Still lay the ground out,
Plan your castles,
Mark the way you wish to travel.
The earth is wide and beautiful,
Choose your fate and seek your way,
By your own light.
God watches all the while,
And guides your footsteps unaware.

And the same poet has given us much comfort in dark, difficult days.

31 · TO MEVROUW ABENDANON-MANDRI

February 18, 1902

We know how to be merry and playful too, just to be young. The Sunday after we got your dear letter we went down to the shore, and last Sunday as well, we were there. We thought of you and we spoke of you. If you could only have been with us, to look at the wild play of the waves, and at the wonderful colors, which stretched before us at sunset. There was a strong wind, more than once our hair was blown down and we had to hold on to our clothes to keep them from flying away. There was not only life in the trees and in the water, there was life in the girls who ran up and down through the waves. We had such a delightful time! Our voices rose above the noise of the water; we laughed aloud. Those were the teachers, the stately princesses, who ran and sported in the waves with blown hair and blown garments. We were so happy, so young, and so gay! Our attendants stood by staring and gaping with wide open mouths.

The next morning we went again to the shore; the sea was no longer blustering, the boundless stretch of water was calm. There were only little ripples playing upon the surface, and the sunlight danced in and out among them like brilliants.

We went into the sea, the ground was even, there were no

pebbles, no seaweed, no slime; we went far out till the water reached our chins. The babu on the shore grew frightened, we could no longer understand her, but she ran up and down like a mad woman, waving her arms and calling us back. We only laughed at her distress. In the distance, she saw our heads sway around as we danced, and our voices sounded over the water, raised in a merry little song.

When we went back to the house, we took with us a lively feeling of hunger, you may be sure. After we had eaten ravenously, Annie sat down to the piano. Out of the fullness of her heart she played a "Danklied" and we sang with her. It was as though we had grown half elf. Now quickly to work. In the back gallery our sewing stood ready; we sat at one table and worked busily, but it was not only the fingers that hurried along, our tongues were not idle and we were chattering and laughing and singing. In the twinkling of an eye, the time had gone by, and we must sit again at the table. At midday we took a little walk and wandered back to the shore.

After our walk, if it is not too dark, we usually drink tea in the garden, among the shrubs and flowers, and under the blue sky, where after a while, a few stars and the pale gold moon come out. When we go in, we have music or we read together. When Annie plays the piano, we sit by her, and sew or write, for it is a delight to be able to work while there is music; the work goes so easily.

Cooking is also on our program. We practice that every day after the rice meal.

You and your husband must come to see us and rest here from that oppressive Batavia. Can you not come now? We shall expect you. Then you can amuse yourselves with our kind of life, which is so restful, so still, so quiet and so peaceful. We will take care of you and we shall have the help of the wind and the sea; and of the birds that greet us every morning with their songs.

Come, dear friends, come, and find fresh life in our modest, still, little place.

. . . .

Of the wedding here, I shall only say that sister was a lovely bride.

She was married in wajang costume and looked beautiful. In the evening, at the reception, she looked like a fairy princess from the *Thousand and One Nights*. She had on a golden crown, with a veil hanging down behind. It was a new idea, but I have no doubt that it will be imitated.

Resident Sijthoff was much interested in seeing sister for the last time as a young girl. He stayed through everything. He would have liked to press her hand in farewell, but that might not be. He could only greet her with his eyes.

As though carved in stone, she sat straight as an arrow, before the glittering golden canopy. Her head was held proudly high, and her eyes were looking straight ahead as though staring at the future that was so soon to be unraveled before her. There were none of the usual tears, but even strangers were affected. Only she and her two sisters were calm. Our emotions had been lulled to sleep by the gamelan music, by incense, and the perfume of flowers. We were unmoved, we had looked forward to our parting as to something frightful, so everyone was astonished. We are still stared at very hard, people are anxious to see how we hold up under the strain.

We talked to the Resident of our plans that very evening. Imagine our speaking at the end of a crowded feast about a cause which is so earnest and so sacred; but it was our only opportunity to talk to him alone, and we had to make the most of it. Alone! all around us there were people, and still more people. Surrounded by evergreens and flowers, with a shimmer of silk, and the glitter of gold and jewels before our eyes, amid the buzzing of a thousand voices, in a very sea of light, we sat there at midnight, with champagne glasses in our hands, to speak of grave matters.

We were afraid that he would laugh at us or at least think us "silly." But we did not let him frighten us. He talked first with me, and then with Roekmini, separately; to make sure that our ideas were our own and not borrowed from each other.

I have a request to make of you, an important one; when you see your friend, Dr. Snouck-Hurgronje, ask him if, among the Moslems, there are laws of majority, as among you. Or should I write myself to his Excellency for enlightenment? There are some things I should be so glad to know about the rights and duties, or, better still, the laws concerning the Moslem wife and daughter. How strange for me to ask! It makes me ashamed that we do not know ourselves. We know so bitterly little.

February 28, 1902

The influence of blood cannot be denied. I attach a certain value to the descent of every one around me, and I have an idea that I shall be blessed by the ancestors of those persons whom I love and honor. I am eager to read the books you have sent me and I hope to be able to understand them easily. Do you not think me a little stupid? I am only a great child, who longs very much to be loved, and who longs too for knowledge and understanding.

Understanding is a very difficult art. Is it not so, dearest?

But when one understands, one judges mercifully, and one forgives.

It is Friday evening; gamelan evening. Our souls are wafted up to the blue heaven of our fancy by the sweet serene tones that are borne to us on the evening wind from the pendopo.

Let us dream as long as it is possible; if there were no dreams, what would life be?

We have taken away all the little trifles and ornaments from our room. It is no longer the joyful girls' room, where we dreamed dreams, where we wept, thought, felt, rejoiced and struggled! Only our bookcase remains unchanged, and our old friends smile at us still in their friendly, confident and encouraging way.

One of our best friends, who is no longer ornamental because he has grown old-fashioned, shows very plainly whenever the door is opened. Our dear, true, old friend. Many people would turn up their noses at him, but we love him because he has never left us, but has rejoiced with us in happy days; and through dark troubled ones, he has comforted and supported us. He is De Genestet. He has been such a consolation to us of late.

March 5, 1902

Do you know who has painted so many wajangs for us? It is one of our gamelan players. The art of painting is part of the air in Japara. Little urchins, buffalo boys, draw excellent wajangs, in the sand, on the walls, on bridges, on the supports of bridges. The wall behind our house is always covered with wajang figures. All the bridge supports erected today are covered with them tomorrow, drawn with charcoal or with a little piece of soapstone by naked, dirty little apes. Favored land, our Japara. You do not know how proud we are of our dear, quiet place.

The grave of the Sultan of Mantingan is half an hour's ride, or somewhat more from here. There is a whole connected narrative about the Sultan's grave, for it is a holy tomb. When the Sultan came back from China, a Chinese followed him and lies buried in the same place; over his grave there is a *patje* tree. Miraculous powers are ascribed to this tree. Barren women, who would gladly have a child, go there and take the Sultan flowers and incense wafers. When a patje fruit falls upon the grave of the Chinese. the woman must take it away, make it into a stew, and eat it; her wish will then be granted. We have been told the names of persons who had obtained their wishes in this way.

You see that the Javanese are a superstitious people fond of myths and fairy tales. It is said that the children with which the Sultan of Mantingan blesses the childless, will all be girls. Poor childless ones! We shall have to look for a holy tomb that will bless the world with boys, for there are all too many women in the world!

It was uphill work to make our artists carve wajang dolls. They were frightened to death for fear the wajang spirits would be angry with them. Father assured them that he would take all responsibility, that all consequences would be upon his own head, and that the anger and wrath of the spirits would smite him alone, the taskmaster, and not the workmen who had merely carried out his will.

It was most difficult to take a photograph in the kampong. A superstition says that one shortens one's own life when one allows a photograph to be taken, and that a photographer is a great sinner; all the portraits that he makes will demand their lives of him in the afterlife.

34 · TO STELLA ZEEHANDELAAR

March 14, 1902

I have already written you about my sister in a former letter. It is such a great loss, we miss our heart and soul sister all the time. Happily we have already had encouraging letters from her. She is such a dear, noble child. She is worth more than the other two of us put together. She likes her new home, and has met with much kindness from everyone. Her new family took her by the hand, and wherever she went she found cordiality and sympathy from Europeans, as well as from her own people.

You know already, from the marriage announcement that was sent you, that her husband is a *patih*; that is one of the highest ranks in our native official world; besides, our brother-in-law is heir to a throne. When his father ceases to reign, he will, of course, succeed him. As the wife of a regent, sister will be able to do a great deal for the education of women, much more than we will ever be able to accomplish. We have great hopes that her husband will support her; at least, he was much in favor of the plans of Heer Abendanon.

He is devoted to his little wife, has a cheerful, energetic disposition and a sympathetic heart. He supports a whole multitude of poor families; that is pleasant, do you not think so? But many Javanese do that; they have much consideration for their poor neighbors. There is hardly a single native official who has not one or more poor families living in his house, or on his support outside. It is not for nothing that India is noted for its hospitality. Are you not satisfied now about sister too?

She is discouraged only because people expect too much of her. She is like her older sister, who never feels her littleness so much as when a certain person in Holland (Amsterdam) sets her too much in the sun.

Truly Stella, you must not do that; I shall be too much of a disappointment to you when the happiest of all happy stars brings me to you. You have much too good an opinion of me, of my character, and of my intellect; they are, if I speak the honest truth, not worth a dubbeltje. But you will never be disappointed in one thing, and that is, in my warm affection for you.

Lately, I had a letter from an old gentleman who had great ideas about my "gentle courage" and "sweet disposition" and my "skill in the Dutch language." I smiled mournfully when I read it and thought to myself "if you but knew."

Yesterday we received letters from Holland, and I said to myself, "Girl, hold your head, this will not be the only disappointment that life will bring you; you may as well realize that the future has a whole multitude of them stored in her lap for you." And yet I am in no wise cast down. Life itself teaches one to be cold and unfeeling.

And now about the proposition from Mejuffrouw Van der Meij. In the first place I thank you heartily, my true comrade, for what you have done for me, and I thank you too for sending me *Belang En Recht*. I went to Father with your letter and asked him to read it.

Father will wait for the coming of Van Kol before he decides the question. I have good hopes of his consent. Yes Stella, I will, but not under my own name, I wish to remain unknown; tell that to Mejuffrouw Van der Meij. But that will not help very much, when they learn here in India of articles by a Javanese woman, they will know at once upon whom to lay the blame. It is tiresome. I do not like to hear my work discussed, especially as I hear nothing but praise. Ah! it is interesting for a Javanese woman to write in Dutch; that is the whole of my easily earned success.

But let me take advantage of that interest whatever its cause. Frankly it has its good side too, for at least I can obtain a hearing.

But how am I to gain friends for our cause by writing for the public unless I say things that will make an impression and will be talked about, till they penetrate to the Parliament itself?

I have always wanted to write something scathing, that tells what I feel, but I do not feel strong enough; I still lack experience, I have yet to see and hear much, and to think over what I have seen. The fruit is not yet ripe, Stella; when it is, I shall no longer hesitate on account of the difficulties.

If we should turn to the Queen, it would not be in her official capacity, and because we wished to obtain the help of the State through royal intervention. We should only ask the Princess for her personal help. If you knew how proud we were, then you would understand what a struggle it has caused us to make up our minds to ask for assistance.

But as you said, when large affairs come up, small ones must go to the wall.

We set our own pride aside before the general good. In the present instance our only chance of success lies in asking for help.

Everyone who has met the Queen assures me that Her Majesty is interested to the highest degree in the welfare of her Indian subjects. And the Queen Mother also takes a warm interest in Indian affairs. We believe it; we are glad to believe it.

At the time of the Woman's Exposition, it was the Queen Mother who sent her personal secretary to the president of the colonial department to enquire about our work, and Her Majesty asked the president, when he was conducting her around, to read to her some extracts from our letters. I feel confident of support, from the Government and from the Queen.

If this support does not materialize, there is only Modjowarno left, but that is not what our hearts wish. Do you know whom I long for in despondent, unsettled weather? For our friend who is far away in the wilderness. Deep in the heart of our inland country, living among headhunters in that distant place, doing good in many ways but above all through his knowledge of medicine. I would fly to him as a bird with wounded wings, and he would stroke my tired head till my sorrow could be stilled, and the peace which he breathes would fall around me. But he too is human, he too must have his despondent moods, his struggles.[1]

Stella, Stella, if I could only throw my arms around you, and let my read rest upon your heart.

1. Kartini refers to Dr. N. Adriani, missionary linquist who was working among the Toradjas of central Celebes.

March 29, 1902

You are right. The separation from sister has been a great grief to us, we have been together so long, and so intimately. People were not wrong when they said that we three had grown to be one in thought and in feeling. We cannot realize that sister has really left us; the idea that she has gone away never to return is unbearable. We try to imagine that she is only away on a visit, and will be back some day.

We miss our Kleintje very much. But happiness will not stand still; this will not be the only hard parting, we know that; many others await us in the future.

> *It is wise from time to time,*
> *When a tender strong bond*
> *Binds and caresses the poor heart,*
> *To tear it asunder with our own hands,*

says De Genestet. But it is easier said than done. Do you not find it so? We receive encouraging letters from little sister. She is happy and pleased with her surroundings. That makes us so thankful, her happiness is our happiness. And now I shall try and tell you something of her wedding

A native marriage entails a heavy burden upon the family of the bride. Days and weeks beforehand, the preparations for the solemnity are begun. Sister's wedding was celebrated very quietly on account of a death in the family. One of our cousins, who was a sister of the bridegroom, died shortly before the marriage. Poor creature. She was still such a young thing, and she left little children behind her. You must know that Kleintje is married to her own cousin. His mother is father's sister. He was here with us long ago, but then she was only a schoolgirl and no one thought of an engagement; though it has happened that children have been affianced and married, and later, when both were full grown, the marriage would be celebrated over again.

The acquaintance of sister and her husband was renewed when the Governor General was at Semarang. It is not customary among us for young girls ever to leave the house until they follow a strange bridegroom; but as I have already told you, we have broken with many traditions, and can do what others cannot, on account of the unusual freedom of our bringing up; and now we are working to break with tradition still further.

No Javanese girl must be seen before her marriage; she must remain in the background, usually in her own chamber; and in December we were at Semarang with sister, and she went openly into the shops to buy some things which she wanted.

A Javanese girl receives no good wishes upon her engagement; the subject is not mentioned before her; still less does she mention it herself. She acts just as though she knew nothing of it. I should like to have read the hearts of our fellow countrywomen when they heard sister speak openly and freely of her coming marriage.

A day or two before the wedding, we commemorated our dead. That is our custom: in the midst of joy we always invoke the memory of our dead. There was a sacrificial meal, during which their blessing was asked for the offspring of the coming nuptials.

This takes place in the bride's family. My brother-in-law and his family came on the day before the wedding. The first thing that a European bridegroom would do on arriving at the home of his bride, would be to go to her. But among us that would be out of the question. The bridegroom must not see his bride until the knot is tied. Even his family must not see her.

On the day of the wedding, the bride was bathed in a bath of flowers, and after that she was taken in hand by the *tukang paès*, a woman whose business is the dressing of brides. The bride takes her seat on a cloth that is especially prepared for the occasion, it consists of pieces of cotton and silk, enough for a kebaja, joined together. This is the property of the tukang paès. At her side are placed sweetmeats besides sirih, pinang nuts, bananas, a jug of water, uncooked rice, a roasted hen, a live hen, and a burning night candle. Incense is burned, and the tukang paès cuts the fine hair from the bride's neck and face; the hair on the forehead is cut, too; even the hair over the ears. And the eyebrows are shaved off with a razor. One can always tell a newly married woman, by the shorn hair across the forehead and ears and by the shaved eyebrows.

At about one o'clock in the day, the toilet of the bride begins. The forehead is covered with soft salve, even to the ears, and the face is whitened, while the hair is dressed in the form of a cap, and ornamented with flowers.

On the headdress are seven jewels, fastened upon spirals, which are constantly waving up and down.

A gold embroidered *kain*,[1] and kebaja of silver gauze, with the usual jeweled ornaments, such as brooches, necklaces, bracelets, earrings, and sleeve-buttons, completed her toilet.

In Java, young girls must not wear flowers in the hair; only married women may do that; one often sees very old women going around with flowers in their hair.

The evening before the wedding is called *widodarèni; widodari* means angel, heavenly being. On the last evening of her maidenhood, the girl on the threshold of matrimony is compared to such a heavenly being, and the evening is celebrated.

You must have seen the photographs of Javanese woodwork at Mevrouw Rooseboom's, and you may remember the picture of an article of furniture with three doors in front. That is called a *kuwadé,* and it is used at weddings.

And a handsome carved kuwadé covered with gold figures on a purple ground, was in the great hall at the back of the kabupaten. All tables, chairs, and benches were removed from that apartment and the floors were covered with a great alcatief.

On both sides of the kuwadé, which was draped and ornamented with flowers, stood two large copper vases, filled with young cocoanut leaves and flowers. These vases are called *kembang majang,* and must not be broken at a wedding.

At about half-past seven in the evening, when all of the women guests had assembled in the kuwadé-hall and were ranged on the ground in two rows, one on each side of the kuwadé-hall, sister came in, led by the hand of our married sister and our sister-in-law, and followed by a woman who carried her sirih box and cuspidor.[2] Sister sat down in the middle of the room, near her family and the most prominent guests. The sirih box and the cuspidor were placed next to her only as a matter of form, for

1. *Kain,* meaning cloth, refers to the large strip of cloth which forms the Javanese skirt, or *sarong.*

2. The sirih box which contained the ingredients for betel-chewing, and the cuspidor, into which to spit after chewing betel, were objects found near every Javanese man and woman of that period. These bowls and boxes were often of gold, silver and tortoise-shell and were beautifully carved and ornamented.

Kleintje eats no sirih; behind her, a little girl waved a fan.

Sister sat with crossed legs before the gold shining kuwadé, motionless as an image of Buddha, between the gravely dressed, solemn looking wives of the native dignitaries, equal in rank to her husband. Tea and cakes were served, every one took a cup of tea and several kinds of small pastries. The bride and the most distinguished guests each had an individual tea service, and a tray of pastries. It was as though a whole carpet of pastries were spread out before the guests, here and there broken by sirih boxes and cuspidors of gold and tortoise-shell, of wood, or of silver. The company was composed entirely of married women. We unmarried ones were not there.

You have certainly heard that among the Javanese it is a great misfortune for a woman to remain unmarried. It is a disgrace as well. Not so long ago, in enlightened Europe it was looked upon in the same way; is not that true? So we must not think ill of the foolish uncivilized Indians.

If the bridegroom has a mother, on this evening she must be at the feast of her daughter-in-law-to-be.

Our masculine guests ate with father in the pendopo, while the bridegroom stayed at home in his lodgings.

Sister was so glad when, at half-past nine, the ceremonial was over, so far as she was concerned. She walked decorously and sedately from the hall, through the throng of women sitting around; but as soon as she was out of sight, and safe in our room all the formality was gone. She was again our little sister, our dear happy Kleintje, and no Buddha image. That evening was sacred to the Prophet. In the mosque there was a great *slametan* (sacrificial meal, celebrated with prayers); the blessing of heaven was asked upon the approaching marriage.

At the meal, only men were present, our women guests, even the regents' wives who had come to sister's wedding, ate at home with us.

Early the next morning, there was a stir in the kabupaten. It looked quite gay, with its decorations of greens and flags. Outside on the highway, there was bustle and noise. The tricolor waved merrily among the rustling young cocoanut trees that bordered the road which led to the house of the bridegroom. In the green covered *paséban*, two little houses on the alun-alun before the kabupaten, the gamelan played lustily.

We were on the back gallery, where stood baskets of *kanangas*, *tjempakas*, and *melatis*. Women's hands were arranging the flowers into garlands, or suspending them on little swings, or tearing the blossoms from the leaves, so that they could be strewn in the way of the bridal pair wherever they might go. The kabupaten was filled with gamelan music and the perfume of flowers. Busy people walked to and fro. In our room, the toilet of the bride was begun. Her forehead had been painted dark before; now it was decorated with little golden figures.

Sister lay down during the operation. Behind the figures there were two borders fastened to the hair—a dark one behind the gold; into this, jeweled knobs were stuck. With other brides the borderwork is made of their own hair; but for sister we had a false piece set in, because the elaborate process is painful, and the poor child had just recovered from a fever.

Above the borderwork came a golden diadem, and her hair at the back of the head was dressed like a half-moon and filled with flowers; from that, a veil of melati with a border of flowers fell, and reached to her shoulders. Her head was again surmounted by the seven jewels glittering on their spirals. Behind these, there was a jewelled flower, from which hung six chains of real flowers, suspended behind the ears, over the breast, and down to the waist. These chains, which were about as thick as one's fingers, were made of white flowers linked together with little bands of gold and ending in a round knob which was stuck full of melati flowers.

Her wajang costume was décolleté in front, so that neck, face, and arms were entirely uncovered. All that was visible of sister except the face, which was whitened, was covered with a fragrant salve. She wore a gold embroidered kain, over which there was a drapery of gold woven silk; the whole was held up by a sash of yellow with long hanging ends of red silk painted with figures of gold. A dark green sash, growing lighter till it was pale green in the center, was bound around the upper part of her body. Little glints of gold showed delightfully through this. Her arms and shoulders were left entirely free. The yellow girdle around her waist was called *mendala-giri*. Sister wore one of gold, three fingers broad and ornamented with jewels; garlands of flowers, with hanging ends, were fastened to it, reaching from behind one hip to the other. Around her neck, she wore a collar, with three wing-shaped ornaments hanging down over her breast and almost to her waist. There were bracelets on her wrists and on the upper part of her arms, shaped like serpents with upraised tails and heads; golden chains dangled from these.

It was between three and four o'clock in the afternoon. In the kuwadé hall the wives of the native nobles assembled in gala attire. From the kuwadé to the pendopo there was a carpet of flowers, over which the bridal pair must walk. The bride was led forward by her sisters and took her place before the kuwadé. The lights were already lighted in the pendopo; the regents stood assembled in official costume, and there were a few European acquaintances who were anxious to see sister for the last time as a maiden. In the alun-alun, and all outside the kabupaten, it was dark with people; only the road which was decorated with flags and green leaves remained free.

A streak of yellow could be seen in the distance; it drew nearer, till there appeared a train of open gold-striped parasols (pajungs), under which the native officials walk on great occasions.

It was the retinue which preceded the bridegroom, who, with the other regents, was in an open carriage, which was covered with a glittering golden parasol. Gamelan music sounded from the pasébans and the kabupaten, to greet the approaching procession.

It reached the kabupaten and halted at the door of the pendopo. The whole company squatted down; the bridegroom got out of the carriage, and was led forward by two unmarried regents. They went into the pendopo, and all three knelt down in the middle of the room to do homage to Father and the other regents. The two regents moved back, still on their knees, and left the bridegroom alone in the middle of the pendopo. The nobles formed a circle around him, within which there was a smaller circle of pious men.[3] Father sat at the head of the regents, and the *pengulu* who

3. This portion of the Javanese marriage ceremony is the only part which is strictly in accord with the Moslem religion. The other two parts of the ceremony, the slametan meal described above, and the "meeting" of the bride and groom described below, are also religious in purpose but the ritual elements and the beliefs represented by the ceremonies are not primarily Islamic, but mainly Hindu and indigenous Javanese. The three doctrines, Islam, Hinduism, and indigenous Javanese religion, are all tightly intertwined into a single creed. For detailed description see *The Religion of Java*, by Clifford Geertz (Free Press of Glencoe, Ill., 1960). Most Javanese, although considering themselves Moslems, have little knowledge of the Islamic rituals, and call in those who do, to perform them for

was to perform the ceremony next to the bridegroom. Father announced to those present the reason for the calling of this assembly, and said that he now sought the assistance of the pengulu to bind his daughter in marriage to the bridegroom.

From the crowd of people in the pendopo there arose a mystic buzzing noise. They were praying.

I was so sorry that I could not be near enough to hear. A teacher who is a friend of ours, sister Roekmini, and I were the only women in the pendopo, which was filled with men.

But we were very glad to be allowed there at all, and to have that much freedom granted us. It would not have been seemly for us to appear among a crowd of men during the celebration of a marriage ceremony. It was a pity, as we should have been glad to hear the betrothal formulas. We could only see that during the betrothal service the pengulu held fast to the hand of the bridegroom, who had to respond after him. The solemnity lasted a quarter of an hour at most; but we did not have a watch with minutes, so we could not tell exactly. It was impressive and still in the pendopo: not a sound could be heard save the mystic droning of the priests.

There was a stir among the crowd of men, and the pious men rose from their knees. The ceremony was over.

The regents stood up; two of them lifted up the bridegroom, and now they started off over the carpet of flowers, followed by the most prominent regents. Back in the kuwadé hall, the bride was raised up by her sisters, and, supported by them, she too started down the road of flowers, followed by Mama and all the women guests. As the bride and bridegroom came within a few steps of each other, those who were leading them fell back, and the bridal pair gave, each to the other, a rolled up sirih-leaf filled with flowers. They took a few steps nearer, and then both knelt down and with them the whole company.

The bridegroom sat; on her knees, the bride moved nearer to him and made a sembah, both hands held together and brought down under the nose; that is our mark of reverence. Then she

---

them. These men, the "pious," or as the Javanese call them, the *"santris,"* have spent some years learning to read Arabic script, to chant the prayers from the Koran, and to have some understanding of Islamic theology. Led by the *pengulu,* the head of an important mosque, they say the prayers for the wedding.

kissed his right knee. Again the bride made a sembah. The bridegroom rose and raised his wife, and hand in hand the young pair walked over the carpet of flowers to the kuwadé, followed by the whole company except the regents, who turned back to the pendopo.

Bride and bridegroom sat before the kuwadé like two images of Buddha; the family and the lady guests thronged around them. Behind the bridal pair sat two little girls wafting their fans to and fro.

In most cases, husband and wife see each other for the first time at this ceremony. At the stroke of half past seven the regents came back, and formed a half-circle on the ground around the bridal pair; the women of their families formed the other half of the circle.

The bride and bridegroom saluted the older relatives with the foot-kiss.

The bride first raised herself on her knees and shuffled forward toward Mama; she made a sembah and kissed Mama's knee, to beg her mother's blessing on her marriage. From Mama, sister went to the aunts, sisters, and cousins—to all those who were older than she—and went through with the same ceremony. Then she went to Father and kissed his knee, in order to receive his blessing; from him she went to her father-in-law; after that to her uncles and cousins. When she had finished kissing the feet of all and had returned again to her place, the bridegroom began the foot-kiss journey. He followed the example of his wife. When he had completed this ceremony, the regents went out, and tea and pastry were served as on the evening before.

At half past eight bride and bridegroom departed. Hand in hand they left the hall. Usually they must go out on their knees; but as both of them had just recovered from illness, they were allowed to walk.

In other families the bridegroom must creep up the steps instead of walking, on coming to the house of his parents-in-law, before he pays his respects to the ladies of the family; that is the perfection of good manners.

The bridegroom went to the bridal chamber, and sister to our room, where we dressed her for the reception to Europeans.

Her bridal toilet, which had been the work of a whole day, was undone in five minutes. Only the headdress and the decorations on her forehead were left unchanged. We young girls ought not to have dressed her alone, but we did it just the same. We thought that it was entirely too stupid for us not to be allowed to touch sister in her bridal toilet. Sister now put on a kain of silk interwoven with gold, and a kebaja of ivory-colored satin with silver embroidery. She wore another jewelled collar; the jewelled flowers in her hair and the diadem were taken off. In their stead she wore a golden crown from which hung a veil. On her head jewelled flowers on spirals were fastened. So veiled and crowned, it was as though she had stepped from a page of the *Thousand and One Nights*. Sister looked like one of the fairy princesses. The costume was very becoming to her. What a pity that she could not have been photographed in it!

The bridegroom appeared in his official dress. Again the bridal pair sat before the kuwadé. At eight o'clock, they went arm in arm to the front gallery, where two gilded settees stood ready for them before a background of palms.

They received the good wishes of the European ladies and gentlemen, standing.

It was called a reception, but at the sound of the music, the dance-crazy feet turned toward the empty pendopo; bride and bridegroom both took a few turns around the pendopo.

It is not customary for young girls to appear at a wedding, but it would have been foolish for us to remain away from sister's feast.

It was not yet twelve o'clock, when the Resident, who was among the guests, toasted the young pair; his speech was answered by Father. Soon after the European guests took their leave, all but the Resident and a few others, among them a lady who is an intimate friend of ours. They remained for the native part of the feast.

After the departure of the European guests, the native nobles, who had absented themselves from the pendopo during the reception, came in and formed a half-circle, before which the bridegroom must give a proof of his proficiency in dancing.

The regents as well as the other officials had meanwhile dressed in more informal costume.

The gamelan played; a dancing-girl entered and began to dance. The Patih of Japara brought, on his knees, a silver waiter to the bridegroom, on which there was a silken cloth. When the bridegroom had taken the cloth, the Patih fell back.

Soft gamelan tones again sounded; it was a prelude, an invitation to the hero of the day to open the feast. The bridegroom rose and went to the middle of the pendopo; he fastened the silken cloth around him and named his favorite air to the gamelan players. The gongs chimed; it was immediately struck up.

I shall not attempt to describe the dance; my pen is inadequate. I shall only say that it was a joy to the eyes to follow the agile dancer in his graceful movements as he kept time to the beautiful gamelan music. Behind him danced the dancing-girl, also singing. The circle of native dignitaries accompanied the music by singing and beating their hands together. Toward the end of the dance the Resident went forward with two glasses of champagne. The gong sounded, and both dancers fell upon their knees. With a sembah the bridegroom accepted a glass from the Resident. He drank it and the Resident emptied his at the same time amid joyful gamelan tones and sounds of general mirth.

A servant took the empty glasses, and the Resident fell back. The bridegroom stood up and again began to dance. Now his father-in-law brought him a health to drink; dancing, they advanced to meet each other, and at the sound of the gong, the young man knelt down to receive the wine glass from the hand of the older one.

After a health had been brought to him by all the regents present, he left them and went back to sit by the side of his wife. Soon after that the bridal pair left the assembly; the European guests went home, but the feast was kept up till early in the morning. The European gentlemen had danced too, and our Assistant Resident acquitted himself excellently.

Mama, our friend, sister Roekmini, and I stayed till the last European guest had gone.

The next day there was quiet in the house. In the afternoon the last ceremony took place. That is the first visit of the bridal pair to the parents of the groom. It is called in Javanese *ngunduh mantu,* which, literally translated, means "daughter-in-law plucking!" The daughter-in-law is compared to a flower which her husband's parents will pluck.

For this occasion both bride and groom should again put on their bridal costume; but that would have been much too wearisome, so the groom was dressed as usual and sister wore a kain interwoven with gold, and a silk kebaja; her hair was dressed in the form of a cap, and on her head was a small sheath in the shape of a cross, which was filled with flowers, and over the whole was a network of melati blossoms, and again the jeweled spirals waved to and fro above her head.

The bridal pair went in a procession, followed by the native officials on foot, to the house where the father of the bridegroom lodged.

Days and weeks after the wedding the newly married pair are still called bride and bridegroom. The bride is a bride until she becomes a mother. There are women, mothers, who all their lives are called *nganten,* short for *penganten,* which means bride and also bridegroom.

The day after the ceremony was spent in receiving visits from both Europeans and natives.

Five days later there was again a feast in the kabupaten; the first return of the holy day which had opened the wedding ceremonies was celebrated.

The young couple left a week after the wedding; they were feted everywhere by various family connections with whom they stopped on their journey home. At Tegal the marriage was celebrated all over again; they remained there a week, and finally they reached their own home at Pemalang.

There you have a description of a Javanese wedding in high circles. Sister's marriage was called only a quiet affair, and yet it entailed all that ceremony. What must a wedding be that is celebrated in a gala way?

We were dead tired after the wedding.

The Javanese give presents at a marriage; things to wear, such as kains, stomachers, headdresses, silk for kebajas, cloth for jackets; and also things to eat, such as rice, eggs, chickens, or a buffalo. These are merely meant as marks of good-will.

Kardinah also received a splendid bull from an uncle. This had to be placed on exhibition with the other presents!

When a buffalo is killed at the time of a wedding—and usually more than one is needed for the feast meals—a bamboo vessel filled with sirih, little cakes, pinang nuts, and pieces of meat must be mixed with the running blood of the slaughtered buffalo. These vessels, covered with flowers, are laid at all of the crossroads, bridges, and wells on the estate, as an offering to the spirits who dwell there. If these bridge, road, and water spirits are not propitiated, they will be offended at the festivities, and misfortune will come of it. That is the belief of the people. Its origin I do not know.

A friend of ours says rightly that the Javanese are a people who are filled with legends and superstitions. Who shall lead the people out of the dusky realm of fairy tales into the light of work and reality? And then, when superstition is cast off, we do not want the poetry to be trampled under foot.

But of what good is my prattling? Let me rather ask you if you have been interested in this epistle, and if you will now forgive me for my long silence?

There is so much that is lovable in my people, such charm in their simple naive beliefs. It may sound strange, but it is, nevertheless, a fact, that you Europeans have taught me to love my own land and people. Instead of estranging us from our native land, our European education has brought us nearer to it; has opened our hearts to its beauties, and also to the needs of our people and to their weaknesses.

Do not let me tire you any longer with the scribbling of a silly Javanese girl; I have written enough.

(Postscript) In some places it is the custom when the bridal pair meet for the first time for the bride to wash the groom's feet as a token of submission before she gives him the knee-kiss. Whenever a widower marries a young girl, or a widow a young man, the giving of the sirih at the wedding is omitted. The one who has already been married hands the other, who carries a watering can, a piece of burning wood, the contents of the can are poured upon the fire, which naturally goes out; whereupon the charred wood is thrown away and the watering can broken into pieces.

The symbolism of this I do not have to explain. It is plain enough. You should have seen sister as she sat there before the kuwadé. She ought to have been photographed, or, better still, painted, because that would have shown the coloring.

She stepped so calmly and sedately down the carpet of flowers; everywhere there were flowers and the perfume of incense; yes, truly, she was much like a Bodhisattva! (incarnation of Buddha).

I cannot hear the gamelan or smell the perfume of flowers and incense, without seeing her image before my eyes.

The people picked up the flowers over which sister had walked and kept them; they bring good luck, it is said, and to young daughters, a husband!

36 · TO MEVROUW ABENDANON-MANDRI

March 27, 1903

It is always said of the girls here that, "they are well provided for, and comfortably taken care of." Have they a right to complain? Well means well-being, happiness, the opposite of misery; and misery is what the women feel, and yet they have no right to complain—they are said to act always of their own free will. But how about their children? What is more wretched than a sad childhood, than children who too early have learned to read the shadow side of life?

I once copied something from a speech by Prof. Max Müller, the great German scholar who was so learned in Eastern tongues. It was almost as follows: "Polygamy, as it is practiced by the Eastern people, is of benefit to women and girls, who could not live in their environment without a man to take care of them and to protect them."

Max Müller is dead; we cannot call him here to show him the benefits of that custom.

37 · TO STELLA ZEEHANDELAAR

May 17, 1902

I cannot tell you how great was my joy when at last I was able to begin my studies. So far it has been but a review of what I once learned at school more than ten full years ago. But there is one advantage in this late study. I can understand now much more quickly and readily than I could in my childhood, still it is a deep grief to me that I am now twenty-three years old instead of thirteen. I could then look forward so far, I could have carried on my studies indefinitely, but now time is limited on account of my age.

First, I am working at Dutch so that I shall have it thoroughly in my head, and then later I must study one or two of the native languages.

There, I have struck so hard with my pen that my penholder is broken through the middle, but even that does not make me give up. Poor pen! I have depended so much upon it and we have worked together happily for so long. I must be a strange creature to lament over a broken penholder!

In April, we went on a journey; we paid our sister a visit. We left our home without the least idea of seeing her again; we went to see another sister, our eldest, who was ill. While we were there, we received an urgent letter from little sister, begging us to come to Pemalang, to see her. We set out early the next morning. How can I describe that meeting to you? It was simply blissful! We did nothing the first few moments but look at one another and hold one another tight. And I was so thankful to see her well. She had never looked so fresh and blooming before. She had roses in her cheeks. And beyond everything, it delighted me to see how her husband valued and honored her.

It is with great pleasure that I have learned to know my new brother-in-law. He is a good, sincere man, with many fine traits. He is very upright, just and true, and has a sympathetic heart. She is his comrade, his advisor, his friend, and a mother as well to his three children, who are as fond of her as if she were their own mother.

The children follow her footsteps everywhere, like little faithful dogs. The oldest child, a boy of seven, had lived with his grandparents. Sister took him in charge and the child is devoted to her now and loves to be with her; though his grandparents did not keep him at arm's length you may be sure. The two others are girls of six and four, she gives them lessons at home: so I might almost call them little pupils, Stella.

He leaves the education of his children entirely to her, and naturally sister will bring up her little daughters in our spirit. Sister has not been able to realize her early dreams, as she had dreamed it, but is the task which she has undertaken less beautiful for that reason?

Our roads have divided, but both of us work for the same ideal;

what matters it which road one takes if it but leads to the same goal?

.   .   .   .

I long to go to Holland for many reasons; the first is study, the second is that I want European air to blow upon the few remaining prejudices that still cling to me, so that they may be wholly driven away. There are not many left, it is true, but some obstinately remain. Only your cold air, Stella, can make of me in truth, a free woman. To mention but one of the persistent little prejudices, I should not be disturbed in the least if I were alone in a room filled with European gentlemen. But I can think of nothing, that could make me, under any possible circumstances, receive alone, even one wellborn Javanese young man, who was unmarried. I think it is laughable, absurd, idiotic, but it is true. I dare not talk to a strange man without a companion, and even if there were company, I should think it tiresome, and should not feel at my ease.

So you see that in spite of my strong ideas of freedom, I cannot get away from the influence of my native environment, which keeps girls strictly secluded. When the idea has been strongly inculcated that it is not modest to show oneself to strange men's eyes, then it is a hard task to break away from it. It must not remain always so, that prejudice must go. How else shall we be able to work together with men? And that is part of our plan. One way in which we hope to accomplish much good.

Only the air of Europe will be potent to separate me from the influence of my Javanese education. Sometimes I laugh at myself and it drives away the foolishness for a little, but it always comes back.

We returned from our journey on the 19th of April. Father came several stations to meet us. He brought a long official telegram from the Resident, which announced that Heer Van Kol would come to Japara the next day. That was a delightful greeting of welcome, and I found something still nicer when I got home—your letter.

All the government officials along the whole line received the orders from the Resident to wait upon Heer Van Kol as he passed through. On Sunday afternoon, at the stroke of three, the travellers arrived. With Van Kol was a journalist, who served him as interpreter and guide, and Father, who had waited for him at the border.

Van Kol had made a resolution never to lodge anywhere except in a hotel, because he knows well the open hospitality of the country. But after he had made the acquaintance of our family, and received a pressing invitation, he stayed with us. Later we heard that it was we who had been responsible for his faithlessness to his resolution. He thought us worthy of scrutiny, he wished to observe the influence of European education on girls of the aristocracy, and could not let the opportunity pass. Happily we did not hear this till afterwards. The knowledge would have made us constrained and self-conscious.

At the table, he talked almost constantly of his wife and children. It was splendid to hear how this great man honors his wife. He met her through correspondence, a point of resemblance there, Stella. He corresponded with her at first about her literary work. It was only by chance that she discovered her great gift, her talent for writing. She was at that time a governess, and was staying with some friends at a villa on the slope of the Pinanggungan (their villa now in Prinsenhage is called after that villa "Lali Djiwa"—soul's rest). One of the party must write a description of the place, and they drew lots to decide which one it should be. The lot fell upon her. She sent the article to a magazine and the editor wrote asking her for more.

Van Kol has been to all of the places where he lived and worked in his early days, and the children who formerly played with his daughter, he found mothers themselves when he went back. But he still remembered them and knew them all by their names.

Stella, we were happier that evening with Heer Van Kol than we have been in a long time.

At first we showed them examples of the artistic work of our people, which called forth expressions of wonder and admiration, and Heer Van Kol made some sketches of them. Some of the company moved away and the chair next to him was empty; I slipped into it.

Then he began, "You have planned to go to Holland? Melchers told me so."

On my answering in the affirmative, he went on, "But it will be difficult for you later, when you come back. The greatest difficulty lies in coming back to the old life."

"Why do you think that?"

He spoke frankly and openly and said, "It would be too difficult for you, if later on, you should marry. After having lived in Holland you would never be able to make yourself contented as the wife of a native official."

He instanced cases of well educated native girls, their friends, who had married Hollanders. They and their husbands were devoted to one another but the Indian cannot be really happy amid European surroundings, and the Hollander can never accustom himself to the Indian life, so there is always an impassable gulf between husband and wife.

I let him finish quietly, before I brought my own ideas to the light of day; "Mijnheer Van Kol, if I should go to Holland, my intention is to be educated for a profession, that of teaching preferably, and when I come back I plan to open an institute for the daughters of native officials. It is to study that I wish to go there."

He looked at me in surprise; his blue eyes lighted up as though to himself he said, "That is a fine idea—a very fine idea." Then to me, "Do you not think it splendid to have an object in life?" There was so much enthusiasm in his voice and in the expression of his eyes, that I felt my heart grow warm, involuntarily my lips formed a word, a name "Stella,"

Stella, if I could only have you here, but then the earth would be too small to hold my happiness. For that was happiness, that moment when I saw that my plans were understood and respected too, by a superior man like Van Kol. It was like the feeling that mothers must have when they hear their children understood and praised.

He asked if I had talked with Mevrouw Rooseboom. No, I had never had the opportunity; both times I had met her there had been a great company, a ball or a dinner. They seemed to have spoken of us at the palace, because Heer Van Kol told me as soon as he arrived that his Excellency the Governor General had said that he knew me.

Annie Glaser goes on her vacation next month to Batavia and to Buitenzorg. She will go for us to the Abendanons' and tell them all that we have in our hearts; she will go too to our friends at Buitenzorg. Could I but go with her!

What we have to do is to present a petition or something of the kind, which Heer Van Kol will write for us from Batavia. The petition will set forth our names, our ages and very briefly what we want to do. And to make sure that he will remember us when he gets to Holland I have at his instigation written to his wife and explained our plans to her.

He was delighted at Roekmini's idea of going to the Art Academy, and also to know that she wished to go through the household school. For indeed it appears that she has not enough talent to ever go very far in her art. He shared our belief that a teacher of domestic science could help our people very much. But he is anxious for her to be able to go to the Academy for a few months before she starts on her domestic studies. He thought it fine that we too should wish to work together and help each other. He said many times over "I think it splendid for you two to want to undertake so much."

I have talked to him about the idea of teaching hygiene and kindred subjects in our schools, and let him understand that I should be glad to take a course in hygiene and nursing, in order to teach them later. He thought that a good idea too.

"In India you could not study that except under great difficulties; in Europe it would be quite easy, there you would have everything under your hand, and you could easily get through in a few years, as you speak and write Dutch very well."

I told him of other reasons why we wished to sojourn for a time in Europe. He sympathized with us there too. And he was one with us in the belief that our ideas would be able to compel a larger following, that we could spread them broadcast, if we worked under the protection of the Government. The Javanese nation is like a great child that loves show and display. It respects everything with which the all powerful Government concerns itself.

We talked of the education, if such it may be called, of the daughters of the nobles. Van Kol knows regents' wives, and knows of their monotonous dull lives.

It was time that something should be done for Javanese girls; he is the last man with whom I should have to argue about the importance of woman's place in society. He spoke of his own noble and highly gifted wife with such love and respect. He called her his counselor and his guiding star.

It touched me deeply to hear this man making himself so small beside his wife. He is small in body, but great in heart and soul. It was delightful to be in his company.

I have been asked to put my ideas in writing in the form of a brochure or letter to the Queen. It would do much good to our cause if she, who is a woman herself, knows of the deep injustice that our women suffer. But I must know what I am doing. As soon as I let my voice be heard, I know that I shall bring down the anger and hate of many of the Javanese men upon my head.

For myself personally I do not fear their hate or anger, but if I should become a teacher I might have to stand before a class without scholars, because no father would trust his children to me. I should have touched the egoism of man.

I have received an answer to my question as to when a Moslem girl comes of age. It is "A Moslem girl never comes of age. If she wishes to be free, she would have to marry and after that be divorced." So we shall have to declare ourselves of age, and compel the world to recognize our independence.

You know that Van Kol came here with a journalist. He wrote a description of the journey that he made with Van Kol, also the visit to the kabupaten is described, and something is told of our conversation with Heer Van Kol. Now people will know whither we are going. I only hope that making our ideas public will do good and not harm. For the first time my name would come out openly in connection with my people. I am proud of that, Stella— to be named in the same breath with my people.

.   .   .   .

Keep this portrait in memory of the triple bond. Poor clover leaf, it was too beautiful, so it had to be pulled apart. It is the best portrait that we have; it is good of all of us. It was made at Christmas time and it is our last portrait, taken together as girls. The sight of the little group makes me sorrowful. Three hearts grew together on one stem, and now one of them has been torn away. Will the wound ever heal? It still bleeds at the least touch.

Oh Stella, you do not know how we miss her. Everything reminds us of her—speaks of her. We feel so old now; the past seems to lie behind us like an eternity, and yet a half year has not gone by since she left us.

May 26, 1902

I have read your last letter over many times; in it you write so sympathetically about the Javanese people. It is very pleasant that you should have such friendly thoughts towards the brown race. If I could only have you here with us there are so many things about my people which I should be glad to show you. Where can one study and learn to understand a people better than in the heart of that people? and here we have a true Javanese environment. You know that all of you would be welcome at any time.

It is charming of you to wish to have me with you, but alas! for the present I may only appreciate your good will. To travel alone to Buitenzorg belongs just now to the realm of forbidden fruit. But who knows when a change may come! So much that seems to us today to be absolutely impossible, appears tomorrow as an accomplished fact. The Javanese are a nation filled with memories and fairy tales, in dreams and fairy tales the most wonderful things happen, and my heart which is Javanese through and through, holds fast to the illusion that there can still be miracles, even as there were in the far distant past.

If you knew of the dreams of some Javanese girls that you know, possibly you might be surprised at them, think them strange, but you would not, I hope, merely shrug your shoulders in pity. You know, do you not, that we are possessed by the idea of going to your country? But you do not know why. What one naturally thinks when one speaks of visiting strange lands, is of seeing and understanding new things, enjoying oneself, and perhaps also of learning accomplishments.

But when we feel so much for the suffering of our people, is it strange then that there should be in us a great longing to do something that will help them? What has that to do with our desire to go to your country? We wish to gather knowledge and bring back to our people the treasures of other lands, of your own country first of all. We do not wish to change the spirit of the native Javanese, but to cultivate the good which is latent in them. That is the goal which we have set before our eyes.

It is such a pity that we live so far from each other. How

nice it would be if we could exchange thoughts and ideas. Things can be expressed so much better in spoken than in written words. But our correspondence is very pleasant to me, we meet at so many points. How gladly I should teach you to know and understand my people. A great artist must rise up in Java to tell of our race in beautiful words to his fellow countrymen. Just as Fielding has written of the Burmese. Now we have only that notorious book by Veth [1] that has brought so many pens into motion, and caused a storm of anger to break forth.

Every land has its own individual faults. India just as well as every other country on this round earth. Poor India, in foreign lands one knows so bitterly little of you, and a book like that of Veth will certainly not gain you sympathy.

Augusta de Wit writes with understanding, and in beautiful language about India. We always read her articles in the *Gids* with much pleasure.

In everything that concerns nature and art, and in "dreams," Borel is delightful. On other subjects he has less good to say, he goes hand in hand with his friend Veth. Have you read what Borel has written about the gamelan? We think it a little jewel. And did you see the article by Martine Tonnet about the wajang orang at the court of Djokjakarta? That too is a jewel. I wish that Borel would go there, he might feel inspired to break into charming poetry. The dance of the Princes of Solo and Djokjakarta must be magnificent. It is the dance of dances it is said. It is a pity that we cannot go to Djokjakarta. We have often been invited, but it would be so wearisome to dress in court costume, and at court everyone must be dressed (like a bride).

Do you know that fairy story by Marie Marx-Koning? We think it very fine. It seems to me that she must be a great admirer of Van Eeden. "T'Viooltje, dat weten wilde," reminds me of "De Kleine Johannes." Do you not like that too? It is so true in thought, and in style it is charming.

I read what you wrote of your little protégé with great interest, and also what you said of the poor in Holland. I hear much of the misery of the poor there when winter comes. Poor, poor simple creatures! I correspond with a Frieslander; she tells me about conditions in Holland, especially in Friesland. In the winter time she has often sat down on the ground beside poor people who lived

1. *Java*, by P. J. Veth, 4 vols., Haarlem, 1896–1907.

in little hovels of straw. The middle of winter, no work, nothing to eat, no fire, no clothes, no warm covering, and crying children. It is bitterly hard.

39 · TO MEVROUW ABENDANON-MANDRI

June 10, 1902

Dutch has always been my favorite study, and many people say that I am thoroughly at home in it. But heavens! fondness for a language is a very long way from knowledge of it. Next to languages I like geology. I also enjoy mathematics, but I am still struggling with the groundwork of history. Not that I do not like history; I think it is interesting and very instructive, but the manner in which it is set down in schoolbooks has little charm for me. I should like to have a teacher who knew how to make the dry parts interesting. What I do think delightful is ancient history; it is a pity that so little of it has come my way. I should love to study the history of the Egyptians, and of the old Greeks and Romans.

We do not wish to make of our pupils half Europeans or European Javanese. We want a free education, to make of the Javanese, above everything, a strong Javanese. One who will be blessed with love and enthusiasm for his own land and people, with a heart open to their good qualities and to their needs.

40 · TO MEVROUW DE BOOIJ-BOISSEVAIN

June 17, 1902

I read in the paper that some Chinese girls had asked permission to stand for the teachers' examinations. Hurrah for progress! I feel like shouting aloud in my joy. Of what good is the preservation of a few old traditions? We see now that the strongest and oldest traditions can be broken; and that gives me courage and hope. I should like to meet the gallant little Chinese girls; I should be so glad to know something of their thoughts and feelings, their "soul."

I have always longed to have a Chinese girl for a friend.[1] I have often wondered about the inner life of such a girl. It must certainly be full of poetry.

At Semarang, a Chinese millionaire has laid out a splendid garden. It lies on a hill and is so beautiful; there are rocks, grottos and tiny hills covered with green ferns. Masses of flowers and miniature fruit trees are interspersed with little parks and winding paths.

There is a lovely summer house in the middle of the lake. The lake has many capes and twisted turns. And in it, guramis and gold fish can be seen swimming around. On the shore, is a hill with a grotto, and a bath house. A winding stair runs through the grotto and comes out on top of the hill, where two miniature temples stand. Fruit trees and flowers of all kinds grow and bloom everywhere; it is a fairyland become reality, only the fairy kings and queens and the silver shining little elves do not come out of the chasms in the rocks to make the illusion complete. The whole idea is like a poem expressed in art. But where is the art that is not poetry? Everything that is good, that is high, that is holy, in a word everything that is beautiful in life is poetry!

We have seen the creator of this wonder place. A deadly dull, commonplace *sjofele baba*.[2] Images in plaster, human dragons, and tigers are scattered among the grass; these too are the creations of his fancy.

It is a pity that at the entrance of the walk that leads to the fairy lake, two figures of European workmanship have been placed; they destroy the harmony.

You have been to Batavia to see the exhibition? [3] Yes, to be sure, and what do you say now of the brown race? What of its art?

Oh I am so proud of my people, they are capable of so much,

1. In 1898, four years before this letter was written, there were 261,000 Chinese settlers in Java, many of whom had made their home there for generations. Most of the Chinese in Indonesia are merchants, although there are some professional men. See G. Wm. Skinner, "The Chinese of Indonesia," in *Indonesia*, ed. by Ruth T. McVey, Human Relations Area Files Press, New Haven, Conn., 1963.

2. *Sjofele*, ragged or dirty; *baba*, a chinese coolie. *Sjofele baba* is a derogatory term.

3. Exposition of Javanese art held at Batavia in that year.

but you Hollanders must lead us. And you will do that, will you not? We are like children, and you are our protectors, who must guide us and help us to be grown up men and women.

41 · TO MEVROUW OVINK-SOER

July 21, 1902

Father and Mother have both given us their full permission. We had expected storms, thunderclaps, and lightning flashes. I cannot yet fully realize it. I had hoped that Father would consent, but I had not dared to dream that Mama would stand by him. We have never been estranged from one another but things are clearer now between Mama and us, this has brought us nearer together. I felt calm at first, but when Mother spoke to us in such a quiet, gentle manner, my calmness vanished. I had so much in my mind that I had not thought over what I should say, but when it came to the point, the words fell as themselves from my lips. Who was it that placed the words ready in my mouth—who?

There is a power higher and greater than all earthly powers put together. Good spirits were certainly hovering near putting the words in our mouths when we stood before her speaking for our ideals. Now I heard Mama say, deeply moved, "Oh child, why have you not trusted me?" We have done wrong, not to have told Mama everything. Poor, dearest mother, we are not worthy to kiss her feet.

I wish that I could tell you what Mama has been to us all these long years, what she still is. Now we realize for the first time the debt that we owe to her. We owe her a world full of love and gratitude; we are so thankful that we are going away from Mama in peace, in the service of that Good that she herself knows and understands. We no longer express our joy openly as formerly, as we did only a little while ago. We are quiet now, but full of silent gratitude.

I had prepared what I had to say to Father with the greatest anxiety. I do not know where I get the calmness and composure with which I spoke to him. My voice sounded strange to my own ears. I was unmoved, but when the permission for which I was pleading was granted, and I saw how much it cost my dear father, the ice-crust melted from my heart. I longed to throw my arms around him and speak words of comfort, but my knees trembled and my voice refused to do my bidding. I sat before him on the ground and looked at him with the mist before my eyes. I felt his pain and I suffered with him. O, some day I will repay for everything.

In my heart the prayer rose "Father, forgive me, O my father, forgive your child, she cannot do otherwise."

It was on the twenty-first of June; I chose that day, your birthday, for the difficult interview with Father. I wished to have you, my little mother, with me in spirit. Good angels surrounded me, my Heavenly Father stood by me in my struggle against my earthly one. When I was alone once more and had gained my desire, there was no joy in my heart; there was only pity and sympathy for the sorrow of one whom I loved. My tears were for him. From the depth of my soul I prayed: "O grant that from this great sacrifice of my parents, flowers will spring up and fruit will grow for our land, and for our people."

On the same day, the twenty-first of June, we wrote to Heer Van Kol at Batavia at his request. The letters contained our names, ages, and a summary of our ideas and wishes.

But we had to have our parents' permission, without that nothing could be done for us.

And now that this stumbling block is cleared from our way, we stand before a second—the financial one. Our parents cannot possibly afford the expense of our education; nor would we ask it of them. Yesterday I received a long and very earnest letter from Mevrouw Van Kol. If I did not need to keep it until it was answered, and if my unaccustomed fingers did not cling to it so, I should like to send it to you, but I shall try to tell you something of its contents. She has given us more than moral support, she has given us part of herself. We feel as though we had received a benediction. We are no longer afraid, we have no anxiety; we are at peace, we trust and we believe. Of what worth are we! We are no more than the dust of the ground. We feel no jubilant, boisterous happiness, but a still, quiet joy. O God, we are so thankful that we have found Thee, that we have come through doubt, unbelief and materialism.

We have thought much of late. We sought the light afar off

and all the time it was near; it has always been with us, it is in us.

Our souls have been working and growing, and we did not know it. Mevrouw Van Kol has drawn back the curtain from before our eyes; we are more grateful to her for that than for all the other things which have been done for us.

Before I received her letter, Mama had said to me, "Who gave you such ideas?" and I answered "God gave them to me." It was only natural that mother should try to hold us back, but when she saw that we would never change, that we could not change, she said to us with resignation, "Well, children, I shall try to think that you are called to do this; that God has sent you for this service."

Mevrouw Van Kol wrote us: "Often we need human beings and their support, but there are many more times, when it is only God that we need. He has called each one of us to do our special work, and he gives us strength and constancy. Believe me, this is what the voice of experience says. You stand now at the threshold of life; at the beginning of your work; when you are in the midst of it, then you too will have had experience. It is only when we have had experience that we become free and strong, true helpers and friends of mankind, depending not upon them, but upon ourselves and upon our Father—God."

Unasked, *East and West* has sent us assurances of its support and cooperation. Mevrouw Van Kol sent us the paper with an account containing a description of the journey of Heer Stoll. And where the writer had spoken of us, the following had been interpolated by *East and West*:

"We trust that Heer Van Kol, who has been a member of *E & W* since it was founded, will not have neglected to tell her that she can count to the fullest on our support in her noble struggle."

After she had seen this article, Mevrouw Van Kol sent a few words to *East and West* about us, so that we might be brought nearer to the heart of the Javanese-loving public which reads *E & W*.

She has asked permission to publish my entire letter in that paper. I do not like the idea, but it is in our own behalf, and she writes further: "How can the friendly public know what is in your heart and learn to appreciate your aspirations, better than from a candid letter, in which the young Javanese lays bare her soul to an older woman from whom she asks support and sympathy? There is not a word in that letter that the public ought not to see, and I know of no better introduction for you to the circle that has the welfare of Java and of the Javanese at heart. I can easily understand your scruples, but overcome them and say "Yes."

I have come to no decision in regard to this. I must first have Father's consent. Father wants me to keep everything secret at present; if the Government says yes, then the world can hear of it. It is very true that we should choose our way with all prudence, but experience has shown us lately that we gain more by publicity than by secrecy. Even if the Government should refuse our request, we should lose nothing. How many petitions are never granted!

.   .   .   .

Let me say now, to set you at ease, that we will always remain what we are, but we fervently hope with you, that it may be granted us to make our own form of religion admirable in the eyes of those who think differently.

We feel that the kernel of all religion is right living, and that all religion is good and beautiful. But, O ye peoples, what have ye not made of it?

Religion is designed as a blessing, it should form a bond between all the creatures of God, white or brown, of every station, sex and belief, for all are children of One Father, of One God. There is no God but the Almighty, say we Moslems, and with us all-believing monotheists, God is the master, the Creator of everything.

Children of one father and for that reason, brothers and sisters, who must all love one another, help and support one another. Ah, if this were but understood. But we are so harnessed down by form that we are sometimes driven against all religion; the followers of another, despise, hate and, sometimes, even persecute them; but enough of this for the present.

Is there a Dutch translation of Lessing's works, and of the life and writings of Pudita Ramabai? I was still going to school when I heard of this courageous Indian woman for the first time. I remember it still so well; I was very young, a child of ten or eleven, when, glowing with enthusiasm, I read of her in the paper. I trembled with excitement; not alone for the white woman is it possible to attain an independent position, the brown Indian too can make herself free. For days I thought of her, and I have never been able to forget her. See what one good brave example can do! It spreads its influence so far.

42　·　TO MEVROUW ABENDANON-MANDRI

July 28, 1902

No cloud lasts for ever; neither is there such a thing as eternal sunshine. From the darkest night the most beautiful morning is born and here I console myself. Human life is a true reflection of the life of nature.

What we must pray for day and night is strength. But the rain which makes the leaf and bud of one plant burst forth, beats another into the earth, where it rots.

43　·　TO STELLA ZEEHANDELAAR

August 15, 1902

Nellie's [1] enthusiastic article in *East and West* has been copied in several papers here. One in *The Echo* also contains an appeal from that paper asking the sympathy and cooperation of all women in India. *The Echo* quoted, just as did Nellie, a few words from my letter, and asked our permission to publish it all—or a part of it. I think it would be better not to publish another letter; one is enough and that from Nellie throws full light upon the question. Hilda de Booij, the daughter of Heer Charles Boissevain, a director of the *Algemeen Handelsblad*, asked if she could publish one of my letters about a Javanese wedding. She sent a copy of this letter home, and her brother advised me to publish it. Such personal letters will show the Netherlanders that the Javanese are in some respects their superiors, in many respects their equals and perhaps in many others their inferiors. So says Heer Boissevain.

1. Mevrouw Van Kol.

I am busy now with an article for *Belang En Recht;*
they will find room for it. If not, I shall send it to some
paper or magazine. We are collecting Javanese fairy tales for Nei.
and sister R. is making drawings for them. Oh, I hear so much
wisdom and truth from the mouths of the people, and it is expressed in such sweet, melodious words. If I only had your language well under my thumb, I should like to translate the beautiful
inspired music, so that it could be understood and appreciated.
We are not so deep by nature that it will break anyone's head to
understand our wisdom. There is no word for selfishness in our
language. Happy language where that word has never penetrated.

I wish that I could teach you my language, so that you could
enjoy its beauties in their original freshness. The deeper I penetrate
the soul of our people, the finer I think it. Among you wise men
and poets are drawn usually from a certain station, and only the
upper classes are educated. The great majority are—may I say it?—
crude. There are some superior spirits among the lower classes;
but the many, Stella? You know them better than I.

But go around with me into kampong and *desa*; let us visit the
small huts of the poor submerged tenth, let us listen to their
speech, seek out their thoughts. They are an unschooled people
always, but music comes welling from their lips; they are tender
and discreet by nature, simple and modest. If I am ever with you
I can tell you much of our gentle people; you must learn to know
and love them as I do. There are so many poets and artists among
them, and where a people has a feeling for poetry, the most
beautiful thing in life, they cannot be lacking in the instincts of
civilization.

Everything that is high and fine in life is poetry; love, devotion,
truth, belief, art, everything that elevates and ennobles. And poetry
means so much to the Javanese people. The least, the very humblest Javanese, is a poet. And what do you think of the deep
respect which children have for their parents? And of the touching piety of the living toward the dead? There is no joyful occasion
where the dead are not called to our remembrance, and their
blessing and the blessing of heaven invoked. In joy and in sorrow,
we think of our dead always.

And the name of Mother—how holy that is! In hours of pain
and doubt, the pale lips always murmur that name. It is Mother,
and again Mother who is called upon, if we need help, if we need

support. The honor of motherhood lies in this, in the calling of her name in deep, sorrowful hours. Why do we not call upon our father—why just our mother? Because we feel from childhood, instinctively that Mother means a world of love and devotion.

Each object that falls out of our hands is picked up with the saying "Oh, Allah, my child." Do I have to explain the meaning of that to you, what it shows?

Stella, I shall work earnestly at your language, so that some day I may be such a mistress of it that I can make all that is beautiful among our people clear and intelligible to the outside world. I want to study my own language hard as well. I want to teach our people to know that white race as I know it in its finer, nobler aspects. They must learn of your nobleness, of your greatness, so that they will honor and love you. I want to do so much that sometimes I wish that I had a double pair of hands. The will is great, but the strength is little. And I must not injure my health, that would be the most stupid thing that I could do. And yet I am often stupid, sometimes sitting and working till late at night and that is not good for me. I may defeat my own object if in the end it should do me harm and I could not overcome my bodily weakness, so I am doing my best to live soberly and sensibly.

44 · TO HEER J. H. ABENDANON

August 15, 1902

Hurrah for our native art and industry! They are well started now on the road to a splendid future. I cannot tell you how pleased I am. We like to admire our own people and it is so easy to make us proud of them!

The future of our Javanese artists is assured.

Heer Zimmerman was in ecstasies over the work that he saw here by the despised brown face: Wood carving, the art of the goldsmith, and textile weaving have reached a high degree of excellence. Our artists here have received a large order from *East and West* for St. Nicholas. We are delighted. Now the clever artist can bring out new ideas and express his poetic thoughts in graceful undulating lines and in ravishing, glowing, changing colors. Oh, it is splendid above everything else to see the beautiful—a spark of God is everywhere, even when things outwardly appear most evil.

There was once a child who went to an old woman who asked her what she would like to have, for the little one had neither sweets, nor ornaments, nor clothes; but the child said "Oh Mother, give me a flower that opens in the heart."

How do you like that? You must see it in the original—the answer of the child sounds so sweet. There is a deep meaning in "the flower tongue." "Njuwun sekar melati ingkang mekar ing pundjering ati." [1] That is what one hears all the time. We are now busy writing down everything interesting that we hear from the mouths of the people. There is no word for poetry in our language. We say "the flower tongue," and is it not well said.

We are learning songs. Not songs of rejoicing—have you ever heard one of that kind from a Javanese? The gamelan never rejoices, even at the most extravagant festivals, its tone is mournful. Perhaps that is well, life is mournful; not a song of rejoicing.

These pages have been written under the influence of sweet and sad singing. It is evening, windows and doors are open; the fragrant breath of the blooming *tjempaka* beyond our chamber comes to greet us with the cool breeze that rustles through its branches. I sat upon the floor, just as I do now at a long low table, at my left was sister Roekmini also writing. To the right of me was Annie Glaser, she too on the floor. Before me was a woman who read from a book of songs. They were very beautiful, and the pure, serene, sonorous tones seemed to carry our souls far away, nearer to the realm of the blessed. How I wish that you could be sitting there with us in that little circle. You would have felt with us and dreamed with us. Dreams! Life is not a dream. It is cold, sober reality, but even reality does not have to be ugly, unless we make it so.

It is not ugly—it is beautiful. We always have beauty within us. This is the reason that I wish that in education, emphasis were laid upon character forming, and first of all upon the cultivation of strength of will; it should be instilled into the child.

But I am wandering from my subject. This time I wanted to write to you about our people, and not about education.

There is an old woman here from whom I have gathered many flowers that spring from the heart. She has already given me

1. "I beg you for the *melati* flowers which bloom inside the heart."

much, and has still more to give, and I wish for more; always more. She is willing, but first I must earn her treasures, I must buy her flowers—why? Why must I pay?

Solemnly the words sounded from her lips; "Fast a day and a night, and pass that time awake and in solitude."

> *"Door nacht tot licht,*
> *door storm tot rust,*
> *door strijd tot eer*
> *door leed tot lust,"* [2]

sounds like a requiem in my ears.

The meaning behind the words of the old woman is: Fasting and waking are symbolical; "Through abstinence and meditation, we go toward the light." No light, where darkness has not gone before. Do you not think that a beautiful thought? Fasting is the overcoming of the material by the spirit; solitude is the school of meditation.

As a child I did everything mechanically without question, because others around me did the same thing; then a time came when my mind began to question, why do I do that, why is so and so? why—why— It is endless.

I would not do things mechanically without knowing the reason. I would not learn any more lessons from the Koran, saying sentences in a strange language, whose meaning I did not understand and which probably my teachers themselves did not understand. "Tell me the meaning and I am willing to learn everything." I was wrong, the Book of Books is too holy to be comprehended by our poor intelligence.

We would not fast and do other things which seemed senseless to us. Every one was in despair, we were in despair, no one could explain the things which were incomprehensible to us. Our God was our conscience, our hell and our heaven too was our own conscience; if we did wrong our conscience punished us; if we did good, our conscience rewarded us.

The years came and went; we were called Moslems because we had inherited that faith, and we were Moslems in name, no more.

2. *"Through night to light*
   Through storm to peace
   Through strife to honor
   Through sorrow to joy."

God—Allah—was for us a name—a word—a sound without meaning.

Now we have found Him for whom unconsciously our souls had yearned during the long years. We had sought so far and so long, we did not know that it was near, that it was always with us, that it was in us.

It had been working in us unconsciously for a long time; but she who opened the door for which we had sought, was Nellie Van Kol. And who leads us now, and shows us the way toward Him? It is Mama. We have been so stupid all our lives; we have had a whole mountain of treasure under our hands and we have not known it.

Foolish, headstrong, pedantic persons that we were, we reproach ourselves now for our own conceit and self-sufficiency. We say to console ourselves: "It has pleased God to open your hearts at last, be thankful for that."

God alone understands the riddle of the world. It is He that brings together paths that were far asunder for the forming of new roads.

45 · TO HEER E. C. ABENDANON [1]

August 17, 1902

Good morning; here comes sister to prattle to you again. It is a splendid fresh morning, and I am sitting here in a cosy corner by the window where I have a view of the garden. Another time I shall try and describe all our surroundings to you. Our home, which is our *dunia* (little world) and our cloister. Now however, I shall continue my talk of yesterday. It is pathetic to see the joy of our elders over the return of the strayed sheep.

Out of pure joy, an old woman here sent us her collection of books, old Javanese manuscripts, many written in Arabic characters. We are going to study Arabic so that we can read and write it.

You know perhaps that Javanese books are very rare, and hard to find because they are written with the hand. Only a few of

1. Son of J. H. Abendanon.

them are printed. We are reading now a lovely poem in the flower tongue. How I wish that you knew our language. I should be so glad if you could enjoy all our fine things in the original. Have you any desire to learn the Javanese language? It is difficult —certainly, but it is beautiful. It is a sentient language; often the words seem to be conscious, they express so much. We are astonished sometimes, own children as we are of the country, at the cleverness of our fellow countrymen. Things of which one could never imagine anything could be made, they express charmingly. Name something in the dark, give out a subject at random, and a simple Javanese will immediately make a rhyme that astonishes by its aptness and clearness. This facility belongs peculiarly to our Eastern people. It is a pity that when the precious gifts were meted out, your sisters should have been neglected. That is not fishing for a compliment, we mean it literally. As one can see, though one fairy gave us wit in stepmotherly wise, another sister fairy has made reparation by endowing us richly with her gift of sensibility. I do not think so very much of her gift myself, and we have to take good care that this virtue does not degenerate into a vice. A certain amount of feeling is good; but you will soon see, if you have not seen already, that it is often hard for your sisters to keep themselves in the golden middle way. It is very difficult for one who naturally goes to extremes. Now that you know all my faults, here is a prayer: try to understand them. Help me to overcome them. Will you not do that? Your sisters know of things in themselves that are not good.

After having had days of rain, we went out one morning to see how our flower children were getting along. We were afraid that they would have suffered from the over-abundant rain, but we found our rosebushes full of green buds. The days came and the days went; our roses were full of luxuriant leaves and of beautiful blossoms. Rain, rain, they needed it, before they could bear those splendid blossoms.

Rain—rain—the soul needs it in order to grow and to blossom. Now we know that our tears of today serve only to nourish the seed, from which another, higher joy will bloom in the future.

Do not struggle, do not complain and curse sorrow when it comes to you. It is right for sorrow to exist in the world too; it has its mission. Bow your head submissively before suffering. It brings out the good that is in the heart. But the same fire which purifies gold, turns wood into ashes.

Now I want to tell you how it was that we happened to get into touch with Nellie Van Kol. Perhaps you have already read something about it in the paper. One evening in the latter part of April, we had a visit from Heer Van Kol. He was sent to us by a Dutch lady, who has much sympathy for the cause of your sisters. It was one of the most pleasant meetings of our whole lives. Already, long ago, he had won our esteem through what he has been to Java, and the Javanese. But the personal meeting secured for him a place in our love. It is delightful to meet superior people. It was a great occasion in our lives, when we met your dear parents, it was a turning point for us; it waked us up to reality. Before that we had only seemed to live, we had been asleep, always sleeping and dreaming. Now we are alive, fighting and struggling, hoping, despairing, suffering and rejoicing, weeping and laughing; that is life. We have climbed to the heights of joy, and we have descended into the depths of misery. I am happy just to be alive.

I have heard from your mother that you sympathize with our struggles and ideas; and you have told us so yourself. So it will certainly please you to know there are others who are interested in our cause; superior people like Heer Van Kol and his wife.

We told Heer Van Kol everything. It was to hear about our plans that he had come, and he promised to support our endeavors with all his might; just as your father has promised to do. Are you not glad that the cause of your sisters has found a warm defender in Holland—in the council halls of the country? He will do everything that he can to help us. He asked us if we would not write to his wife; she would prove a true, faithful advisor. He spoke of his wife with such love and respect; he called her his guide and his counselor. It touched us to hear a man— and such a man—speak thus of a woman. Would that there were more such men—who would see the highest in woman and honor her for it.

I did not let the grass grow under my feet; immediately after he had left, I wrote to his wife. Was it instinct—I wonder! for when I was writing to her I had no feeling at all that it was to an utter stranger, which was the fact. It had been the same way, when I was talking to her husband. As though she had been my mother, I blurted out without reserve, just what I felt. It was easy to be frank with her husband, for he was so modest, so friendly, met us so cordially, and was so fatherly towards us. I am glad that I followed the voice of my heart and wrote at once to Mevrouw Van Kol. We received a letter from her at once—and such a letter! We feel ourselves rich in her sympathy. God has given us as a gift, the heart of a true friend, and through that friend's heart, he has found us himself. If I could only tell you how happy we are.

"We will find the right human friends, when we cease to seek for support among men, but depend upon ourselves and upon our Father—God." We are deeply grateful to Nellie for that. Again she says: "The loveliest and best among us are but weak blundering creatures; nestle on your Father's heart, he will heal your wounds and dry your tears."

In the days since I have begun this letter something very unpleasant has happened. Before our acquaintance with Nellie, it would have plunged us into despair, but now it is different. We do not seek consolation from men—we hold fast to His hand, and then the darkness becomes light, and the storm wind a gentle breeze.

We are not afraid, we are never afraid, wherever we may be, there is a Father that watches over us, who judges us with love. We are ready for anything. For there is no light where darkness does not go before—the dawn is born out of the night.

Now that we have found Him, our whole lives are changed, our work seems nobler, higher. What do you think of all this, Edie?

I know one thing for certain, that you are glad for your sisters. I have still other things to prattle about, and then I must let this letter go; otherwise it will grow stale, and it is too long already. Perhaps it seems very formidable to you. Honestly, tell me the truth? Candor must be the basis of our friendship. Do not be afraid to tell me something because it might give me pain, when you know that it would be wholesome for me.

From you we did not expect anything else, but that you would not allow the workmen under your orders to be beaten. We share to the fullest your ideas in the matter. I cannot bear to see any one struck; it hurts me so to see the beast in man, unfettered, hot tempered, the man made lower than the beast.

We cannot understand how men, and even women, can go to

see an execution, it is worse than heartless. You know very well that unfortunate convicts are often beaten with rods; they are cruel people that willingly encourage the infliction of such punishment. It is bad in the Javanese, but still worse in the European, when he so debases himself. I have seen, a certainly not stupid, in fact a highly educated European, at a festival of the people, let first a child, and after that a woman, and a young girl, make the acquaintance of his stick in a most frightful manner, because the blunderers had not been deft enough in getting out of the great man's way. I ground my teeth together to keep from crying out aloud; each blow pierced me through the soul.

It is not the idea of pain that makes me abhor bodily punishment, but the deep humiliation that the victim must feel. And also the harm it does to the one who punishes. Physical punishment embitters, but never cures. That is our conviction.

As children of a ruler in a community where the idea is fast rooted that a Raden Mas or a Raden Adjeng is absolutely a being of a higher order, to whom a God-like reverence is due from the people, we have, oftener than we wished, been among scenes that made us tremble with exasperation. At such times we are struck dumb and stand still as death, we can neither speak nor smile, indignation and pity hold our mouths fast closed. An acquaintance of ours once said "We must do it well; how otherwise will our little handful be able to keep peace and order among thousands? Had they not been afraid of us, they would long ago have hunted us from the land, and driven us into the sea."

Obedience through fear: when will the time come when the God-like rule, which is called love, will penetrate millions and millions of hearts? One thousand nine hundred and two years ago the beautiful law of love was preached, but how many thousand years must pass before love will come into its own? Not only among the elect, but among the multitudes?

Your mother knows the whole history of our lives. Has she ever told you of our childhood years, when we lived under the despotic sway of older brothers and sisters? Among us it is a law, the younger ones must submit to the older in everything. That was not for sister Kartini; even in her early years, the desire for freedom had awakened. The result was that I was somewhat out of harmony with my older brothers and sisters, because I submitted to them only when I saw a reason in what they thought good. So

I stood there a child of twelve years, alone against a hostile power. Bitter, bitter tears were wept by us as children.

Do you know who has always been our friend, our help and our support? Kartono. But most of the time he was not at home, he was at Semarang. Our friendship is quite old you see; it goes back to our earliest youth. My eldest sister married, my older brother went away, and then we began a new life. The watchword was "Freedom, equality and fraternity." We wished to be loved—not feared.

It is not a boast, but everyone knows that our little ones would rather be with us than with the others. Love is the bond which binds us together. And how our little ones love us! They have taught us much. Those who embittered our childish years, were also our teachers, for they taught us to avoid being like themselves. Another proof that sorrow justifies its existence.

Those who formerly opposed us, now come to us with love and friendship. They do not tell us so in words, but deeds bear witness. In every letter, our sister asks us to come and visit her. Our presence does good, both to her and to her house, she says always.

God is great, God is powerful! Could not that bit of our life history, become the life history of two peoples, of the Hollanders and of the Javanese? Would it not be possible for nothing but mutual love and respect to bind the Netherlands and Java together? How this happy state of affairs has come about in our own family, I do not know; I protest, I do not know. Many times the question has been asked us, but we only know that we have much love in our hearts and that is the whole secret I believe.

Now, best brother, I hope sincerely that this long discourse will not frighten you away from a further correspondence with your sisters. And that you will take it as a proof of our good intentions, when we say that we look upon you as our brother and our friend. We hope that many letters from Sawah Luntu with Japara as destination will be forthcoming. Tell us about everything —your work—your life and your environment.

It is a pity that photography is such a luxury, for we should be glad to take some peeps, for the benefit of our friends, into typical Javanese customs. We, as children of the country, can go everywhere here with a freedom that would not be allowed to you.

August 20, 1902

Lately we have received some people from Batavia who admire the art of our people, and who wish to do much for it. They were heads of the governing board of *East and West* in India, who wished to have examples of native art for Santa Claus (Sinterklaas), and were anxious for Japara to be well represented. We have been busy with that work. It is such a pleasure to us to be able to work for the furtherance of our people's art. We think it a great privilege to be the avenue through which some of these expressions of their soul find a way into a new world. Works of art that compel wonder and admiration are made by the despised Javanese, whom the world in its simplicity has patronized.

When one looks at the splendid examples which we have, and after that sees their simple creator, and the primitive tools with which he works, one is filled with reverence for his work, and feels instinctively that here one is face to face with a true artist. Once when we were in ecstasies over something which he had made, we said to him "Oh, where did you get such beautiful designs?"

The lowered eyes were raised, and with an embarrassed laugh, he answered "From my heart, *bendoro*." [1] We were delighted at his answer, and afterwards we laughed so at ourselves, because we had sat upon the steps, and he was in a respectful attitude upon the ground, humbling himself before us, to whom he was a hundredfold superior.

.   .   .   .

It is splendid that through the untiring efforts of yourself and some others, the eyes of the Netherlands are beginning to be opened to that important part of a child's education—reading. Holland may well congratulate herself that she possesses such noble strength, which sets itself with heart and soul toward the forming of the mind and spirit of her youth. And in that respect the Dutch child is far more fortunate than the Javanese, who possesses no books except schoolbooks.

We were still children when an inspector of native education

1. *Bendoro* means "master," and is used to either men or women of the aristocracy.

asked us to write little narratives of native child life which were to appear in small illustrated books. We had not the least idea when we wrote the sketches, that some day the pioneer of the noble movement in Holland to give the children good literature, would ask us to bring a little stone for the building of that tower, which is rising so high in the pure air, a tower full of clear, undimmed windows, looking on all the expanse of heaven—which she is erecting for her loved ones—the youth, the men of the future. We are busy now collecting fairy tales, fables, games and songs for her. It will not be easy to write down the fairy tales and the little games. In the first place though we love music very much, to our great sorrow we know nothing about it, because we have never had an opportunity to study it. The greatest difficulty lies in this, we have an entirely different musical scale from you, and in it there are chords for which we seek in vain in European music.

Only last week, we talked with a man who has spent twenty years collecting songs and poetry of all kinds among the Indian people. He has collected all conceivable forms, even rhymes and jingles. Now he is so anxious to have some Javanese songs in his collection. But so far, he has not been able to write them into music on account of the difficulty of which I spoke.

But gamelan music is very difficult, and the children's songs and rhymes are simple. We tried some of them on the piano and they went quite well. It would seem as though an invisible telephone cable ran from here to Lali Djiwa and back again; otherwise we do not see how it can be that so many things of which you spoke in your letter were already answered in ours before we received it. In my letter which crossed yours, you will find many of your questions answered. We had even written you of the songs, games and fairy tales. It will be so unfortunate if we cannot give the songs, for the charm lies in the music. As children, we did not enjoy our fairy tales, if the narrator could not sing.

We have been having a heated controversy about the influence of books. Our adversary thought that idealism was all nonsense; poetry was silly, a book nothing—not of the slightest value.

We were delighted the next morning, when we opened the *Amsterdammer* to find your delightful article on the influence of books. We are novices, triflers, our judgment is worth nothing; but now we have an authority on the subject.

He is a very peculiar man, and it interests him to strike at our innermost convictions. He likes to try to analyze our deductions. He is a man of many good qualities, but so weak. Through him, we see still more plainly why a child should first of all be educated in strength of will. Without strength, all other good qualities are of little worth.

I cannot tell you how thankful we are that you have shown us the way to true happiness—to true freedom—to God. Those who serve God are free—they are bound to no man. To be dependent upon others is to be in bondage to them. Where is true happiness? It is not far away, but it is so difficult to find the road thither, we cannot go by tram, by horse or by boat, and no gold can pay the cost of the journey. It is hard to find the way, and we must pay the fare in tears and heart's blood and meditation. Where is the road? It is in ourselves. In the world we find much that delights us, that transports us, so that we think we have found the long sought happiness. But even as the thought comes, we find by bitter experience that what we hold to our hearts is empty dross.

True, lasting happiness dwells within, and is called soul's peace. We have learned of that from you. God is jealous, it is said. He will not suffer us to pray to any other gods but Him, and He punishes with bitter disillusion those who create gods for themselves, and pray to them with reverence.

So we think, "Thou shalt have no other gods before me," a command of love. In it, there lies an earnest admonition that man is man and but a fallible creature. Alas, if that commandment were only understood, so much suffering would be spared us.

Mother says that she would like to meet you, to thank you personally for the miracle that you have wrought in her children in opening their hearts to the Father of Love. You ask what had turned us into unbelievers: the things that we had seen lurking under the mantle of religion, and Oh, the intolerance of so many strong believers.

We were children. How can one understand the thoughts of a child? We did not know, could not understand that it is man who does evil, using God's name to cover his wicked deeds. We asked and still ask for that matter, not what is your belief? but what is the conduct of your life? Righteousness was our God. Now we know that God and righteousness are one.

. . . .

We are reading a beautiful poem; it is in the flower tongue. There is no word for poetry in our language, so we say flower tongue—and is it not expressive? All our books are in poetic meter and can be either read or sung. Do you remember the cool, bright tropical evenings, when everything was quiet, and the stillness was only broken by the rustling of the wind through the tops of the cocoanut trees? When the fresh evening breeze brought you on its breath the sweet perfume of kemuning, tjempaka, melati. Did a dreamy song never reach you then? the song of a Javanese, who sings to his family and to his neighbors—of love—heroic deeds, and glittering pageantry—of beauty and of wisdom; of mighty men and women, princes and princesses of the long ago. It is that loveliest hour when the Javanese, tired from the hard day's work, seeks rest in song, dreaming all his cares away, wholly lost in the shining faraway past, whither his song leads him. "The Javanese are a people who live in the past," a young friend of ours says rightly. "They are lost in the blissful dreams of their eternal sleep." That is true, but we are alive, we must live; and life always goes forward.

Our friend says, too: "Your people must be awakened to a practical realization of the outside world." Many things that are dear to us will then be driven into the background, but should we for that reason, delay the awakening?

Dreams are splendid, but what would become of us if we dreamed forever? We must make ourselves nobler, by trying to make our dreams real.

There is so much charm in the Javanese people. You have been the means of making us realize it anew in the last few days. This collecting of fables brings us into contact with many kinds of people, and it is a great pleasure to find out their ideas. They tell them to us in simple language, but they tell them so graciously, and we are moved by their truth and wisdom. I wish that I could send you some of their beautiful thoughts in our own soft musical tongue. Translated they are no longer what they were.

We tell you too much about our people, do we not? But what a question, it answers itself. We know that you are glad to know of them and that you love them sincerely. We believe with you that the essential thing is the spirit, and not the world. We are so rich, and so happy with the spirit friends that we have, is it selfish to want to learn from each one of them? To improve ourselves by correspondence with those who nourish and broaden our minds?

We think it abominable to receive and to have to answer letters about nothing, epistles that make one ask "Why were they written?" We are certainly privileged to be in touch with so many superior minds.

Deep in the heart of Celebes we have a noble friend. We admire him sincerely for his great work. It is always a holiday for us when we receive a letter from Dr. Adriani. His letters are as interesting as they are learned. We met him when we were visiting the Abendanons. Mevrouw brought us together, knowing how much we should value the acquaintance. When we are distressed by the heartlessness of others, the mere thought of him is a consolation. The selfishness of people hurts us; often it is boundless. It is such a delight to meet now and then, among lukewarm or indifferent people, many without heart or head either, a being who is all enthusiasm and heroic strength.

.   .   .   .

We are so sorry that you did not know us in the full glow of our triple bond.

We were three souls welded together—one in thought and feeling—living side by side in life as sisters. Storms passed over the young heads, storms raged in the young hearts!

I think of your "In order to reach our ideals, we must lay down many illusions." From the death of young spring blossoms, the strong fruit ripens. It is so with human life—is it not? From the death of young illusions, sometimes mature ones rise up, which ripen and bring forth fruit.

We have laid down a great illusion. It was a bitter, miserable hour; we buried it in our heart's blood, but still we felt as though we were being rushed along as by a river, which was carrying us forward to fresh, strong life.

We know that many tears must be shed to water the young fruit and bring it to full growth. We are beginning now to understand what Mr. Abendanon meant when he told us that through his wife. What was formerly dark to us has meaning now. Yes, we shall only be able to move slowly. The journey is long and the way steep and difficult. The idea of personal suffering does not trouble us, but if it should react upon ourselves, and in that way, impede our cause, it would be terrible.

I think of a certain evening not long ago, an acquaintance took both of us to a concert at the playhouse at Semarang; it was the first time that we two had ever, in our whole lives, been alone in the midst of a great sea of humanity, without sister, without father, without mother; both of us absolutely alone, with all those strange faces. We had the same thought: "So shall our life be in the future; we two alone on the great sea of life! But we are comforted, there is a God who will watch over us."

On the twentieth of this month, we were at Tandjong Priok, in thought. We saw the *Willem II* steam away from the coast of Java, carrying as a precious freight Java's great friend and warm supporter, to the distant Netherlands. He is already known in the parliament of that country, so that when he speaks in the interests of the millions of children in this land, his words will have authority, and weight. Take him safely, *Willem II,* for the sake of these lands, and for the sake of his dear family.

And now, true best counselor, our highly honored and dearly loved friend, we thank you many times for your letter. It did us much good in every way. It encouraged us to earnest meditation—strengthened us and opened up new vistas of thought to us.

47 · TO MEVROUW ABENDANON-MANDRI
September 2, 1902

It is presumptuous for us to play "mother," and with children who are older than we; but what does age matter? Everyone needs love, the graybeard as well as the child.

Should a woman only exclusively through marriage be able to come to her right, to the full awakening of the best gifts of her soul?—because the highest and most sacred glory of woman is motherhood. But then must a woman be obliged to have a child of her own in order to be a true mother—a being who is all love and sacrifice? If that is true, how pitifully shallow is the idea of the world that it is only a piece of oneself that can love better than oneself. There are so many who are called mothers only because they have brought children into the world, but beyond that they are not worthy of the name. A woman that gives all the love that is in her heart to others, with no thought of herself is, in a spiritual sense—mother. We set the spiritual mother higher than the physical.

We hope and pray fervently that later if it is granted us to realize our ideals, and we stand at the head of a school, our children will not call us "mother" as a matter of form, but because they feel that we are mothers.[1]

. . . .

We hope that Anneka will find cordial, affectionate people at Buitenzorg, who will make up to the poor lonely child for the lack of a mother and of a home of her own. Anneka lived our Javanese life with us here. I wish that you could have taken a peep at the little corner behind the door, where Anneka sat on the ground with us in such a sisterly manner. One evening she sat by us in our chamber, at the low table where I am now writing; she sewed, we wrote. There was still a fourth in the circle—a friend of ours. She read aloud or rather sang to us. You know of course, that all of our books are written in poetic meter, flower tongue as we say, and they are meant to be sung.

Doors and windows were open. Outside the chamber there bloomed a tjempaka tree; its perfume came to us on the soft wind. The voice was gentle and tender, the song was sweet to our listening ears. It carried our souls back to the far distant past, to the golden age of barbaric splendor, and of men and women who were wise and beautiful and strong.

We bit our penholders absently—much oftener than we made them fly over the white paper, and amid these wholly Javanese surroundings, there between brown children of the sunny land, sat a pale daughter of the West. Oh how gladly would we have you, even so, among us.

We have learned the songs too, and if we were not bashful, we would sing and dream before you.

Yesterday Annie did something typically Javanese. She was so anxious to go away from Japara, we said to her "Ask the help of the Sultan of Mantingan, promise him an offering of flowers if your wish comes true." So she did.

Day before yesterday evening we spoke of it, and the next morning she went with us to make her offering. We went there with a band of priests to the holy grave, and we took flowers and incense with us.

1. It is the custom in Java for students to address their teachers not by their names but as "mother" or "father."

Anneka went with us into the building over the grave and sat with us on the ground at the foot of the tomb. Incense burned, and a mystic buzzing rose at first softly but gradually louder from the priestly choir. It was solemn and impressive. We sat with lowered heads and listened to the murmur of the mystic prayer, while blue clouds of incense rose upwards.

One of the priests creeping forward on the ground brought Anneka's flowers and laid them reverently on the grave of the Sultan, and after that on the other graves. Next to me I heard a sob. It was Anneka! Barefooted as a mark of reverence, she had come with us into the building. For it is our custom to look upon the dead as holy, and to show them reverence.

We then went to the little stream behind the churchyard to wash our feet. We asked the priest for Heaven's blessing for Anneka.

Dearest, we should so love to have you here, so that you could live our native life with us. There is so much that is touching in our Javanese life, especially in the honor that we show to our dead and to our parents. Nothing ever happens in our lives of any importance, either of joy or of sorrow, that we do not think of our dead. Anneka will remember Japara when she sits high and dry at Buitenzorg, although she may be a thousand times better off there than here. They that have known Japara, who have seen its soul, can never forget it. They must think of it again and again, whether it is with love or whether it is with hate.

Yesterday at midday we went to the wood-carving works; it was very interesting. There were fifteen people, men and apprentices, at work. The work they do is severely simple but it is in the highest degree effective.

Sister Roekmini must naturally go to work with them, and she sat down with the wood carvers on a bench as naturally as though she had been there all along.

We have made the acquaintance of Frits Reuter; he is a writer who draws one's heart. He is so wholesome and spontaneous. What do you say to reading one book through from seven o'clock in the evening to three o'clock in the morning? It is not sensible, but it can be forgiven when one is in good company. If it was your intention by your present to make us love your great poet of the people, then you should certainly be satisfied with your work.

We have also enjoyed Vosmaer's [2] beautiful *Inwijding*. It was our first acquaintance with this Netherlander, and we thank you heartily for introducing us to him; it is one of the pleasantest introductions of our lives. After reading *Inwijding*, we received a book on Greek mythology, with pictures of all the gods and goddesses; it is delightful to look at the plates and read the descriptions after *Inwijding*. Oh! to see all that beauty with one's own eyes, and to experience the emotion that thrilled the souls of Sietska and Frank. No, no, we must not desire so much. We are only thankful that there is someone endowed with the power of words, who has made it live and breath, and that we can understand his language.

48 · TO STELLA ZEEHANDELAAR

October 11, 1902

I feel some anxiety as to who will carry on our work in directing the wood carving after we have gone away. Our little sisters are too young, and there is the financial responsibility as well. If a European comes here, naturally our artists will be exploited merely for his own profit; the one who devotes himself to this work should be disinterested and have in his heart a love for art and a love for Java.

. . . . . .

The world says everything spontaneous must be suppressed, and everything that differs from it, is necessarily soiled and smirched. In all ages, the way of the idealist has been hard. No deviation from the set type is suffered. Anyone who is not like the rest of the world is tormented all his life, unless he throws away his own coat, and in its stead draws on the coat of custom.

. . . . . .

I do not want to promise you anything, Stella, for I am not sure that I should be able to keep my promise. Do you think Modjowarno so frightful? Which would you prefer, that we should go crazy here at home, or that we seek healing for the

2. Carel Vosmaer. Poet and art critic. Author of *Amazone*, and the translator of Homer into Dutch hexameters.

wounds in our souls there? If we are disappointed in our plans, we are determined that we will not remain any longer cloistered and imprisoned here for petty, futile reasons. We will not submit to conditions which we detest and despise with all our hearts. The enemy abroad does not frighten us, but the enemy in our own country eats into our souls. Nothing can help us but God.

Now do not say that you will be cast down and sad, when you receive a letter telling you to address me at Modjowarno. The idea has no terror for me. It is true that we shall go there with lacerated hearts, but that will not be the fault of Modjowarno, and even there, all will not be lost, Stella. You have often encouraged me to use my pen—I shall still have that, and there I shall have nothing to lose and nothing to venture save myself. Here I should venture much, if I said what I really think. If I became a teacher, I should be striking my own calling dead, because those whom I had offended would gird on their armor and hunt me down.

I have already said that we would not go to Modjowarno, save with deeply wounded souls. Do you know the effect that would have upon my pen? Nothing speaks so to the heart like suffering. And even I have made eyes grow wet. You know me too well, I hope, to accuse me of vanity when I say that. It is only to show you how very much the worth of a pen rises when one has heart's blood for ink.

A few months ago, some one wholly unknown to me burst out crying when she read some words of mine. She felt how I had suffered when the words flowed from my pen. She was so affected that she wished to begin work at once for the alleviation of the misery of which I had written. The next day she even offered to help us; alas, only to withdraw the offer a few days later, through the working of reason.

People think that they are pleasing me, when they assure me that I write "splendidly." What does it amount to? I want what I write to make a lasting impression, Stella, and I can only do that when I have had experience. When my heart has been written upon, then—only then—will what I say be of worth.

October 12, 1902

During the last year I often heard something about myself, which distresses me. I am a coquette. Do not spare me, but answer outright; am I a coquette? and if so, in what way? I am seriously troubled, for I dislike anything that is inconstant.

Someone, no slanderer, says that I speak with my eyes. Is that true? I have asked my sister to watch me well, and to tell me what they see in me that is strange, what there is in the play of my eyes. And my truth-loving little sister says—she is always conscientious—that my eyes dance as if they were saying much when I talk long, never mind with whom. Believe me, when I say that I do not do it intentionally; that I have no thought of pleasing; and if what she says is true, it is unconscious and in spite of myself.

It is a strange sensation, when one has always thought oneself a serious, candid girl, to hear all at once that one is a coquettish creature. I was astonished and distressed; I had never given the matter a thought, and would not be guilty of such conduct knowingly.

I am told that I must modestly (hypocritically) cast down my eyes. I will not do that. I will look men, as well as women, straight in the eyes, not cast down my own before them. I know very well that we shall be made to promise, perhaps under oath, when we go from here, that we will not bring to our families the terrible disgrace of sharing our love and sorrow with a European; on that point they can be at peace.

We would never think of such a thing; inevitably it would be wreaking destruction upon the whole cause. For our own sakes, we could not; we, who wish to set ourselves up as examples.

You know how very little I care for what "they say," but in this case it shall never be said, "There, you have the whole thing; see what comes of it. When a man gives his daughters European educations, they marry Europeans." That would do incalculable injury to the cause, and that may not be.

And yet actually what do we do but share our love and sorrow with Europeans? What am I doing at this moment? Do not

Europeans live with us in our inmost hearts? And do we not share the inner life of Europeans?

Much, yes everything, can be taken away from me, but not my pen—that will always be mine. Do not let them provoke us too much, the most enduring patience can give way. We may be driven to the use of that weapon, even though it should rebound and wound ourselves. You may be assured that we will make good use of it if we go to Modjowarno.

We long for comfort from our true friends, we have grown cold; we want to warm our frozen hearts on your hearts. We complain about the egoism of others, but what of ourselves? It is pure egoism to share our pain and suffering with others, and to ask for love when we know that for us love is inseparable from sorrow.

Do you not think we have gone back sadly? We have grown hard and unfeeling, and we are often afraid of ourselves.

O God, give us strength, help and support us; and from you, dear, I ask forgiveness for the sorrow I have caused you by this letter. But to be silent is not good—it is not honest. Forgive me, and love your brown children.

50 · TO MEVROUW ABENDANON-MANDRI
October 27, 1902

In spite of all that we have suffered, we know that we are fortunate, for there are many poor creatures in even more miserable circumstances than ourselves, who without friends, without a single confidante—must struggle on alone through life never hearing a cordial sympathetic word; never meeting an understanding look, or receiving a warm pressure of the hand. We feel that we are richly blessed in the possession of love and friendship such as yours.

If you will always love and trust us, little Mother, you will make us happy. We thank you again and again, for your love and sympathy. You see we are answering your letter at once, and we shall put it away and keep it as a sacred relic!

We pray and entreat you, think no more about our happiness. We have told you so often that it is not our own happiness we seek, but that of others.

When we go to Europe, we do not expect to gather roses for ourselves.

I protest we expect nothing of Europe—nothing of the "happiness" of which European girls dream, nor do we expect that we will find much friendship and sympathy there, or that we will feel at home in a strange environment. We hope only for one thing, to find there knowledge and enlightenment. It will not matter if we do not find it gay in Europe, if we but receive there what we seek.

We do not expect the European world to make us happier. The time has long gone by when we seriously believed that the European is the only true civilization, supreme and unsurpassed.

Forgive us, if we say it, but do you yourself think the civilization of Europe perfect? We should be the last not to see and appreciate the great good that is in your world, but will you not acknowledge that there is also much that brings the very name of civilization into ridicule?

We complain about pettiness and smallness of soul in our own surroundings; do not imagine for a moment that we think that in Holland we shall not find pettiness too.

You know better than we, that among the thousands that are called civilized by the world, only a very few are that in reality. That a broad mind is not possessed by every European from whom it might be expected. And even in the most elegant, exclusive and brilliant salons prejudice, intolerance and short sightedness are no infrequent visitors.

We do not think of Holland as an ideal country, not in the least. Judging from what we have seen of the Hollanders here, we can certainly reckon upon much in that small, cold country that will wound our sensibilities and bitterly grieve us. We Javanese are reproached as born liars, wholly untrustworthy, and we are called ingratitude personified. We have not only read this many times, but we have heard it spoken aloud, and that was a fair test of the speaker's delicacy of feeling.

We only smile when we read or hear such pleasantries, we think to ourselves of European society life which often gives glaring proof of the truth and sincerity of those who sit in high places and look down with scorn upon the lying, untrustworthy Javanese.

We came in contact with Europeans very little until a few

years ago; the first occasion on which we found ourselves in a European crowd, was at the time of the coronation of Her Majesty. How admirable was the comedy play of the European world behind the scenes!

At that festival, my reverence for Europeans received its death blow. We saw two ladies in earnest speech, intimately holding one another by the arm, their heads confidentially close; we heard affectionate words here and there; good friends, thought we. A gentleman came and broke up the tête-à-tête. As he walked away with one of the ladies, we heard her say: "Such a cat."

While the remaining lady said to another nearby, "That unfortunate creature, she rigs herself up so ridiculously." Just a little while before she had declared that the dear one was charmingly dressed.

We received blow after blow that evening, through this, and other heart-rending little scenes. We saw red, fiery men's faces—"gentlemen" who spread the horrible breath of alcohol around them when they spoke. And, oh, the noise and racket everywhere! We grew cold to our very hearts, and longed eagerly to get away from these "civilized" surroundings. If we had been base, and had told what these friends had said of one another, a formal civil war would have broken out!

Soon after that a girl wrote us of a visit which she had paid to an alleged friend. She had been so charmingly, so cordially received. A little after, we met this "friend" and thanked her for her kind reception of our little friend. She said, "I think her a sullen girl; she always looks so sour and waspish."

Innumerable times we have witnessed fantastic kisses between persons whom we knew hated one another. And it was not the despised *nonas* [1] who did this, but white people of unmixed blood; educated, and brought up with every advantage. We saw too how harmless, simple nonas were held up to ridicule by clever, educated Hollanders. "The Javanese is a born liar—wholly untrustworthy." We leave the accusation there. We only ask that when a child sins through ignorance, and a full grown, thinking person commits the same sin deliberately and with calculation, which of the two is the most guilty? We think sometimes with reason, what is civilization? Does it consist in a commanding tone, or in hypocrisy?

1. A half-breed woman, child of a native mother and European father.

Oh, what do we do? what have we said? Forgive us, little Mother. You know that it is not our intention to grieve you by being honest. Is it not true that honesty is the basis of our friendship—of our love? Often it is not polite to be honest. We do not enjoy being impolite; we are Javanese, to whom "politeness' belongs as a natural heritage.

We think that you ought to know our opinion of some things in your civilization. Because you seem to think that we look upon the European world as our ideal. It is not always there that we have found true education, and we know that you must think the same thing. True education is not the exclusive property of those who have had the advantage of books; it is to be found as well among the people upon whom a majority of the white race, convinced as it is of its own excellence, looks down with disdain. Our people have faults, certainly, but they also have virtues which could very well serve as examples to the civilized nations. We have degenerated, gone backward you see, or we would not have lost what a superficial glance can recognize as one of the peculiar qualities of the Javanese people—modesty.

Father said to me once, "Ni, do not imagine that there are many Europeans that really love you." Father did not have to tell me that, I knew it very well myself. We could count upon our fingers, and we would not have to use two hands either, those who are really our sincere friends. Most of them pretend sympathy for effect, or through calculation, with some end in view. It is amusing; if one looks at the humorous side of such things, then one is not distressed.

People often do such foolish things. Do not imagine that I do not see that many of those who now talk about native art only do it to make themselves agreeable to me, and not because they have any real appreciation of it. Before me everyone is enthusiastic. Is it from conviction? But that does not matter, the result will be good, and through such people the real friends of Java and the Javanese may be reached.

We know why *The Echo* is glad to publish our articles. It is because we are a novelty, and make a fine advertisement for that paper. The Dutch *Lelie* placed its columns at my disposal, and time and again the directress has asked for letters from me. Why? For the advertisement. Letters from a true daughter of the Orient, from a real "Javanese girl," thoughts from such a half-wild crea-

ture, written by herself in a European language, how interesting!
If in despair we cry aloud our miseries in the Dutch language,
again it is so very "interesting." And if—which may God forbid—
some day we should die of our broken hearts—then it would all
be so terribly "interesting." Oh, there are people who think that
only the interesting is desirable.

．　　　．　　　．　　　．　　　．　　　．　　　．　　　．

There is much that is beautiful in the Javanese religion. It is
only a pity that it is not taken more as a symbol.

People take the things that wise men preach literally. They
abstain from food and sleep; as now interpreted, it means that
one must eat and sleep as little as possible and all will be well
in this life and in the life hereafter. The great idea that is back
of it, they pass by. That is "It is not eating and sleeping that
is the aim of life."

I am a child of Buddha, and it is taught that we should eat
no animal food. When I was a child, I was very ill. The doctors
could not help me, they could suggest nothing. Then a Chinese
convict,[2] who had been friendly with us children, begged to be
allowed to help me. My parents consented, and I was healed.
What the medicines of learned men could not accomplish was
done by "quackery." He healed me by giving me ashes to drink
of the burnt offerings dedicated to a Chinese idol. Through
drinking that potion, I became the child of that Chinese divinity,
Santik-Kong of Welahan. A year or so ago we made a visit to
the holy one. There is a little golden image before which incense
is burned day and night. In times of epidemic it is carried around
in state to exorcise the evil spirits. The birthday of the holy one
is celebrated with great brilliancy and Chinese come from far
and near. Old Chinese residents have told us the legend of the
golden image, which for them really lives.

Our land is full of mysticism, of fairy tales, and of legends.
You have certainly heard many times of the enviable calmness
with which the Javanese meets the most frightful blows of destiny.
It is *takdir*—foreordained, they say, and are submissive. The fate
of every man is determined, even before he sees the light of life.
Happiness and misery are meted out to him before his birth. No
man may turn away that which God has decreed. But it is the

2. Formerly in Java convicts were released from prison to work the
government lands.

duty of every one to guard against misfortune as far as possible; only when it comes despite their efforts, is it takdir. And against takdir nothing in the world can prevail.

That tells us to be steadfast and to push forward and to let happen what will happen, to submit calmly to the inevitable, and then to say it is takdir. That is why our people would not set themselves forever against that which had actually happened. Brought face to face with a fact, they are face to face with takdir and are submissive. God give us strength.

We are in deep sorrow. We are preparing to go away from our loved ones. To break loose the bonds which until now have been our happiness. But better a sound little hut than a castle in ruins, better a strong little skiff than to go in a splendid steamboat and be driven upon a reef.

For a long time now I have had to go to bed without Father's good-night greeting. Until a few months ago, Father never went to bed without stopping first outside our chamber door, and putting his head inside to see his little daughter once more and to call her name before he went to rest. If the door was locked, he knocked, softly; his little daughter must hear and know that she was not forgotten.

Gone now is that dear, dear time. I have had much love—too much—all to myself. For when one has had too much, then there must be another, who goes lacking. Now it is my turn to do without. I have bathed long enough in the overflow.

It is hard for me, but for him, my father, I hope and pray fervently that he may be so fortunate as to banish me from his heart utterly. My poor, dear loved one will then be spared much misery. I shall always love him dearly in spite of everything; he is more to me than ever, and I am thankful for all the happy years that have gone by. But for my poor father, it would be better had I never become a child of Buddha, he would then possess me wholly. Even though it were only in memory.

What Nellie said is true: "Life brings more cruel partings than death." Those whom death takes away from us in the bloom of love and friendship remain more surely ours in spirit than those whom life leaves to us.

My dearest father, that he should find this out in his old age and from his favorite child! May God forgive me, but it is not he alone who has suffered and who will suffer; we too have striven and suffered. We pray God fervently that in the course of time he may see the truth and will learn to be proud of his little daughters. That we may atone to him in some measure for the deep disappointment we are causing him now.

51 · TO MEVROUW ABENDANON-MANDRI

November 21, 1902

When we love, is it not our earnest wish that the object of our love should be happy? and those are happy who love and are loved in return. I am not speaking here of the love of man and woman; that is a delicate question and one that I am not capable of judging. But I mean a love which one can feel for many; and never mind how much for one, for another in just the same measure.

Is it selfish when we expect those whom we love and who love us in return, to rejoice in our happiness, even when it consists in the giving of our hearts to another?

52 · TO HEER E. C. ABENDANON

November 21, 1902

Three of the four shelves of our bookcase are plumb full of books; the fourth we keep free for photographs and other souvenirs, so that we have all of our friends before us. You are between Mama and Brother Kartono. A little further away is Dr. Adriani, the learned man who is such a friend of humanity. Then comes a charming little creature, a pure, fresh, unspoiled flower of nature, whom we love very much. Papa, too, has a place of honor. You are in good company truly. And we have you with us—every day. In fact, the day has not begun for us until we have seen our friends and looked into their dear, true faces.

We have an idea that we shall see you just once, and that the meeting will be brief. A meeting—a brief greeting and then a—

parting; all in a few moments of time. We shall catch, as it were, a glimpse of one another, and then vanish forever—each from the other's ken. It is silly, but we have this idea and are not able to get it out of our heads. But why do we yearn for the personal, bodily meeting when the spiritual meeting is so pleasant? We ought not to need anything more—is not the spiritual the best in us?

.   .   .   .

What do you think of Japara-made fire-screen? It is splendid, is it not? Hail to all noble friends of Java, who brought the art of her people, and with it the beauty of their souls, into the light! We hope fervently that the interest now taken will not dwindle as has that in all too many other things, and that it will not prove only a fleeting fashion.

No, it shall not do that, although we realize the majority of those who now show interest in our art do so only because it is the fashion; but those who gave the movement its first impetus did so from sincere conviction, and that will prevail in the long run.

You see, I should enjoy living so many different kinds of lives. I should like to be in a mining district—among mine workers; or in a native Christian community, among native Christians. In a Chinese or Malay camp, or what not. But above all I should like to experience life, as it is lived in desa and kampong among our own people; that has always had a great charm for me. I know that my people would then grow still nearer to my heart. One cannot learn the soul of a people without living and working among them. The love that I have for our people is only a foretaste of what I should feel under more intimate circumstances. We try to come in contact with the people as much as possible. When we go out alone, we always stop and pay a visit to some of the kampong houses. In the beginning they looked at us with strange, unfriendly eyes, but it is not so any longer.

A child's hand is quickly filled, so too is the hand of a childlike people. They are very sensitive to kindness and also have a quick sense of humor. Under the influence of a ready word which will bring a hearty laugh, a sullen laborer is changed into a cheerful human being. Every day for some months, we have had a gang of workmen from the irrigation department on our place. They are busy building an addition to our house. We are going to have a splendid pendopo at our rear. During the rest hour, we often go and talk a little with the work-folk. Picture your sister, sitting on a heap of sand, surrounded by workmen who have almost no clothes on their bodies and who are smoking straw, or eating rice. Naturally we must begin the conversation, for an inferior would rather be silent a whole day than to speak first to his superior.

They work under the supervision of an Indo.[1]

He is good to his people, who come and go freely in his presence, and are always treated with consideration. We often hear them make little pleasantries with the *tuan*, a certain indication that the *baas* is good to them.[2] If they receive orders to work overtime, we never hear them grumble. That is pleasant, is it not? And this *sinjo*[3] might well serve as an example.

1. Indo is the usual term for an Indo-European, a person of mixed Indonesian and European descent. Under the Dutch, these persons occupied many of the lower supervisory and clerical jobs.

2. *Tuan* is the Indonesian term meaning "Mr.," "sir" or "master." In Kartini's time it was employed mainly in addressing foreigners. *Baas* is the Dutch term for "boss."

3. *Sinjo* is an Indonesian term of address used for men of mixed Indonesian and European descent.

53 · TO MEVROUW ABENDANON-MANDRI
December 12, 1902

We think that your little table is the most beautiful of all the carved work that our Singo has done. A short while ago he was saved as though by a miracle, from a great calamity. Eleven houses near his own were burned to the ground. The cocoanut tree in his little garden was all ablaze, but by great good fortune his house remained uninjured. The whole village ran out to see the miracle and asked the lucky owner of the only remaining house, what *ilmu* or *djimat* he had to protect him.[1] For they thought, of course, that he had saved his house through some magic spell. No, he had no *ilmu* or *djimat* nor magic spells, he had only "Gusti Allah" who had spared him for his own purposes. The day after the fire, the man came to us, and fancy! he thanked us for the

1. *Ilmu*, as used here, means spiritual or magical powers. A *djimat* is a magical amulet or talisman which has the power to protect its wearer from danger.

preservation of his dwelling. He insisted that it was the power of our prayers for him that had kept his house from misfortune. Such naive and simple faith is touching.

I asked myself if it would be right to take away from these poor souls the simple faith that makes them happy. What could I give them in its stead? The stupidest person can tear down, but it is quite another matter to build up.

We have found so many charming qualities in our humble friends.

We were turned away for a long time from all religion, because we saw so much uncharitableness under its mantle. We learned, at first slowly, that it is not religion that is uncharitable, but man who has made what was originally Godlike and beautiful, bad and ugly. We think that love is the highest religion, and must one be a Christian in order to love according to that heavenly command? For the Buddhist, the Brahmin, the Jew, the Moslem and even the heathen can lead lives of pure love.

A little while ago I received a letter from Dr. Adriani in which you would be interested. I told him what you had done for us, and he is so glad for our sakes. "What Mevrouw Van Kol has made you see," he wrote, "is the substance of all religion, the recognition of God as a person, not as goodness, but the Good."

There are many earnest things in his letter, I wish that I could read it to you and talk about it with you; I must answer it. Somewhere he says, "But I can see no other way. Christianity alone does not bring one happiness; only the personal love of God does that, of which Christianity is the symbol."

54 · TO MR. J. H. ABENDANON

January 14, 1903

My brother; my little brother, will positively not become a *prijaji*,[1] and enter the service of the Dutch East Indian Government. If Mevrouw has told you something of my letters, you will know that I am not sorry, but am rejoicing with brother in his decision.

1. A *prijaji*, as Kartini uses the term here, is an employee of the government, and traditionally, a member of the King's court and staff.

We think it splendid that brother has not for an ideal that which thousands of his fellow countrymen have always looked upon as most desirable, as the very height of good fortune—to be a little prince, glittering with buttons, under a gold striped parasol. It is a great joy to us that pomp and ceremony have no charm for him, and that he has realized so young that he wishes to go another way from the one that has always been followed, and trodden flat, by the feet of thousands.

I should have liked for him to dedicate himself to the service of suffering humanity, and to have studied medicine. That is perhaps part selfishness in me. I should have been glad to see him become a doctor because it is such a beautiful calling, and it would have inevitably taught him to understand our ideals. He could have done so much to further the mutual respect between the European and native elements. He could have taught his people to trust the European methods of healing, and he could have called the attention of the European world to the simple native methods whose value has been many times proven.

I spoke to little brother about the Doktor-djawa School, but he had no inclination in that direction, and we do not wish to press him.

55 · TO MEVROUW VAN KOL

January 17, 1903

For three long weeks not a drop of rain has fallen. It is boiling hot as it has never been before, even in the driest east monsoon.

Father is in despair. The young rice in the fields is turning brown. Oh, our poor people! So far they have had enough to eat here and they do not know the most frightful of all calamities which a land can suffer—famine. But what has not been, may be; and this great drought in the time of the wet season presages anything but good. What will happen if it keeps up? For several mornings the wind has blown as it usually does first in May. Has the turning point been reached, has the dry season begun?

It is frightful, everyone looks on helpless. It is hard to see everything that has been sown and planted turn brown and die, without being able to turn a finger to help it, and the great heat harasses the body too; one feels dull and listless.

What do you think of such a complaint from a child of the sun? Oh, how frightful for the people who are working out in the fields, if for us in here it is so scalding hot, and this is the wet season (west monsoon). Do not be chary with your cold; could you not spare a little of it? You may take as much of our warmth as you wish.

56 · TO HEER E. C. ABENDANON

January 27, 1903

I have been thinking of the time that is past, the old time when I sat with your father and your dear mother by the sea; those were moments of delight, such as one never forgets. The last time too that we sat with your father by the shore, and he talked to us of our plans, will always live in our memory.

It was splendid to speak heart to heart with one whom we knew to be such a noble, sincere friend. And what was the result; I could not sleep the whole night, I tossed about in my bed with your father's earnest affectionate words still in my mind and in my heart. That was what we had needed, what we had longed for; an earnest affectionate word, spoken face to face. The next morning early, your father had to go away, to our great sorrow. We went with His Excellency in the carriage past the way where we had talked on the sand; the result of that talk is that very soon, with the full consent of our parents, we are going to present a petition to the Government through the Governor General, asking it to give us an opportunity to help the Javanese woman of the future by completing our education at Batavia. Are you not startled, Brother? I do not know what you will think—that we are fickle? To strive with all our might at first to go to Holland, move heaven and earth to get there, and when at last, thanks to the work of our friends, we can go—to say "I am going to stay." What do you think of such instability? But is it not better to turn back and acknowledge one's mistake than to persist in a wrong course for the sake of consistency?

Do you know when that idea of going to Holland first took such a fast hold of us? It was in the December days of 1901, when we suffered without knowing why. Then there came to us a wild longing to go away—far away. Away, away—away into another atmosphere—to another land, where we should breathe a different air, and all our soul's wounds should be healed, where we should be strengthened in spirit and perhaps also in body. Strengthened and born anew, we would come back to work for the regeneration of our people. While we were away, people would cease to think of us. Alas, that it would seem so good to be forgotten. We should be forgotten by those for whom we would work, whom we so longed to help.

O, poor illusions! You know that it has always been one of our dearest dreams to be educated for our work, in Holland. But Father's last severe illness has made us think deeply. We understood at last as we stood over his sick bed how fast his dear heart was bound up in us. But I still ask myself, should we have come to this decision if your father had not been here and talked with us? I do not know, but there is no doubt that our parents have to thank your father for much, and we ourselves are very grateful to His Excellency too.

Sister and I have talked and pondered over your father's words for a long time. The result is that our going to Holland is still in the air—has flown to the moon—but that we hope to go to Batavia with all speed.

This is all personal. More important is the effect which our decision will have upon our cause. In the first place, if we go to Batavia we can begin to study at once, while if we go to Holland, we must wait a long time. I think always of your father's words, "Why not do what can be done at once—something will have been accomplished then, while in Holland everything would lie far in the future." Your father spoke of the wounded man who called for help; someone came to him and said, "No friend—I cannot help you now, I must first study, and learn how wounds should be dressed." Then the someone went away, and when at last he had learned the art of binding wounds, the man who had called to him had long been dead.

Then your father spoke of a pearl lying deep in the sea. You know that it is there but you do not know precisely where. You wade out into the sea and try to find it. The water comes up to your lips, someone calls to you and says—"Friend, do not do that, go no further. The water already comes up to your lips; if you are drowned, still you will not have the pearl. Get into a boat, measure and fish for it."

Your father said we could open a school at once without having to pass a single examination. There is nothing in the law that compels one to pass examination before teaching native girls. We could get some European teachers to help us, that would be as we wished, but do you think it would be well for us to open it at all without adequate preparation? It is true that in "our school" (how pleasant that sounds) we want to give more of a moral than an academic education. If it is not erected by the Government we would not have to follow the prescribed paths, and we want the whole idea of our school to be the education of children, not as though they were in a school, but in a home, as a mother would bring up her own children.

It must be like a great home community. Where the inmates all love one another and learn from one another, and where the mother is not a mother in name but in spirit, the educator of the child's soul and body.

We have thought much about that other idea of your father's, but in this way: if we are not able to study, but have to remain at home, could we not take the little daughters of regents here, as many as the kabupaten would hold? Let them go to school outside, but give them their moral education here with us. We could lead the young hearts through play and help to form the young characters. During the hours when those children would be at school, we could take other little children of native officials here in our own neighborhood and teach them elementary branches, handiwork and other things. All the while unperceived, we would be knocking at the little hearts, and trying to get nearer to the little souls. But if we find that we can open a school, then we had rather study first. Do you not think we are right, Brother? The school would be at Magelang or at Salatiga. Your father has talked with ours about it, and there is no objection at all. That would be almost as good as going to Holland. It would be splendid —Hé Brother?

Our grandfather in the past brought up the sons of other nobles. Grandfather had a tutor for his children, and he took the sons of the Pangeran of Solo and of a regent of middle Java to be educated with his own sons. So you see there is nothing new under the sun; our idea which is called startlingly new, is old, inherited from our grandfather. Our plan of education—our spirit, has descended from him. Grandfather was a pioneer; we are only carrying on his work—they were good people, both grandfather and grandmother.

Your father has told us that according to form, a note must be presented in which our plans and ideas are set forth plainly and exactly. It must be written from the heart, not at all as though it was intended for the Governor General. We should like your father to read the note first, but His Excellency does not think it necessary. We must write simply, just as we feel.

57 · TO MR. J. H. ABENDANON

February 1, 1903

I must thank you once more for your advice. Your talk did us a tremendous amount of good. Why should I not acknowledge to you that we had never looked at things in that light before, and had never dreamed that if we went to Holland we might endanger our own cause. Our "friends" would be only too glad to spread abroad the report that we had grown to be wholly "*blanda*," [1] and many parents would shudder at the mere thought of entrusting their children to us. You have opened our eyes; we are grateful from our hearts.

This morning we were taking a drive and we witnessed a naive example of native faith. It was out in the fields. Men and animals were uniting in prayer to the All-Highest to bathe the thirsty earth with blessed rain.

In the foreground sat the pengulu and *santris*,[2] behind, the pious women in white garments and around them hundreds of men, women and children. Sheep, goats, horses and buffaloes were bound to stakes. A pengulu stood before them and led the service, praying in a loud voice. Most of the people fell in with "Amin-amin," in

1. Dutch.
2. Those who have been to an Islamic religious school or who attempt to observe the ritual obligations of Islam with strictness.

which chorus the bleeting of the sheep was blended.

This ceremony is called *"sembajang istika."* They prayed for three days and three nights. You can imagine the delight and gratitude of the people, because now it has rained. Their prayers were effectual and do you know what they say now? We cannot get the idea out of their heads that we had a share in it.

Before this at other places the people had held "sembajang istika," but never a drop of rain fell. Chance willed it that we should be present at the solemnities here, so our simple people drew the conclusion that we gave strength to that last prayer and supplication which, plainly, was heard and answered.

Such childlike, confiding faith is touching.

I wish so often that I had a photographic apparatus and could make a permanent record of some of the curious things that I see among our people. There is so much which we should like to preserve, so that we could give to outsiders a true picture of us Javanese.

It would mean so much more than mere written description if they would see the whole scene on the padi—the buffaloes and the *botjah-angongs* [3] included. I could then write what I, as a child of Java, think and feel about these things.

You know that I am always glad to be able to do anything for you, and when you ask a favor of me, it is a joyful occasion. I am also glad to do what I can for *East and West*. I feel that I am only doing myself a service, for it is for our people, and I and my people are one. So dispose of my time as you will, with a quiet mind, and do not be afraid that you will be asking too much of me. I only ask your forbearance when something that you have ordered does not come quickly enough.

I have talked with the goldsmith about going to Solo to learn to work in tortoise shell there. He is eager to go; already he can make little combs, he has the tools for that, but he does not understand polishing very well; he could learn that at Solo. He is also anxious to learn to work in horn and mother of pearl. That too could be learned there.

But the revival of our art is just beginning and naturally all of these things cannot be done at once. I have had a pleasant letter from Dr. Pijzel, one of the editors of *Eigen Haard*. I also received some copies of my article on wood-carving. The illustrations are

3. Boys who herd buffaloes.

reproduced beautifully. Do you not think so? I have one set of them made on very fine paper. Do you know what I think so splendid? That the very first time that I write for the public under my own name, "Moedertje" should introduce me. Though it is even as pleasant that the little article should be in demand. We have heard that in the Minahassa, a native girl has "crazy" ideas just as we have. You see we are not the only simpletons. If the nobles here disdain us, and we are rejected by the people too, then we can fly away and seek that sister soul. Far away from the whirl of the markets, in some forgotten place, together we will find work for the head, the heart and the hand. In the great wide world somewhere there must be a place for us.

My eldest sister has been here, but she went away yesterday, not back to Kendal, but to Kudus to visit her mother-in-law and to try to arouse the latter's interest in our cause. Someone goes now to plead for us who herself once bitterly opposed us. When she was coming here, we did not plan an elaborate speech that would soften her heart. We talked to her simply, just as we felt, and it was sweet and strange when our sister with moist eyes said tremulously "Good, may you carry out your plans and meet with success. I shall pray God to bless you."

We asked her, "Will you still cling to us if others revile us and condemn us?"

And she answered, "Even the loudest talkers will be silent some day." Sister thinks that her mother-in-law will help us, and that her husband too will have sympathy for us.

But how are things here at home? Formerly we must never speak to others about the subject nearest our hearts, now they bring it up themselves. We talked not long ago with a stranger about several things. My heart beat with joy and happiness when I saw Father standing next to me the whole time. "I am his child in spirit too," sang my heart! Father invited the stranger to come here so that we could exchange our thoughts and ideas. He thought it would be good for us. Oh, is my dream to really become reality? Are we going on our way with our parents' full blessing? Before we had an opportunity to write to the Heer Sijthoff, we received a very cordial letter from him last week, reproaching us for our obstinacy. A few lines further on, he declared that we had forced his respect and promised to give us his support. When we need it, we have only to ask him.

58 · TO MEVROUW ABENDANON-MANDRI

March 4, 1903

I have been laid low by sickness; for days they watched over me anxiously—I was in the most frightful pain. Thank God, that is now behind me. And the suffering is a thing of the past. I was freed from my pain by such a strange remedy; we have preserved it and given it to all of our family. Later, it may do our children good.

Yesterday I began work again. And today for the first time, I went driving. Father's pleasure was touching. Naturally I sat next to him, and he held on to me tightly as if he were afraid of losing me. It was a delightful hour, the precious memory of which will be with me always.

59 · TO MEVROUW ABENDANON-MANDRI

March 9, 1903

We have received word that the tortoise shell will be here before many days. And then the goldsmith will go with it to Solo. Now all three branches of the artistic industry of my birthplace are growing and thriving. And we are still looking for others that can be spurred back into life. The people know that our aim is their well-being, and they show their appreciation by working with eagerness and enthusiasm. I am thankful that they understand that we have their good always before our eyes; otherwise everything that we might do for them would be useless.

It is splendid to see life waking and stirring around us. They are beginning to grow vegetables on a large scale, even in the kampong, around the Malay quarter. Everything goes so well. The goldsmith has taken more boys as apprentices, and there are some clever youths that want to be educated for the wood carving trade also. I have noted one thing with great pleasure; among the apprentices, there is a boy from the *kota*,[1] and consequently not a child of

1. Town.

Blakang-Gunung, the wood carving village. We have to seek out other apprentices, but this boy from the kota came of himself and asked us to take him.

The little ones here will carry on our work when we are gone. We can lead them from a distance so long as they need leading.

. . . . . .

Someone complained to us about ingratitude among our inferiors. We told him that if he were distressed at the ingratitude of the people, it was his own fault.

He looked at us with his great eyes and said; "My fault, when people are ungrateful to me?"

"Yes, your fault, when you allow yourself to be distressed by it. For we must never do good with the thought of gratitude before our eyes. We must do good simply because it is good, and because only in so doing will we fulfill ourselves." I believe that to be happy ourselves, and to make others happy, we must understand. The more we understand the less bitterness we feel, and the easier it is to be just.

He asked us too, "What would happen if you should meet someone in whose presence your heart would beat?"

"I should be happy and thankful because that would indicate that I had met a companion soul, and the more companion souls we find, the better it is for our cause, and that of those whom we love."

"You will never meet a companion soul."

That was said forcefully. What did he mean? Does he place our men too low—or me undeservedly high. If he but knew, I had just received an enthusiastic letter from a young—and to me unknown—companion soul. I shall send the letter to you. It is from a student of the Native Artisans School. A spontaneous expression of sympathy about the article that appeared in *Eigen Haard* which you induced me to write. It is so like a young boy—young in its glowing enthusiasm, but through it a spirit speaks that is far from commonplace; there is candor in every line.

That is a luxury which writers can enjoy: unknown people feel that they are friends when they strike a sympathetic chord. I love to think that it was you who induced me to make my own name known to the public, and such an introduction from one whom I admire deeply is like a benediction.

If that article has met with success, I attribute it to the fact that it first saw the light through your hands. There were many things that had to be included in that introduction, but in none of them did it miss its mark. Its success has meant much to our artists, and since its appearance many questions have come to me about our wood carving.

60 · TO STELLA ZEEHANDELAAR

April 25, 1903

It is stupid and unpardonable that we did not write to you as soon as the great decision was made that we were not to eat the fruit of the noble work which you and others have done for us. No one could be more surprised at this determination than we ourselves. We had been prepared for anything, but we had never expected that we would say of our own free will, "We want to stay." But do not think of us, think of the cause and what will be best for that; it is there we must rest our case.

Do not think that our feelings have changed, they have not. When our request was on the way to the Governor General, we believed firmly that for the sake of our future pupils, education in Europe was an absolute necessity. But after that another truth was impressed upon us: "At this time, it would be far better for the cause if we remained in India."

You know that it is our dearest wish to complete our educations in Europe. Can you realize what it will cost us to give up the idea on the very eve of its realization? We have been through a terrible struggle. But we threw aside our own desires, when we found that the cause could be served best in a different way. We saw this as soon as we ceased to think of ourselves, but only of our cause.

The people for whom we wish to work must learn to know us. If we went away, we should become as strangers to them. And when after some years, we came back, they would see in us only European women. If the people do not like to trust their daughters to European women, how much less would they be willing to trust them to those who were worse in their eyes, Javanese turned European.

Our aim is our people; and if they should be set against us, of what good would the help of the Government be? We ought to strike as quickly as possible, and place before the public as an accomplished fact a school for native girls. Just now they are talking about us, and we are known over the whole of Java. We must strike while the iron is hot. If we went away, interest would grow lukewarm and after a time dwindle away altogether. Now we can make ourselves personally known to our people. Seek to win their sympathy, teach them to trust us. If we had their sympathy and their trust then we should be at peace.

We have not entirely given up the idea of going to Holland, Stella. We could still go, always, and if we should go from Batavia, it would be better than from here. Our parents would then be accustomed to having us at a distance, and after they had once gotten used to the idea, it would not be so hard for them if the distance were made greater.

For us too that would have a good side. Consider this: we have never been away from home, and if we were suddenly taken from our warm little nest, from our own country, and placed in another environment far from all who loved us, the change would be great.

But that is only a side issue. We knew that all along, and had never seen anything against it. The main question is the danger to our undertaking itself. We had never looked at the other side; from defiant courage, or courageous defiance, call it what you will —carried away by our enthusiasm, we thought little—or not at all—of the temper of the public. Yes, we thought it to our credit to defy it, and to hold our own ideas high against the world. Not disturbing ourselves one way or another about its approbation, so long as we ourselves were convinced of the holiness of our cause. We still think that is right, but in this instance we may not live up to our ideal. For now everything depends for us upon the good will of the public. Always we wish to work for the good of our people, and we must not set them against us by crushing with relentless hands the ideas upon which they have thriven and grown old through the centuries.

Patience, the wise have said to us all along. We heard them but did not understand. Now we are beginning to understand. Stella, now we know that the watchword of all reformers must be patience. We cannot hasten the course of events, we only retard them when we try to push forward too hastily. If the public should be aroused against us, the whole cause would be held back. People would be unwilling to give their daughters a liberal education, for education would be held responsible for such impossible creatures as we.

Patience! patience, even unto eternity. Stella, I was so miserable when this truth penetrated at last. We must curb ourselves in our enthusiasm, we will not pass our goal without seeing it. Mevrouw Van Kol wrote to us that before we can realize an ideal, we must first lose many illusions. The first illusion that we have thrown aside is not to give ourselves to the public frankly just as we are. No, that may not be. The public must not know what we are really fighting—the name of the enemy against which we take the field must never, never be cried aloud—. It is—polygamy. If that word were heard no man would trust his child to us. I have struggled against this, for it as though we began our work with a lie.

We hoped to make ourselves known just as we were, and that even so, from conviction that we were right, parents would send their children to us. It would be impossible.

We have not yet begun our work and yet we have seen our illusions dwindle away one by one. Oh Stella, do not make the loss of this great illusion harder to us by your sorrow. It is hard enough as it is. You have always known that it was my dearest wish to go to your country and to gather wisdom there for my own people. Let us never speak of it again.

I thank you, in the name of my parents too, a thousand times for all that you have done for us and—for nothing. No, Stella, your work is not lost, the work of you all. Though we may make no use of its fruits now, it will be of great good to our cause, attention will have been drawn to it.

Before this, questions relating to the education of the Javanese people have always been brought up by those who had some interest of their own at stake.

Now the interest is free from ulterior motive; would that have been the case if you had not drawn the attention of the liberals to us? Would the Government have been ready to help us if you had not worked for us? I thank you a thousand times for your great love. In the name of my people, I thank you sincerely. Great good will come of your work for the Javanese. Be sure of that.

Our plan is, if our request is answered favorably, to go at once to Batavia. Roekmini will study drawing, handiwork, hygiene and nursing. In drawing, she will have lessons from the teacher at the Gymnasium, and she will take the course in hygiene at the Doktor-djawa school. I shall take a normal course, continuing the same studies with which I have already been working here for several months.

61 · TO MEVROUW ABENDANON-MANDRI
July 4, 1903 [1]

Whatever the future may have in store for us, I pray that we may always remain confident and gay and full of faith.

I have said so often to others, "Do not despair, do not curse your cross, weary one. Through suffering comes power." Now it is my fate to apply what I have been preaching.

But I will not think any more of strife or suffering, of care and of anxiety. It makes my head so tired, and my heart so sick. I will smell the perfume of flowers and bathe in the sunshine; they are always here to comfort us.

Moeske, we have begun our work. We thank your husband for his advice to begin at once, just as we were. We had not dared to hope that it would begin so easily.

We started with one pupil, quickly the number jumped to five, tomorrow morning eight will come to the kabupaten, and soon there will be ten. We are so pleased when we look at our little children. They are such a fresh unspoiled little band; they always come exquisitely neat, and they get along so amiably together. They learned to trust us quickly; while they pay all due respect to form, they are still as free and unrestrained before us as though there were no such thing as rank or difference of degree.

The day before yesterday the djaksa of Karimun Djawa [2] brought a daughter to me. Picture it, Moeske, they send their daughters away from home and let them eat with us here in a strange place.

1. Written with a pencil after an illness.
2. A group of islands off the coast of Japara.

Yesterday, a young mother came to me in great distress. She said that she lived too far away; if it were not so, she would be so glad to come and study with us herself. As that cannot be, she wants to provide for her little daughter the education which she has not had the opportunity to gain. Her child is not yet a year old; as soon as she is six years old, her mother will send her to us, wherever we may be.

The children come here four days in the week, from eight to half past twelve. They study writing, reading, handiwork and cooking. We teachers do not give lessons in art unless the pupils show a special aptitude for it.

Our school must not have the air of a school, nor we that of schoolmistresses. It must be like a great household of which we are the mothers. We will try and teach them love as we understand it, by word and deed.

In our own youth, we were guided by that simple precept which is universally understood: "Do not unto others what you do not wish done unto yourself."

Mevrouw Van Kol has told us much of your Jesus, and of the apostles Peter and Paul.

Of whatever belief or race a man may be, a great soul is a great soul—a noble character, a noble character. I have read *Quo Vadis,* and I have been thrilled with admiration for the martyrs to their faith, who amid the bitterest suffering still looked faithfully and trustingly toward the Highest and proclaimed His praise in beautiful song. I have suffered with them and I have rejoiced with them.

Do you know *We Two,* by Edna Lyall? That is a very fine book. It treats of atheism and Christianity, of true Christianity and of its frightful perversion, of which, alas, there is so much in the world. The atheist, Luke Raeburn, is a great figure, and Erica Raeburn too is a noble character, who from a zealous atheist becomes a sincere and believing Christian. They were a father and daughter who loved each other devotedly, and depended each upon the other.

We read too the *Soul of a People.* That is about Buddhism and is also a beautiful book. We are anxious now to read something about Judaism (do you not say that?). Perhaps Zangwill's book *Dreams of the Ghetto* will be what we seek.

62 · TO MEVROUW VAN KOL

August 1, 1903

A few words to announce to you, as briefly as possible, a new turn in my life. I shall not go on with our great work as a woman alone! A noble man will be at my side to help me. He is ahead of me in work for our people; he has already won his spurs while I am just beginning. Oh, he is such a lovable, good man, he has a noble heart and a clever head as well. And he has been to Holland, where his bride would so gladly go, but must not for her people's sake.

It is a great change; but if we work together, and support and help one another, we may be able to take a far shorter road to the realization of our hopes than could either alone. We meet at many, many points. You do not yet know the name of my betrothed; it is Raden Adipati Djojo Adiningrat, Regent of Rembang.

And now, adieu! Soon I shall write again, and I hope at greater length.

63 · TO MEVROUW ABENDANON-MANDRI

August 1, 1903

I want to make myself worthy of the highest title, and that is, Child of God. Have I not told you often that we were done with all personal happiness?

Now life comes to demand that promise of me. I have said that nothing could be too bitter or too hard for us, if it would but enable us to add one little grain of sand to the building of that great structure, the happiness of a people.

Now I have been tested—: what am I worth?

Yesterday was again an exciting day for us. We received a communication from the Department of Education, telling us if we did not wish to make use of the opportunity granted us to be educated as teachers, to send a statement accordingly in writing to the Governor General. How must the statement which has been asked for be worded? Briefly and to the point, that I no longer wish to make use of the offered opportunity because I am engaged to be married; or because now a still better opportunity has presented itself to me of working for our people at the side of a noble man, whom I respect, who loves the people with me, and who will ably support me in my work. I shall be of much greater service with him, than we two, as women standing alone, could ever be.

And Roekmini does not wish to take advantage of the opportunity because she may not, nor does she wish to even if she could, go alone. She will reach her goal in a different way.

Then I wish to express my respect and gratitude to the Government for having taken the interests of Java to heart, and because when a child of the people asked for aid, it lent an ear to her request, and was willing to meet her halfway in her regard for the future welfare of her race. Holland has now grown nearer to us. We are convinced now that the Netherlands wishes the happiness of India. That is no hollow phrase. We mean it.

All of my friends among my humble fellow countrymen have always wished and prayed this for me, "that Bendoro Adjeng Tini might go nowhere but to a kabupaten."

And the simple-minded hearts rejoice now because their dream is to be realized, they are happy because their wish for their bendoro is coming true. You see how my simple friends triumph. "Vox populi vox dei." If that is true then it is under the guidance of a higher power that my path in life has taken a different direction from that which I myself had planned.

"May you be a blessing, a refuge to many, the tree in whose shade they find refuge from the heat of the day." That is what many old people here pray for me. May I live up to the expectations of these who are simple of heart.

A great task lies before me; unquestionably it is hard, but if I succeed, and bring it to a good end, I shall serve our people as I could never have served them in any other way. If my work is well done, it will be a lesson that will have a powerful effect upon our cause, because to my fellow countrymen my future will be the most beautiful and desirable in the world.

The mere fact of my marriage will do good; it will interest the parents, spur them on to educate their daughters, and impress them more than could a thousand inspired words. It stands for a fact that beauty and riches are to be despised before gifts of the heart and mind.

I remember my own words, when some one asked me how the idea of education could be impressed upon our women and girls. The Javanese people are just like other children by nature: they are children of the sun, worshippers of splendor and brilliancy. Very well, gratify that wish, give them what their hearts desire, but at the same time give them something that is true, that is of real worth.

Now we shall not infringe too harshly upon the customs of our land, our childlike people can still have their pomp and splendor. The freedom of women is inevitable; it is coming, but we cannot hasten it. The course of destiny cannot be turned aside, but in the end the triumph has been foreordained.

We shall not be living to see it, but what will that matter? We have helped to break the path that leads to it, and that is a glorious privilege!

Do not be uneasy; my betrothed will not cut my wings short; the fact that I can fly is just what has raised me so high in his eyes. He will only give a larger opportunity to stretch out my wings; he will help me to broaden my field of work. He appreciates your Meiske for herself, and not as a possible ornament for his home.

64 · TO MEVROUW ABENDANON-MANDRI

August 8, 1903

Do you know what day this is? It is the third anniversary of our meeting. Three years ago today, three simple, childlike girls received a costly gift from heaven, the gift of a friend after their own hearts! The childlike girls have grown to be women, life has furrowed wrinkles in the still young faces; their hearts have been through fire. Have they wasted and gone to ashes, or have they come forth from the fire purified?

. . . .

Just now we have company; at the table where I sit there are five of us working. Justinah the wise woman came this morning and will stay until next week. We think her a treasure. She spends her time here usefully, teaches embroidery and is so severe when we are careless. When we make a mistake, she immediately pulls everything out. How rich I felt this morning when she laid her hand trustingly on my shoulder while I explained something or other to her. Now she feels at home with us. I look with so much pleasure into her fine intelligent eyes; they say so much.

She is a desa-child. Oh, how full of love is her calling! You would enjoy meeting her. She listens with attention when one speaks, and then asks such intelligent questions. If you ever come to our neighborhood again, I hope to be able to take her to you. This clever little woman has already attended forty-eight women in childbirth, and she is such a young thing still, with all a child's eagerness.

The Regent of Rembang comes on the seventeenth of this month. I have asked him to bring his children with him. I am so anxious to make the acquaintance of my future family. The children are to be my future, and I shall live and work for them, strive, and suffer, if need be, for them. I hope that they will love me. I have asked their father to give the entire control of his children to me. My dream is to make them feel, insofar as it is possible, that they are my own children.

There are others that call themselves my children; the Under-Collector here, a rich regent's son and heir, said, "Make my child your servant, let her scrub the floor, draw water, anything that you will, if you will but let her stay with you." I listened with a smile on my face, but I felt like crying.

I said nothing, promised nothing, but only prayed silently that I might lock all the little children entrusted to me safely in my heart, and nourish them with my love.

I am only going to take one child with me to my new dwelling —a girl of eight or so, who has been given into my care by her parents. She is the daughter of a teacher and has been to school. She is a lovely child, clever and quick. If she shows any inclination at all, I shall educate her for some profession. Now she receives lessons from my sister in handiwork. In Rembang there are women and children of gentle birth who have been educated. I shall try to gain their interest in our work later.

My future sister-in-law is already "tainted" by a Western education; that will be pleasant for me. My days at home are numbered; only two more short months and my future protector will come for me. He and his younger brother, the Regent of Tuban, have been here. The day is set; it is the twelfth of November. The wedding will be very quiet, only our families will be present and neither of us is to wear bridal dress; he will be in his uniform, as I have already seen him. That is my wish. His children are not coming, to my great disappointment. They are still too little, and the journey is tiresome.

65 · TO MEVROUW ABENDANON-MANDRI

August 25, 1903

I shall find a rich field of work at Rembang, and thank God, there I shall not stand alone. He has promised to stand at my side and support me; it is also his wish and his hope to support me in my efforts to help our people. He himself has already labored diligently for their welfare for years. He too would like to help in the work of education, and though he cannot give personal instruction himself, he can have it done by others. Many of his various relatives are being educated at his expense. He expects me to be a blessing to him and to his people; may he not be disappointed! I am very grateful for one thing: his family share his ideas and approve of his choice. They look upon me as the future rearer of their children, and I really hope to serve in that capacity; I do not think of anything else.

Sometimes I forget that I have lost so many beautiful illusions, and I think that I am still following my calling, only along a different way from the one that I had mapped out for myself, and I shall think that always. It gives me peace and helps me to be cheerful.

Nothing is perfect, and nothing may ever be perfect in this world. I had hoped and prayed that I might become the mother and sister of many, and God has heard my prayer, though it is a little different from what I meant.

It is one of his dreams, too, to be able to raise up our people. He is truly good to his people and to the officials under him; they eat out of his hand.

Day before yesterday a collector was here and spent the whole evening talking to Father about his daughter. He wishes me to undertake her education. His wife has already spoken to me and now he came to talk to Father.

I am asked to take other children from here. I do not know whether I shall be able to take them all; it is hard to refuse, but I will promise nothing. We shall first see how it goes. We shall wait some days before coming to the hard duty of making a decision, and meanwhile I shall not speak of it save under stress of urgent necessity. I will be forgiven when they see that I do not refuse from pride, but from expediency and out of consideration for others; perhaps for the sake of their own children too.

Fortunately Rembang is a quiet little place, and it is good that he cares as little as I for amusements.

I am delighted that the Resident there is interested in our cause, so that I shall not go as a stranger. And there will be my great friend, the sea! It lies not more than a hundred feet from the house.

When they told him that I was much interested in the art and kindred industries of our people, he said that there were gold-smiths and wood carvers there; they only needed a little directing. And listen to this: it is something very pleasant. Perhaps our good friend Singowirio will go there with me; you know whom I mean, the man from Blakang-Gunung.

He could not have followed his bendoro to Batavia, but now that the plan is somewhat different he is anxious to go. We are planning to take him. But capital and leadership are needed first of all, before our artistic industries can be placed upon a practical basis. A large workplace ought to be built, and many apprentices and artisans taken to work under regular supervision in our immediate neighborhood.

If we only had the money, we could build a workplace, buy material, employ workmen and train apprentices. Singo could be placed at the head of the establishment. I believe that in less than a year, or two years at most, the capital thus invested would be doubled.

I should have been glad to begin here, but both of us had our eyes upon Batavia. When we were gone our little sisters would have had to take the responsibility for everything, and that would have been too hard for them. Now it is different, we could take the responsibility, if we had the necessary money. I am convinced that our artistic industry has a great future.

Not long ago, while we were on a little journey, we met the Heer Brandes, brother of Doctor Brandes. He expressed much interest in the art of our country. When I told him of a little shop for the products of native art at Semarang, he set out immediately to look for it. You must understand that the people of Semarang are opposed to sending the products of their own neighborhood to Batavia. *East and West* wishes to open a little shop at Semarang. But again money is needed, and *East and West* cannot give very much as yet. When I told Heer Brandes this, he said, "Oh, do not worry about that, the money will be found if you will only take care of the other side."

I said, "But there must be someone of discrimination who will stay at Semarang."

"That will be found too, and your only care will be to see that beautiful things are produced."

I have received a short letter from him. He has spoken to various friends about the plan, and they were all much interested and have promised their financial support. I spoke to him of our other idea in regard to the art of wood carving. At once he asked how much money we would need for that. I did not mention any certain amount: I must first ask those who know, how much the workplace would cost, how much the wood, and what wages would have to be paid out to the workmen every month. The workplace could be very simple at first. The great difficulty is that there must be a force of fifty men kept steadily working, and there would have to be money with which to pay them, because they could not afford to wait for their wages until their work was sold. Rembang would be an excellent country for wood carving. It is the land of *djati* and there is also much *sono* there.[1]

Singo himself thinks the idea excellent, if we only had the money!

If everything goes well, what a retinue I shall take with me, even though I am a modern woman. I shall certainly have a strange bridal dower.

The Regent of Rembang is marrying a whole kota. What business has he to put himself between the people and their bride? Oh, heavens! I shall strike an unfortunate time, for I shall arrive in

1. *Djati* is teak wood. *Sono* is another type of wood.

the busiest time of the year, *Puasa* or *Lebaran,* the "New Year." [2]
I have said all along that I would not allow my foot to be kissed.
I could never allow anyone to do that. I want a place in their
hearts, not outward forms.

I cannot think of the future without my Roekmini. How shall
I get along without her and she without me! When I think of her
my eyes stay wide open the whole night long.

66 · TO MEVROUW ABENDANON-MANDRI

October 19, 1903

Do you know what has happened? At his earnest request, the date
has been changed. The wedding will not be on the twelfth, but on
the eighth of November, and on Wednesday the eleventh, at about
five o'clock, I shall leave my home.

67 · TO MEVROUW ABENDANON-MANDRI

November 3, 1903

Your girl is alive again, she is alive. Her heart glows and thrills,
and it is not burning pain or bitter, dumb despair that makes the
strings vibrate; love is sounding the chords. Why did I complain,
ungrateful that I was, with such a rich treasure within me?

Love is greater than all else! And she is richest who gives most.
And I shall give, as a rich father's child, with a full hand. What
has been given me, I shall give back with interest. Oh, there are

2. *Puasa* is the Javanese name for the Moslem month of fasting,
Ramadan. In Java, the days immediately following this month of abstinence and prayer, *Lebaran,* are festive days. While not exactly a New
Year in the calendrical sense, there is a feeling of beginning again, of re-
newal. During these holidays everyone dresses in new clothes and goes
calling on their parents, grandparents, and on certain social superiors.
During these formal visits, the caller asks the forgiveness of the host for
past offenses, and shows his deep respect with a low sembah, and, in
Kartini's time, by kissing the knee or even the foot of the higher person.

so many that hunger and thirst after love!

Strange and wonderful things can happen in life. He and Father were drawn together from the very first moment that they set eyes upon each other two years ago. He and Father have been friends ever since; and he has visited us often.

It was one of his poor little wife's wishes to come and see us, with him and all of the children. Both of them called my father, "Father." She was so anxious to make our acquaintance; alas, before her wish could be granted, death took her away.

Shortly before her death, he saw his wife in a dream; she was deep in fervent prayer, and the prayer that was sent up to to All-Highest was that she and Raden Adjeng Kartini might meet and be friends through all eternity. Since that time, I have never been out of his thoughts.

Yes, he has suffered much; when she went away it was a deep blow to him, for he loved her very dearly.

And his hope for himself is that Father's treasure—his *wasiat djati*,[1] as he calls me—shall help him to forget his grief.

May I not find a little message from you when, on the eleventh, I enter my new home for the first time? It will be as if you had raised your dear hand to bless me.

68 · TO MEVROUW ABENDANON-MANDRI
November 7, 1903

My dearest Moedertje:

This is the last greeting from your little daughter as a young girl, on the day before her wedding. Tomorrow, at half-past six, we are to be married. I know that tomorrow my whole heart will be with you. Goodbye, my dearest. Greet your husband heartily for me, and remember that you will always have the deep affection of

Your own little daughter

K.

1. True legacy.

69 · TO MEVROUW AND MIJNHEER
ABENDANON

Rembang, December 11, 1903

My Dearest, Best Friends:

You do not know with what affection this, my first letter from my new home, is written. A home where, praise God, there is peace and love everywhere, and we are all happy with and through one another.

I regret so deeply that through the press of circumstances I have not been able to write to you before. Forgive me. The first days were so frightfully hard; then our children were ailing, and at last I felt the reaction from the wearisome days through which we had passed. I was far from well and was obliged to take care of myself. Now I am again fresh and happy. Once more it is the old irresponsible, hare-brained creature of other days, who can look forward to the future with smiling eyes.

Do I have to express myself still more plainly, dearest? I bless the day on which I laid my hand in that of him who was sent by the All-Father to be my comrade in the journey through this great and difficult life.

Everything that was noble and beautiful in my eyes I find here realized before me. Some of the dreams that I still dream he has carried out years ago, or he dreams them now with me. We are so entirely one in thought and ideas that often I am frightened. You would both love him if you knew him. You would admire his clear brain and honor his good heart. I have thought so often that the noble should live for the people, and I have wanted to preach this aloud. Our nobles would not care to hear it, but he, my heart's king, has gone before me.

It is just a month today since my husband brought me here to his country, and led me into his house, now our home. The Queen could not have been more warmly welcomed. All of Rembang made festival; even on the border, every house was decorated with flags; the very hired carriages on the highways bore the tricolor. The enthusiasm of the people was so spontaneous and genuine, the expressions of sympathy came so warmly from their hearts. The people were gay and rejoiced because their beloved ruler was happy. Again and again my husband took me out on the balcony—the people must see his new *Gusti-Putri*.[1]

I sat on a stool near him, silent, my eyes full of tears and my heart overflowing with emotion. There was happiness, there was gratitude, there was pride; pride in him, that he had gained such a warm place in the hearts of the people; gratitude because one of my dearest dreams was realized, and happiness because I sat there at his side.

And our children—how can I tell you of these delights? I felt drawn to them at once; they are such dear, unspoiled creatures, and every day they grow closer and closer to my heart. Their father has laid a good foundation to their education; it began just as I always wished education to begin—in simplicity and modesty. My little treasures do not hold themselves above the most humble person here in the house; everyone is alike to them. The field is prepared, I have only to go forth and sow.

In January I hope to be able to open our little school. We are looking for a good teacher, and till we have found one, I shall have charge of the lessons myself. If unforeseen circumstances should intervene and I be prevented in any way, one of my sisters will carry on the work for me, till I am able to take charge of it again.

Several parents have already asked me to teach their children. Our idea is to open a school for daughters of the native officials here, if we can get a suitable teacher. If we could find a good governess, then she could care for the mental development of our children and also for the formation of their characters.

When everything is in good working order, could we not hope for a subsidy from the Government? The expenses of the school would be as low as possible; the children would receive their board and lodging free from us. Shall I write a letter about it?

The parents are full of confidence and are asking us to take their children. This is now our opportunity. We must begin. After a while I shall write to you at greater length about our plans. I have the fullest confidence that a girls' school, held by us at our home under the direction of a European teacher with me as headmistress, would succeed. We have great plans, and we would give anything to be able to talk this over with you and your husband face to face.

1. Queen.

I am writing this at five o'clock in the morning. The children are awake and hanging over my chair; mother must give them bread and milk.

You must see our youngest just once; he is not yet two years old, but so intelligent. As I sat here, he came with a little footstool; it was too heavy for him to carry, so he dragged it to mother; mother's feet must not hang. Then the darling child climbed on my lap. When I call the children to me, they fight to see which one shall reach me first, and our little sister brings me the spoons and forks.

The one who is naughty must not come to mother. They have the greatest fun when they bathe with me, and I too enjoy this more than anything else. It is such a pleasure to see the fresh, laughing little faces.

And now I am going to talk about myself. I have not thanked you yet for the many expressions of love which we have received from you of late. I was made so happy by the letter from your husband and yourself, which I received at Japara; my warmest thanks to you both. And you, Moedertje dearest, I kiss you heartily on both cheeks for your welcome greeting, which I found upon my arrival.

70 · TO MEVROUW AND MIJNHEER ABENDANON

December 16, 1903

Today I feel a great peace. A whole history lies behind it. And this letter must not go until I have told it to you.

Guess who has been staying here and who went away only this morning? Mevrouw and Heer Bervoets, from Modjowarno. They had been to Japara to see my parents, who sent them here to us. It was an inspiration of Father's, and we bless the happy chance which led those good angels here.

I had been anxious for a long time to make the acquaintance of this noble couple. My wish has been granted, and in what manner! I have always thought of them with sympathy, but now deep gratitude is mingled with the sympathy.

Day before yesterday, my husband was cheerful and wide awake the whole day. At noon the Bervoets came, and he was so well that one would have little thought that a few hours later he would be lying desperately ill. Much interested, it was past midnight before we took leave of our guests. An hour later, my husband was suffering from a violent indisposition; the sickness came suddenly, and in less than three minutes it was so severe that he hardly expected to see the morning. How I felt, you can easily imagine. I had Doctor Bervoets called. He had expected to leave the next morning at eight, but neither he nor his wife had the heart to go away and leave us in so much trouble; they would go at one o'clock instead. But even then they saw that my husband needed constant medical attention, and our doctor was away on a journey.

It was an acute case of colic; an illness from which my husband had never suffered before in his life. Yesterday at midday he began to mend, and fell asleep. You can imagine how thankful I was. This morning at eight o'clock, our new friends went away. My husband is improving steadily and is only very weary. At this moment he is sleeping quietly, and has been for a full half hour. God grant that he may soon be entirely well!

It is so strange that in her last days his first wife should have thought of me. She longed to know me, and to become friends with me. Her dream was to go to Japara and to take her children to me; she hardly laid my portrait out of her hand, and even on her last sickbed she had it by her.

After she had departed, and her earthly pain was over, every one here, even the native officials, have had but one wish, which has now been granted since the eighth of November. That is why there was such general rejoicing when we came.

My husband received your letter with great pleasure. The horse trappings for *East and West* are ready. They are now packed and as soon as he is better, they will be sent. He has also several kinds of peacock feather cigar holders, and we are looking for some examples of real Lassemese sarongs. We shall then see what we can do further for *East and West*.

My husband thinks the idea of moving the Japara wood carvers here excellent. He supports me warmly in that, just as he does in all my other projects. A handcraft school for natives has been one of his dreams all along.

My husband is anxious for me to write a book about the sagas and legends of Java. He would collect them for me, and we could work on them together—a wonderful prospect.

There is so much that he wants to do with me; on my writing-table several articles from his hand are already lying.

71 · TO MEVROUW ABENDANON-MANDRI

Rembang, March 6, 1904

My Own Dearest Moedertje:

I wish that I could throw my arms around your neck, I long from my soul to tell you of my great joy, to make you a sharer in our splendid secret. A great, sweet happiness awaits me. If Gods so wills it, toward the end of September, there will come one sent from heaven to make our beautiful life still more beautiful, to draw the bond closer and tighter that already binds us together. Mother, my mother, think of the little soul that will be born from our two souls to call me mother.

Can you picture it? I a mother! I shall make you, old Moedertje, I shall make you a grandmother! Will you come later on to see your grandchild? I shall not be able now to go to Batavia. Our plan was first to go on a journey this month, to take a month's holiday. Now we must give up the idea. I am not able to travel, and when our little one is here, then, too, I may not travel. So I shall see Batavia no more, at least while you are there. And what would it be worth to me without you and Mijnheer? My husband is so glowingly happy because of this new life which I carry under my heart. That alone was wanting to our happiness.

72 · TO PROFESSOR AND MRS. ANTON

Rembang, April 10, 1904

Highly Honored Friends:

It must have seemed strange to you to have heard from me in reply to your cordial letter, and to have had no word of acknowledgment for the splendid presents with which we have been so greatly pleased. If every thought sent to you had become a deed, what an array of letters you would now have! Forgive me, dear friends, that no word has gone to you before this.

The change from a simple young girl to a bride, a mother, and the wife of a highly placed native official—which means much in our Indian life—is so great that I could think of nothing at first but of how best to fulfill my new duties. But that was not the only reason. Shortly after our wedding, my husband was taken very ill. After that I myself began to ail. Even now the Rembang climate does not agree with me. We live flat by the sea, but what at Japara was an advantage, is here at Rembang a plague. Here we must have a care for the sea wind, which is very unwholesome, because it must first blow over coral reefs and slime before it reaches us. But let me thank you, also in my husband's name, most gratefully for the magnificent presents which you sent to us at the time of our marriage.

The interesting painting and the colored photograph of Jena hang in our sitting room, where my husband, who is a great lover of statues and pictures, keeps his art treasures. I look at them so often with great pleasure and then many loving, grateful thoughts fly to my friends in Jena. How charming of you to want to give me a "boomkoek," the German national cake, which no single festival in your country must be without. That you were not able to express the thought in deeds, makes no difference to me. I appreciate it just as much as though it had become an accomplished fact.

And now I must tell you about my new life. You will be glad to hear of that, will you not? Because you take such interest in your Javanese friend, and have been so concerned about her future. God be thanked, your fears for me have proved groundless. A young wife writes you these lines, a wife whose happiness beams in her eyes and who can find no words adequate to express it.

My husband (and it is known through the whole of Java that I am different from others; yet he has bound himself to me) is not my husband, he is my best friend.

Everything that I think has been thought by him too, and many of my ideas have already been expressed by him in deeds. I have laid out for myself a full life. I have planned to be a pioneer in the struggle for the rights and freedom of the Javanese woman. I am now the wife of a man whose support gives me strength in my efforts to reach the ideal which is always before my eyes. I have now both personal happiness and also my work for my ideal.

I know that you will both be pleased to know that your little Javanese friend of the turbulent spirit is now anchored in a safe haven. I wish that you could see me in my new surroundings. You know how little I cared for luxury and worldly position; they would have no value in my eyes, were not that it is my husband who gives them to me. But they are means by which I may reach my goal more easily. The Javanese are deeply loyal to their nobles. Everything that their officials desire is readily accepted by them. So now at the side of my husband I shall reach the hearts of the people much more easily.

The success of the plans for our school shows that I have their confidence.

We began to teach at home in Japara, and now our younger sisters are carrying on the work there. Our little school now has one hundred and twenty pupils, daughters of native officials. My sisters give them instruction. But here too I have begun our work; my own little daughters were my first pupils. So you see that the little Javanese are beginning to realize the dream of their girlhood.

73 · TO MEVROUW ABENDANON-MANDRI

Rembang, June 28, 1904

We do not go out often, and we entertain very little, yet my life is always full. Splendid! I divide my days between my dear husband, my housekeeping, and my children—both my own and the adopted ones. And these last take the largest share of my time and attention. When their father is at work, then the children work with me from nine until twelve o'clock. At half past twelve, father finds a troop of clean-faced but very hungry children. At half-past one the little ones are sent to bed,[1] and if father is in bed, and I am not too tired, I work with the young girls. At four o'clock I preside at the tea table. When the little ones have drunk their milk and have bathed, they can drive the fowls to

1. In Java it is customary to take an hour's rest in the afternoon.

the coops, or walk with us, or play in the garden. We amuse ourselves for a little, and prattle about everything or about nothing.

When our little troop comes in, then we are done with play. Father sits down to read the paper, and they range themselves around mother. I sit in a rocking chair with the two smallest on my lap, a child on each arm of the chair and the two eldest at my knee. We tell stories; soon afterward suppertime comes around. We eat early with the little ones, the smallest of all sits next to mother. The little fellow has taken upon himself the task of lifting the glass cover for mother. No one must take that little work away from him, and if he is not allowed to do it, he knows it is because he has deserved a punishment.

At eight o'clock the little treasures are sent to bed. And we parents sit up and talk to each other till Klaas Vaak drives us to the *pulau kapok*,[2] and this is not so late as at Japara, for we get up very early in the morning.

Sunday is a holiday for both of us. We begin it always with a walk; after that I teach my girls cooking, and then the mother and wife can do the things for which she has not had time during the week. It is not much that I can do, for my husband is happier when I sit by him. He charms me sometimes with beautiful gamelan music and songs. I think it is delightful in my husband to add the songs. For the gamelan music alone makes too great an impression upon me. It takes me back to times of which I must not think. It makes me weak and sad.

So the days fly by, calm, quiet and peaceful as a little brook deep in the forest.

If the child that I carry under my heart is a girl, what shall I wish for her? I shall wish that she may live a rich full life, and that she may complete the work that her mother has begun. She shall never be compelled to do anything abhorrent to her deepest feelings. What she does must be of her own free will. She shall have a mother who will watch over the welfare of her inmost being, and a father who will never force her in anything. It will make no difference to him if his daughter remains unmarried her whole life long; what will count with him will be that she shall always keep her esteem and affection for us. He has shown that he respects women, and that we are one in thought, by his desire

2. Klaas Vaak is the Dutch version of "the sandman"; *pulau kapok* is an Indonesian phrase meaning "kapok island," i.e., the bed.

to trust his daughter wholly to me.

Oh, if you only knew the things that slander has spread abroad about me! What I heard before my marriage was praise compared to what I have since learned. My husband must indeed have had courage, to offer me his heart, his hand, and his name. He had heard many things concerning me, but never a single word of praise; still, in his heart there was a conviction, which nothing could shake, that we were the bearers of new ideas, which were incomprehensible to the great multitude, who scorned us because they could not understand. When his first wife was still living, he would always take my part when they dragged my name through the mud. She had been so anxious to know me, and during her last illness she slept with my portrait in her hand. And he had a premonition that some day I should play an important role in his life. Everyone here in the house had been interested in me. So there are premonitions, secret longings, that come often as forerunners of what will happen in the future. Only I alone did not think, did not dream that this would be my future existence.

I am not giving my little ones any vacation; they will have one in September when my child is born. For the first fortnight I must rest, and then my baby will go into the schoolroom. I have already prepared a corner where baby can sleep, while mother and little sisters and brothers study. Now we shall have something *à la* Hilda van Suylenburg—a mother who with a suckling baby goes out to work.

74 · TO MEVROUW ABENDANON-MANDRI

Rembang, June 30, 1904

When shall I ever be able to write to you as of yore? From all sides come reproaches that I write so seldom. But I cannot do anything else; I have undertaken a great task, and it is my hard duty to carry it through to completion. The children are doing their best, and I have now twelve, among them several who are full grown.

I am busy now with the outfit for your little grandchild. My sisters are eager for a girl, and my husband for a son. If it should be a girl, then I shall have to love her doubly, for everyone here is anxious for a boy.

75 · TO MEVROUW ABENDANON-MANDRI
Rembang, July 17, 1904

My own Dearest Moedertje:

My love for you and my interest in everything that concerns you must not be measured according to the number of my letters to you.

With the best will in the world, it is almost impossible for me to write to any one at all, now especially, when I am struggling against bad health. I have been quite sick: I caught a cold and suffered severely. That is now past, thank God! but I still have to take care of myself. And I must—I will be well, for our child's sake.

How much a child costs its mother! All the tedious suffering is still to come. Oh Moeske, I must take care of myself, and be prudent in everything. For a month past, I have only received members of the family, who can come into my room. I write this in a long chair. I cannot sit up straight comfortably.

Mama was with me last week; the dear one, nothing is too much for her where the welfare of her children is at stake. Just so she went to Pamalang when Kardinah was sick, and just so she came all the way here when my husband in his distress telegraphed for her. My husband is looking forward to the approaching time with great apprehension. He cannot bear to see me suffer, poor dear one; he really suffered more than I when I was so sick. He would turn the whole world upside down to spare me suffering and pain.

Rembang, August 10, 1904

Moeske Dearest:

I think of you so much! Above all do I think of you now, always with a feeling of tenderness, but at the same time, a deep sadness.

Sadness because you are so far from me, and will be even further removed beyond my reach. Why must it be that just those souls that are most closely akin should be separated so far from one another? I am so unhappy when I let myself long for you. I sit still, looking straight ahead, neither hearing nor seeing what is happening around me. I live in the past, that sweet and that bitter past, when I was so eager for suffering, and where your love is interwoven always like a garland of light. I suffered and I rejoiced. My heart is full of sadness, but also of gratitude, for the happiness which your love has brought me. I never cease to thank God for having brought you to us.

. . . . .

Why is it that the Javanese is so poor, they ask? And at the same time, they are thinking how they will be able to get more money out of him. Who will that money come from? Naturally from the little man for whose woe and weal we express such extreme concern that a whole commission is named to inquire into the cause of his retrogression; "What makes the Javanese so poor?": when grass cutters who earn 10 or 12 cents a day are made to pay a trade tax. Every time a goat or a sheep is butchered a tax of twenty cents is paid. A *saté*-merchant [1] who butchers two every day must pay this tax, which amounts to one hundred and forty-four florins in the course of a year. What is left for his profit? Barely enough to live on.

I learned much of this at my parents' house, but here where my husband shares every thought with me, where I share his whole life, his work and his troubles, I have come to know of conditions of which I was not only in ignorance, but the very existence of which I did not dream.

There is so much crying injustice, and he who loves righteous-

1. *Saté* is a dish composed of meat strung on a stick and roasted.

ness and holds office must suffer indeed. He must see much, and do much himself that is against all principles of right.

Goodday, Moeske; perhaps this will be my last letter to you. Think sometimes of your daughter who loves you and your husband so dearly, and who presses you now to her heart.

77   ·   TO MEVROUW ABENDANON-MANDRI
Rembang, August 24, 1904

Dearest Moedertje Mine:

After all, that was not to be my last letter. I have been afraid, but perhaps it will be for the best that my time is coming quickly. I feel it, Moedertje; it is very probable that your grandchild will be born sooner than we first expected him.

Greetings, my dear one. Think well of me, both of you; in my heart there is a prayer which says, "God keep my dear friends."

Your own little daughter

KARTINI.

78   ·   TO MEVROUW ABENDANON-MANDRI
Rembang, September 7, 1904

My Dearest Moedertje:

How can I thank you for the precious little frock that you have given our baby. It has all the more worth in our eyes because we know under what circumstances you have worked this present for your little grandchild. We heard through Roekmini that you made it yourself after your return to Batavia. To think that you, who were indisposed yourself and had so many cares upon your shoulders as always, but especially at that time when you were under great pressure, could still take such delicate and patient stitches for our child. Your friendship must indeed be great, and your love for me deep and sincere. I looked at the little frock yesterday with wet eyes and a grateful happy heart, and often I feel I must look at it again. It tells me so much, Moedertje dearest. It has made your daughter so happy.

Later your little grandchild can wear the figured ornament around his neck, when the dress grows too small for him. I shall keep it for him till he can understand me, when I tell him of the great love which God has given to his mother, so that the little ornament will be even more precious to him than it is now to me.

My husband said to me yesterday, when we received your present, "Go, wife, and write to Moedertje right away, or it may be too late," and I have followed his advice and, at the same time, the voice of my own heart.

Our little one is not here yet, but it may be any moment now. I feel that his coming is very near.

Thank you so much for your encouraging words, dear. The thought that far from here there is one, a part of my soul, who hopes and prays for me, makes me strong and does me unutterable good.

People who have seen me during these last days think me unusually cheerful. And why should I not be cheerful when such great happiness awaits me? What matter all the hours of pain, when they are the price of such sweet happiness? I long so for my little treasure, and it is sweet to know that many whom I love are with me in thought in these last days. Do I not know how at my dear home, hour by hour, they think of me, hope and pray for me?

When so many hearts pray the same prayer, heaven will not be deaf to it. Moeske, I am so firmly convinced that all will go well with your daughter; naturally you will be notified at once as soon as the great event has taken place.

Oh, if you, my good angel, could but stand at the cradle of my child, how blissfully happy I should be! I know that you will love our child even though it should grow into a greater simpleton than its mother. If it is only not too sensitive, all will be well— hè, Moeske? And that will not be unless the evil spirits watch by its cradle. But your talisman will take care of that and protect your little one from evil spirits.

My mother has been with me for two weeks, and there is also an old grandmother who has come to be with me during the hard hours that are coming. I am waited upon, spoiled, and watched over like a princess.

The layette and the little bed are in our room all ready for the coming of our treasure.

And Moeske, how are you, my little Grandmother? How is Mijnheer getting along? Oh, I hope that you will both be in the best of health when this reaches you. How is Edie? Is he still in China? I read his article in *Elsevier's* magazine with much interest. How well that boy can write! Ask brother Edie if he still remembers me. I have always regretted so much that I have never met him personally and now the chances of that have gone by forever.

When you write to him give him a cordial greeting from sister Kartini. Tell him of my great happiness, and that my husband and I both think of him with sympathy.

How delightful is the odor of the little fruit which is our true native perfume! I have put it away with the baby's frock, in a chest with other garments, so that they will be perfumed delicately. My treasure must smell sweet.

Good-night, dearest Moederjte; accept again sincere thanks from us both. Greet Mijnheer heartily for us, and feel yourself softly kissed by your own little daughter.

KARTINI.

[This was her last letter. On the 13th of September, her son was born, and four days later, she died suddenly, being just twenty-five years old. She was deeply mourned by all who had known and loved her.]

THE NORTON LIBRARY

Rostow, W. W. *The Process of Economic Growth.* New introduction. N176

Rowse, A. L. *Appeasement.* N139

Russell, Bertrand. *Freedom Versus Organization.* N136

Russell, Bertrand. *The Scientific Outlook.* N137

Sachs, Curt. *World History of the Dance.* N209

Salvemini, Gaetano. *The French Revolution.* Tr. by I. M. Rawson. N179

Shway Yoe. *The Burman: His Life and Notions.* Introduction by John K. Musgrave. N212

Simms, William Gilmore. *Woodcraft.* Introduction by Richmond Croom Beatty. N107

Sitwell, Edith. *Alexander Pope.* N182

Spender, Stephen. *The Making of a Poem.* New intro. N120

Stauffer, Donald A. *The Nature of Poetry.* N167

Stendhal. *The Private Diaries of Stendhal.* Tr. and ed. by Robert Sage. N175

Stovall, Floyd, Editor. *Eight American Authors.* N178

Strachey, Lytton. *Portraits in Miniature.* N181

Stravinsky, Igor. *An Autobiography.* N161

Summerson, John. *Heavenly Mansions and Other Essays on Architecture.* N210

Taylor, F. Sherwood. *A Short History of Science and Scientific Thought.* N140

Tolles, Frederick B. *Meeting House and Counting House.* N211

Tourtellot, Arthur B. *Lexington and Concord: The Beginning of the War of the American Revolution.* N194

Toye, Francis. *Rossini: A Study in Tragi-Comedy.* New introduction. N192

Walter, Bruno. *Of Music and Music-Making.* N242

Walter, W. Grey. *The Living Brain.* N153

Ward, Barbara. *India and the West,* Revised Edition. N246

Ward, Barbara. *The Interplay of East and West: Points of Conflict and Cooperation.* New epilogue. N162